Processing Mortgage-Backed Securities

Louis J. Karcher

New York Institute of Finance

Library of Congress Cataloging-in-Publication Data

Karcher, Louis J.
    Processing mortgage-backed securities / Louis J. Karcher.
        p.   cm.
    Includes index.
    ISBN 0-13-723685-9
    1. Mortgage-backed securities.   I. Title.
HG4655.K37   1989
332.63'244--dc19   88-38857
                                                                    CIP

This publication is designed to provide accurate and authoritative information in regard to the subject matter covered. It is sold with the understanding that the publisher is not engaged in rendering legal, accounting, or other professional service. If legal advice or other expert assistance is required, the services of a competent professional person should be sought.

From a Declaration of Principles Jointly Adopted by
a Committee of the American Bar Association and a
Committee of Publishers and Associations

Printed in the United States of America
10 9 8 7 6 5 4 3 2 1

New York Institute of Finance
(NYIF Corp.)
70 Pine Street
New York, NY 10270-0003

To my wife, Rosemary, and my boys, Steve and Mike, for their confidence, encouragement, and patience during the long hours spent away from them while writing this book.

Contents

17
Principal and Interest (P&I) Processing

Appendix
PSA Guidelines to Reduce Daylight
Overdraft and Payments System Risk, *306*

Acknowledgments

I want to take this opportunity to acknowledge the efforts of Dennis Paganucci of the MBS Clearing Corporation, Sam Wood of Daiwa Securities America Inc., and Tonya Young of Kidder, Peabody & Co., Inc. Each of them was extremely helpful in contributing to various segments of the book and also spent considerable time editing the final version. I am very grateful to them all. I also want to thank Jim Dennean of Paine Webber Inc. who was my original mentor on Wall Street and who is always available to share his valued knowledge.

Introduction

When this book was first conceived, it was with the thought that it would be used exclusively by the banking and brokerage professionals who are responsible for the systems and operations support in the mortgage-backed securities industry. As writing continued, however, it became obvious that the information the book contained would be useful to a far broader range of interests than originally believed. The book's primary audience remains unchanged, but there are two additional groups who might find this material both interesting and useful.

The material in this book is significant to *the managers and senior executives* of financial organizations because it covers what this group must consider daily: control of the assets of the firm and its customers. The book emphasizes the types of broad control necessary to administer this product successfully. Processing mortgage-backed securities is controllable when the pitfalls are known and the proper measures are taken to prevent them. There are ways to avoid the tremendous losses of receivables that have at times been associated with the product.

And the book is of interest to the layperson—the individual who may have considered buying mortgage-backed securities but who has been hesitant because a simple explanation of the product has not been provided. Now, the information is incorporated into this book in easy-to-understand terms.

Whoever the audience is, however, there is no question that mortgage-backed securities are unique instruments in the following ways:

❑ The way they are originated.

❑ The flexibility of their structure or format.

❑ The fact that they are secured by a variety of assets ranging, for example, from single-family homes to shopping centers.

❑ The manner in which they return both interest and principal to the investor.

❑ The fact that principal and interest payments usually fluctuate.

❑ The fact that they are traded on the basis of a yield-to-an-average-life rather than on a yield-to-maturity or to first-call date.

To the systems and operations professionals who support mortgage-backed securities, what is the natural implication of a product such as this? The knowledge required to support mortgage-backeds must transcend that which is required to support the more traditional equity and debt instruments, and this is the primary reason this book has been published.

The book also is unique in its scope. Many excellent publications are available that deal with mortgage-backed securities. However, they have been written for use by sophisticated investors and by people involved in the trading of mortgage-backeds. This book focuses on the knowledge required by systems and operations professionals oriented to mortgage-backeds. The book explains why and how the mortgage-backed securities market evolved. It defines the products that systems and operations professionals are expected to service. The definition of the products is an especially important topic from the systems analyst's viewpoint because there are many factors that must be understood in order to create a security master file that will adequately meet everyone's requirements.

After addressing the origin of the industry and its products, the book guides you through the back office support operations that, for more than any other product, play a significant role in the overall profitability of the brokers, dealers, and institutional investors who participate in this marketplace.

This market segment is interesting, complex, changing, and growing. It started with the idea of using a basic mortgage loan to collateralize and create a mortgage-backed pool certificate. The market then used the securitized mortgages to collateralize and create new types of bond issues. It then took various types of consumer debt and used it to collateralize and create asset-backed securities. And then . . .

There is no doubt that there will be new products and/or variations of the original themes. There is no doubt that there are and will be tremendous opportunities for the person who takes the time and makes the effort to understand this product. It is my hope that this book will be a valuable tool for all persons actively involved in the support of this segment of the securities industry and also for those persons personally interested in understanding mortgage-backed securities processing.

1

The Origin of the Mortgage-Backed Securities Industry

Early in 1970, a new product was introduced into the securities marketplace. The Government National Mortgage Association (GNMA) issued the first mortgage-backed security (MBS). The necessity and philosophy that led to the development of this product can be easily understood if you compare the needs of an individual to finance a home with those of a corporation to finance its business. So, let's begin by discussing an individual's home financing requirements.

The basic component of a mortgage-backed security is the common mortgage. A mortgage is a loan granted most commonly to an individual by a bank or thrift institution for the purpose of buying a home. The first thing that a prospective homeowner must do is to obtain a contingent loan commitment. Before the mortgagee (the lending or thrift institution) actually consummates the loan, however, the borrower must be able to secure, usually through the services of a lawyer, certain documents. These documents must include a description of the house and property, an acceptable assessed valuation of both, a title search showing any outstanding liens or other limitations (for example, an easement), and an engineer's report attesting to the general physical condition of the structure.

After these preliminaries have been completed, the mortgagee and the homebuyer formalize their agreement at what

is known as a closing. It is at the closing that the loan to the
homebuyer is legally finalized, the title to the property changes
hands, and the property is assigned to the lender as collateral for
the loan, or mortgage.

This is the typical scenario followed when an individual
secures a mortgage. But mortgages are not restricted to individuals or to single-family housing. Mortgages are issued on
all types of property: single-family homes, multifamily homes,
mobile homes, and special projects such as a shopping center. The
type of loan is an indicator of the basic collateral that secures it.
The loan must be repaid within a specified period, which is known
as the *term of the loan*. In return for the loan, the mortgagor (borrower) agrees to compensate the lender for the use of its capital—
that is, the borrowed amount. This compensation is in the form
of interest paid on the outstanding principal amount of the loan.
Normally, mortgage payments are made monthly and usually
consist of a portion of the principal and interest (P&I) on the outstanding principal (amortized) amount of the loan. It is ad-
vantageous to both the borrower and lender if some manner of
insurance is available to back up the basic collateral. So, the key
factors in any mortgage are the following:

❑ Purpose or underlying collateral.
❑ Rate.
❑ Term or maturity.
❑ Insurance.

The most common purposes associated with mortgage loans
have been indicated. Interest rates are fixed or adjustable, and
monthly payments are fixed or variable. The final payment of a
mortgage loan is usually due in 15 or 30 years, although there are
many different maturity terms depending on the type of loan and
on the borrower's individual preference. Qualified individuals
can obtain a favorable rate of interest by insuring their mortgage
through the FHA, the FmHA, or the VA (each a government
agency).

Let's leave the topic of mortgages for a moment and look at
the evolution and ramifications of corporate borrowing. Consider
the standard debt instrument, or bond, that investors buy daily.
It, too, is nothing more than a loan, but it is on a much larger scale.

Debt issuance by a single major corporation can amount to hundreds of millions, even billions, of dollars. What are the consequences of borrowing billions of dollars to operate a business conglomerate versus borrowing $100,000 to purchase a home?

The first and primary consideration for our purpose is the source of this amount of capital. Few single institutions are able to advance the sums of money needed by corporations. More important, none will. The risk is too great. Banking and thrift organizations' policies specifically define limitations as to the amounts of their capital that may be invested (loaned) to either a single entity or to an industry endeavor in general. The banking industry carefully avoids overconcentration in a single field and overcommitment to a single corporate client. This type of concentration would put the lending institution in jeopardy should the corporation or industry fail and become insolvent.

Corporate and industry financial needs are satisfied through the capital markets of the nation and the world. *Capital markets* is a term associated with the accumulated funds (capital) of the investing public, which includes individuals, corporations, and institutions. The marketplace is tapped most frequently through the services of an intermediary known as an investment banker. Corporations seeking to raise capital for their operations will seek the advice of one or more investment bankers. Together they will determine the amount of capital required and determine the best way to obtain it. This capital is frequently raised through the issuance of corporate debt.

Take, for example, the needs of the fictitious A. B. Sea Corporation. The firm requires $250 million to develop and market a new high-tech product. Their investment banker structures an underwriting for the issuance of $250,000,000.00 A. B. Sea Corp. 10.75% fixed-rate bonds due 07-15-2019. Part of the agreement that the investment banker makes with the corporation is to purchase the bonds directly and guarantee payment of the bonds to A. B. Sea. Simultaneously with making this payment to the corporation, the investment banker will sell the bonds that it will have purchased to its own customers and to other investment firms. This is a gross oversimplification of the investment banking function, but it demonstrates what happens. An enormous amount of capital is provided to the A. B. Sea Corporation from the thousands of customers and contacts of the investment banker.

There are two important facts to consider in the foregoing example. First, the ultimate source of A. B. Sea's funding capital is virtually worldwide. Second, because thousands of investors have each supplied a portion of the $250 million, the risk is spread. Each investor's risk is limited to the amount of his or her own investment in the corporation. Through a network of numerous investment banking firms, corporations and other organizations seeking operational funding have access to the trillions of dollars available from the millions of investors who comprise the capital markets.

There is more to the risk question. Risk is a double-edged sword. If a corporation that issues a bond becomes insolvent, there is the possibility that a substantial portion of an investor's funds (loan) will not be recoverable. That's *capital risk*. A second type of risk that is associated with the lending of funds is the risk associated with the inverse relationship that exists between current interest rates and current bond prices, known as *interest rate risk*. Should general economic conditions result in an increase in interest rates after an investor purchases a bond, the market value of that bond will decrease to reflect current market conditions.

Let's use the A. B. Sea Corporation's 10.75% bonds to illustrate what happens. At the time of the offering (underwriting), the interest rate associated with these bonds was a reflection of current rates in the market for similar investments. Economic conditions at the time dictated that debt investments should yield 10.75%, and therefore A. B. Sea's bonds were sold at par, or $1,000 per bond. Each bond carried a 10.75% "coupon." Table 1–1 illustrates the effect of rising interest rates. Investor A buys 10,000 of the original offering at par. As long as that investor owns the A. B. Sea bonds, he or she will receive $1,075 annually in the form of interest income. This is known as the *nominal yield*; the amount received will not change. After 14 months, interest rates have risen to 12%. Investor B purchases A. B. Sea's bonds at this time in the secondary market and expects to receive a yield of 12%. But the bonds carry a 10.75% coupon. Consequently, Investor B will not pay par but, rather, a lower price that will result in a 12% *current yield*. The purchase price that provides the current yield can be approximated by dividing the annual interest (coupon) amount by the current interest rate. However, the result of this calculation is merely a "ballpark" estimation of the current market value. It does not take into consideration the far more complicated mathematics needed to take discounted and premium prices into consideration in the computation of an overall yield to maturity.

TABLE 1–1. The Inverse Relationship Between Interest Rates and Bond Prices

Investors A and B each purchase 10,000 A. B. Sea 10.75% 7/15/19.

Investor A buys at par; Investor B buys 14 months later at 895.834/bond.

Purchased	Price	Gross Cost	Annual Income	Nominal Yield	Current Yield
A 10,000	1.0000	10,000.00	$1,075.00	10.75%	10.75%
B 10,000	.895834	8,958.34	$1,075.00	10.75%	12.00%

Pricing: Annual coupon per bond / current rate / 1,000 = aproximate price
$107.50 / 0.12 / 1,000 = .895834 of par

Proof: Invested amount × current interest rate = annual income
$8,958.34 × 0.12 = $1,075.00

RISK AND THE SECURITIZATION OF MORTGAGES

If you consider the two risk factors associated with debt investments, you will begin to realize why the needs of the traditional mortgagees and the resources of the capital markets complement each other. The needs are twofold.

First, there was a need on the part of the traditional originators of mortgage loans to download the risks of both capital risk and interest rate risk. Remember that in the late 1960s mortgages were exclusively long-term, fixed-rate loans, and interest rates were beginning to rise. With money becoming more expensive to obtain and with large amounts of low-rate mortgages outstanding, the banking industry would soon be in serious trouble.

At about the same time that interest rates began their precipitous climb, there was an urgent need to expand the source of capital available to potential mortgagees. This is best explained using the following scenario. Envision an economic boom in a particular geographic area. Associated with this economic expansion is an influx of people. A sudden and strong demand for local capital develops; funds are needed for the corporate enterprises associated with the economic prosperity and for mortgages for housing. An inbalance has been created between regional capital supply and demand. It becomes necessary to develop an alternative or supplemental method to finance housing and building developments in order to keep the economy in its forward momentum. The alternative method must accomplish the following:

- ❑ Provide constant availability of enormous amounts of capital.
- ❑ Limit, or download, the risks associated with interest rate fluctuations.
- ❑ Limit capital exposure risks.

The solution to each of these situations is to use the investment capital of institutions and individuals. Ample capital is available, and investment by the public spreads both the capital and interest rate risks through a broad range. But how do you get an individual investor or institution involved in financing a mortgage? Would you, as an individual, finance a stranger's home? Of course, the answer is "No!" Aside from the fact that you probably do not have sufficient excess capital to finance a $100,000.00 mortgage, you would have serious concerns about a default on the part of the mortgagor and about collecting your payments on time. But if you financed only a portion of someone's mortgage and if you were guaranteed timely monthly payments and repayment in full at the maturity of the mortgage, then would you finance a stranger's home at current mortgage rates? The answer now becomes an emphatic "Yes!"

THE MORTGAGE SECURITIZATION PROCESS

Companies, national governments, and municipalities have been financing their operations for centuries through the capital markets. Evidence of such loans has always been the bond certificate, which is a debt security. Today, there are many agencies and issuers actively engaged in the creation, marketing, and sale of mortgage-backed securities (MBS). Historically, the Government National Mortgage Association (GNMA) was the first entity to create debt securities collateralized by individual mortgages. The GNMA is a federal agency that was created by congress in 1968 for the purpose of expanding the amount of capital available to the housing market.

In general, public investments are evidenced by securities; GNMA became the first agency to securitize mortgages. This was accomplished by consolidating (pooling) a group of mortgages and submitting the mortgage documents to GNMA for review. The mortgages submitted had to be government guaranteed (insured), have an aggregate value of at least $1 million, be of the same type and maturity range, be less than 12 months old, and have the same interest rate. After reviewing and approving the documents associated with each mortgage loan, GNMA authorized its transfer agent, Chemical Bank, to issue a certificate representing that particular pool of mortgages. Every pool of mortgages has a unique number, separate and apart from the certificate number. GNMA guarantees to the registered holders of the GNMA certificates timely payment of all interest and principal due on the pooled mortgages. It receives its fee for this guarantee, and the issuer (the banker that originated the underlying mortgage loans) is responsible for the marketing and servicing of the new security.

This is the foundation of the MBS market. Let's recap the steps that go into the creation of a mortgage-backed security. The following five steps will assist you in conceptualizing the general mortgage securitization process:

❑ A number of similar mortgages (those with rates, maturities, and underlying collateral that are the same or similar) are combined into a single group. The cumulative outstanding principal amounts of the mortgages become the principal or face amount of the group.

❑ The documents associated with the group are put in trust and assigned an identification (*pool or group*) number.

❑ An MBS certificate (a debt security) is issued with a face amount equal to the combined principal value of the mortgages in the pool. The mortgages that have been bundled together, so to speak, serve as the underlying collateral for the debt security. Thus the name, *mortgage-backed security*.

❑ The MBS certificate is sold to investors. Each investor is entitled to a *participation* in the cash flow associated with the underlying mortgages to the extent of the percentage of the original certificate that he or she purchases. The usual minimum investment is $25,000.00 which can be increased in increments of $5,000.00. Each certificate is imprinted with the identification number of the group of mortgages collateralizing the issue, and each certificate has its own unique certificate number.

❑ Monthly payments of principal and interest are made by the individual mortgagees to the original mortgagors. These payments are *passed through* to the holders of the MBS certificates and prorated according to the holders' percentage of ownership in the entire pool. The amount of the interest that passed through is reduced by a nominal fee that is split between the bank that services the MBS and the agency that guarantees, or issues, the MBS. The total amount withheld as fee income is usually 0.5%.

The italicized words are terms you will constantly hear in discussion about MBS. There are many different MBS programs and issuers, and each has its own unique characteristics that are discussed in the following chapters. Therefore, it is important to understand that some of the information in the foregoing five steps may not always apply. Also be aware that the entire securities industry is trying to eliminate physical certificates. This subject is discussed later in the book. At this point, it is enough to say that *physical* mortgage-backed security certificates, for the most part, will soon no longer be issued to the public. Evidence of ownership will be accomplished by what is known as *book entry*, or journal entry, as opposed to the old physical, or definitive, form.

2

The Distribution Cycle of Mortgage-Backed Securities

You now understand the philosophy behind pooling groups of mortgages and using that pool as collateral for the debt instrument known as a mortgage-backed security. How do the securities so created find their way into the securities markets?

Again, be alert to the numerous variations of the cycle about to be discussed. Regardless of the method used to create a particular MBS, the concept remains unchanged. Three principal entities are involved in the issuance and sale of mortgage-backed securities:

1. Mortgage bankers.
2. Guarantors (issuers) of the securities.
3. MBS dealers who market and sell the securities.

Let's examine the functions of mortgage bankers, which are the lending institutions that specialize in supplying mortgage loans to the public. After issuing these mortgage loans, they then indirectly sell them to investors in security form, using a cycle of events and interrelationships that are the topic of this chapter. Remember that they are bankers. As such, they have the same concerns and risks associated with all lending institutions: the source of their working capital and its profitable utilization.

The source of capital in the mortgage banking industry (MBI) differs from that of commercial banks, which to a great extent use the demand deposits of their customers. The MBI borrows most of its funds from the commercial banking industry. A typical mortgage banker has an extensive line of credit with a number of banks known in the mortgage industry as *warehouse banks*. These warehouse banks lend funds to the mortgage bank, which in turn lends the funds to homebuyers. Both the mortgage banker and the warehouse bank are earning income because the interest rates escalate throughout this lending chain as shown in Table 2–1.

TABLE 2–1.

Income/Expense	Warehouse Bank	Mortgage Banker
Cost of Funds	5.75% (rate paid on demand deposits) [a]	8.00% (rate paid to warehouse bank)
Income	8.00% (rate charged on loan to mortgage bank)	10.00% (rate charged to mortgagors)
Profit (spread)	2.25% (income on loan)	2.00% (income on mortgage)

[a] Indicated percentages are theoretical for illustrative purposes only; actual rates and spreads may be higher or lower.

If the mortgage banker's only source of cash were the funds borrowed, it would soon exhaust its credit line at its warehouse bank. That would limit its profit potential to the spread it could achieve on a capital base equivalent to its credit line. This impediment is removed by creating cash flow, which is accomplished by converting outstanding mortgage loans into securities for sale to the public. The need for this cash flow is the essence of the market for mortgage-backed securities.

The steps in the cash flow and distribution cycle are as follows:

❑   The mortgage banker borrows large amounts of cash from its warehouse bank(s) to satisfy the borrowing demands of its customers.

❑ Potential homebuyers obtain a mortgage loan from the mortgage banker.

❑ After writing a number of loans, the mortgage banker pools similar loans. It requests one of the major MBS issuing agencies to create a mortgage-backed security, collateralized by the mortgage loans.

❑ Simultaneously, the mortgage banker contacts various MBS dealers and obtains a standby commitment from an MBS dealer to purchase the soon-to-be-issued securities.

❑ The issuing agency completes its review of the submitted mortgage loans. It assigns a pool, or group, number. If necessary, it instructs its transfer agent to register a physical certificate according to the instructions of the mortgage banker.

❑ The mortgage banker executes the standby agreement by selling the new MBS to the dealer with whom the agreement was written.

❑ The mortgage banker delivers the MBS to the dealer, who pays the contracted amount of the purchase to the mortgage banker.

❑ The mortgage banker uses this cash to repay its outstanding loan(s) with the warehouse bank(s). This payment has the effect of replenishing the mortgage banker's line of credit to an amount equal to the payment. The mortgage banker can now make additional loans, and the cycle is repeated.

❑ The dealer sells the new MBS to its customer base, who become the ultimate owners of the securitized mortgages. These sales are the source of the funds that flow back through this cycle.

❑ The investors receive a monthly pass-through of the principal and interest (P&I) payments made by the mortgagors to the mortgage banker who originated and continues to service the individual mortgage loans.

This cycle is graphically depicted in Figure 2–1. This cycle satisfied a 1968 congressional mandate and has resulted in a multi-trillion-dollar industry. Through this cycle, individual homebuyers are linked to individual investors, and an endless

FIGURE 2–1. The Cash Flow and Distribution Cycle of the Mortgage-Backed Securities Industry

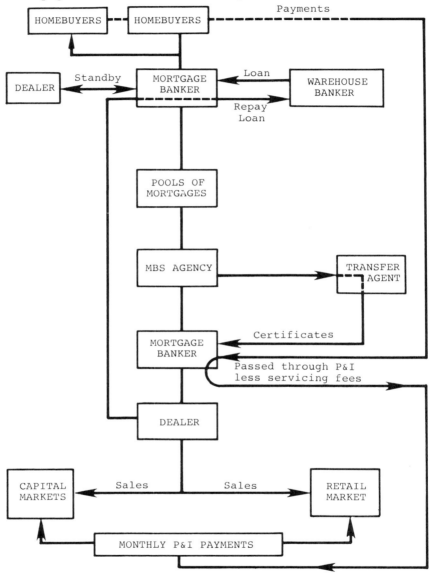

chain of loans, mortgages, investments, loan repayments, and more mortgages is realized. Although this means that most mortgages are now being financed by the investing public, the entire process is invisible to the homeowner. At no time are you, as a homeowner, aware that your mortgage may have been pooled with other mortgages and is now part of the underlying collateral for an MBS. To you, it remains unchanged, and you will continue to make your payments directly to your friendly neighborhood banker as though the entire process did not exist.

3

Guarantors and Issuers of Mortgage-Backed Securities

The guarantors and issuers are the MBS agencies through whom the mortgage banker converts its whole loans, or individual mortgage loans, into an MBS. As is obvious from the title of this chapter, these agencies can play a dual role. As guarantors, they provide the investor with an additional level of security by guaranteeing the performance of the mortgage banker who originated the request for an MBS. As issuers, they may buy whole loans for their own portfolio, or they may originate mortgage loans. In either case these mortgages, which are part of the portfolio of the agency, serve as the collateral for the MBS of an agency when acting as a direct issuer. Under these circumstances, the guarantor status is implied. The major agencies involved in the creation of MBS are:

❑ The Federal Home Loan Mortgage Corporation (FHLMC or Freddie Mac).
❑ The Federal National Mortgage Association (FNMA or Fannie Mae).
❑ The Government National Mortgage Association (GNMA or Ginnie Mae).

Mortgages are the common denominator whether you talk about Ginnie Mae (GNMA), Fannie Mae (FNMA), Freddie Mac (FHLMC), or a private issuer of mortgage-backed securities. However, it will be useful to briefly discuss the main differences between these "issuers" through the use of the following matrix.

	GNMA	*FHLMC*	*FNMA*	*Private Issuer*
Ownership	Govt. agency	Federal Home Loan Banks	Publicly owned	Self-owned
Packager	Approved mortgagees	Freddie Mac	Fannie Mae	Banks and real estate dealers
Mtg Gty	FHA, FmHA, VA	Conventional FHA, VA	Conventional FHA, VA	Conventional
MBS Gty	U.S. Govt.	Freddie Mac	Fannie Mae	Per terms of pool insurance
P&I Gty	F&T, [a] P&I	F&T Interest Prin gtd in yr	F&T, P&I	F&T Interest Prin eventual [b]
Issues	Pass-throughs	PCs, CMOs	MBS	Various

[a] F&T: full and timely.
[b] Payment will be made up to amount recoverable by insurance.
Note: Issues listed are primary products; listing is not all inclusive.

In addition to the basic differences between the issuers, another point of consideration is the primary differences between the various programs offered by the issuers. Page 36 provides a clear illustration of the variety of programs offered by FHLMC. Each has certain advantages that appeal to a particular investment segment. Some considerations include the paydown stability offered by the geographic diversity of the mortgages underlying programs such as the GNMA II Jumbo Pool program and FHLMC's Giants and certain Cash programs. Some investors will be interested in programs which will fully pay down in 12 years, others might want a seven-year paydown, and others yet a shorter paydown period. Therefore, 30-year MBS, 15-year MBS, and "A" Tranche CMOs and REMICs would be appropriate. Still some may be looking to obtain a fixed rate of income while others want adjustable rate instruments. Each program has been designed to fill a particular niche in the marketplace. The following pages attempt to identify the differences in the major programs. Although much of the information is the same from one program to the next, it has been repeated for your referencing convenience. The information that is unique to a specific program has been set in **boldface**.

Contents:

GOVERNMENT NATIONAL MORTGAGE ASSOCIATION (GNMA)

PRODUCT: GNMA ADJUSTABLE RATE MORTGAGES (ARMs)

ISSUER: FHA approved mortgage lender (e.g., commercial bank). **Single issuer.**

GUARANTOR: Government National Mortgage Association *(GNMA).*

INTEREST RATE: **Rates can vary monthly depending on the market.**

ISSUE DATE: First day of month (e.g., 10/1/1987).

DAYS TO FIRST PAYMENT: **45-day delay.**

PAYABLE DATE: **Fifteenth** of the month (e.g., 11/15/1987).

PAYMENT FREQUENCY: Monthly.

PAYMENT AGENT: Individual issuers send checks to investors.

RECORD DATE: Last business day of the month.

MATURITY: **30 years** (e.g., 10/15/2017).

PREPAID LIFE: **12 years** (e.g., 10/15/1999).

CREDIT RISK: None. Government guaranteed.

LIQUIDITY: **Fair secondary market.**

MINIMUM PURCHASE: $25,000.

DENOMINATION: Increments of $5,000.

QUOTED: In increments of 1/32 of 1% of par.

ROUND LOT: $1 million.

MODE OF ISSUANCE: Physical and wireable:

Physical = > 7.50 < 12.49 $\left.\right\}$ as of 1/89
Wireable = < 7.49 > 12.50

LAST CERTIFICATE ISSUED: Still issued.

CERTIFICATE AVAILABILITY: Still available in physical range. Available in wireable range if requested.

FACTOR PUBLICATION DATES: **Twice monthly**—6th and 12th of the month.

SOURCES OF FACTOR INFORMATION: Tape, diskette, or hardcopy by *The Bond Buyer.*

SPECIAL ASSIGNMENT RESTRICTIONS: Cannot split a tail for a face quantity of less than $5,000.

METHOD(S) OF CLEARANCE: Wireable and physical.

CLEARANCE SIZE: $50 million maximum per piece.

TRF AGENT: Chemical Bank.

TRF FEE: Normal—$10 per certificate.

Rush (24 hours)—$20 per certificate + $5 per pool.

PRODUCT: GNMA I, 15 YEAR

ISSUER: FHA approved mortgage lender (e.g., commercial bank). **Single issuer.**
GUARANTOR: Government National Mortgage Association (GNMA).
INTEREST RATE: **Mortgages must have the same rate.**
ISSUE DATE: First day of month (e.g., 10/1/1987).
DAYS TO FIRST PAYMENT: 45-day delay.
PAYABLE DATE: **Fifteenth** of the month (e.g., 11/15/1987).
PAYMENT FREQUENCY: Monthly.
PAYMENT AGENT: Individual issuers send checks to investors.
RECORD DATE: Last business day of the month.
MATURITY: **15 years** (e.g., 10/15/2002).
PREPAID LIFE: **7 years** (e.g., 10/15/1994).
CREDIT RISK: None. Government guaranteed.
LIQUIDITY: **Good secondary market.**
MINIMUM PURCHASE: $25,000.
DENOMINATION: Increments of $5,000.
QUOTED: In increments of 1/32 of 1% of par.
ROUND LOT: $1 million.
MODE OF ISSUANCE: Physical and wireable:
Physical = > 7.50 < 12.49
Wireable = < 7.49 > 12.50 } as of 1/89
LAST CERTIFICATE ISSUED: Still issued.
CERTIFICATE AVAILABILITY: Still available in physical range. Available in wireable range if requested.
FACTOR PUBLICATION DATES: **Thrice monthly**—6th, 12th, and **19th** of the month. Included on GNMA I tape.
SOURCES OF FACTOR INFORMATION: Tape, diskette, or hardcopy by *The Bond Buyer.*
SPECIAL ASSIGNMENT RESTRICTIONS: Cannot split a tail for a face quantity of less than $5,000 **on a physical security.**
METHOD(S) OF CLEARANCE: Wireable and physical.
CLEARANCE SIZE: $50 million maximum per piece **for wireables.**
TRF AGENT: Chemical Bank.
TRF FEE: Normal—$10 per certificate.
Rush (24 Hours)—$20 per certificate + $5 per pool.

PRODUCT: GNMA I, 30 YEAR

ISSUER: FHA approved mortgage lender (e.g., commercial bank).
Single issuer.
GUARANTOR: Government National Mortgage Association (GNMA).
INTEREST RATE: **Mortgages must have the same rate.**
ISSUE DATE: First day of month (e.g., 10/1/1987).
DAYS TO FIRST PAYMENT: **45-day delay.**
PAYABLE DATE: **Fifteenth** of the month (e.g., 11/15/1987).
PAYMENT FREQUENCY: Monthly.
PAYMENT AGENT: Individual issuers send checks to investors.
RECORD DATE: Last business day of the month.
MATURITY: **30 years** (e.g., 10/15/2017).
PREPAID LIFE: **12 years** (e.g., 10/15/1999).
CREDIT RISK: None. Government guaranteed.
LIQUIDITY: **Good secondary market.**
MINIMUM PURCHASE: $25,000.
DENOMINATION: Increments of $5,000.
QUOTED: In increments of 1/32 of 1% of par.
ROUND LOT: $1 million.
MODE OF ISSUANCE: Physical and wireable:
Physical = > 7.50 < 12.49 ⎫ **as of 1/89**
Wireable = < 7.49 > 12.50 ⎭
LAST CERTIFICATE ISSUED: Still issued.
CERTIFICATE AVAILABILITY: Still available in physical range. Available in wireable range if requested.
FACTOR PUBLICATION DATES: **Thrice monthly**—6th, 12th, and **19th** of the month.
SOURCES OF FACTOR INFORMATION: Tape, diskette, or hardcopy by *The Bond Buyer.*
SPECIAL ASSIGNMENT RESTRICTIONS: Cannot split a tail for a face quantity of less than $5,000 **on a physical security.**
METHOD(S) OF CLEARANCE: Wireable and physical.
CLEARANCE SIZE: $50 million maximum per piece **for wireables.**
TRF AGENT: Chemical Bank.
TRF FEE: Normal—$10 per certificate.
Rush (24 Hours)—$20 per certificate + $5 per pool.

PRODUCT: GNMA BUILDER BUYDOWN

ISSUER: FHA approved mortgage lender (e.g., commercial bank). **Single Issuer. Secured by mortgages where funds have been provided to reduce borrowers' monthly payments in the first years.**
GUARANTOR: Government National Mortgage Association (GNMA).
INTEREST RATE: **Mortgages must have the same rate.**
ISSUE DATE: First day of month (e.g., 10/1/1987).
DAYS TO FIRST PAYMENT: **45-day delay.**
PAYABLE DATE: **Fifteenth** of the month (e.g., 11/15/1987).
PAYMENT FREQUENCY: Monthly.
PAYMENT AGENT: Individual issuers send checks to investors.
RECORD DATE: Last business day of the month.
MATURITY: **Up to 20 years** (e.g., 10/05/2017).
PREPAID LIFE: **12 years** (e.g., 10/15/1999).
CREDIT RISK: None. Government guaranteed.
LIQUIDITY: **No secondary market.**
MINIMUM PURCHASE: $25,000.
DENOMINATION: Increments of $5,000.
QUOTED: In increments of 1/32 of 1% of par.
ROUND LOT: $1 million.
MODE OF ISSUANCE: Physical and wireable:
Physical = > 7.50 < 12.49 ⎫
Wireable = < 7.49 > 12.50 ⎭ as of 1/89
LAST CERTIFICATE ISSUED: Still issued.
CERTIFICATE AVAILABILITY: Still available in physical range. Available in wireable range if requested.
FACTOR PUBLICATION DATES: **Twice monthly**—6th and 12th of the month. Included on GNMA I tape.
SOURCES OF FACTOR INFORMATION: Tape, diskette, or hardcopy by *The Bond Buyer.*
SPECIAL ASSIGNMENT RESTRICTIONS: Cannot split a tail for a face quantity of less than $5,000 **on a physical security.**
METHOD(S) OF CLEARANCE: Wireable and physical.
CLEARANCE SIZE: $50 million maximum per piece **for wireables.**
TRF AGENT: Chemical Bank.
TRF FEE: Normal—$10 per certificate.
Rush (24 Hours)—$20 per certificate + $5 per pool.

PRODUCT: GNMA CONSTRUCTION LOAN (CL)

ISSUER: FHA approved mortgage lender (e.g., commercial bank). **Secured by one mortgage representing a single loan on a project under construction. Provides for conversion to a Project Loan at maturity.**

GUARANTOR: Government National Mortgage Association (GNMA).

INTEREST RATE: **Mortgages must have the same rate.**

ISSUE DATE: First day of month (e.g., 10/1/1987).

DAYS TO FIRST PAYMENT: **45-day delay.**

PAYABLE DATE: **Fifteenth** of the month (e.g., 11/15/1987).

PAYMENT FREQUENCY: Monthly.

PAYMENT AGENT: Individual issuers send checks to investors.

RECORD DATE: Last business day of the month.

MATURITY: **150% of length of construction period.** Usually matures upon and is redeemed by issuance of a Project Loan.

PREPAID LIFE: **75% of length of construction period.**

CREDIT RISK: None. Government guaranteed.

LIQUIDITY: **No secondary market.**

MINIMUM PURCHASE: $25,000.

DENOMINATION: Increments of $5,000.

QUOTED: In increments of 1/32 of 1% of par.

ROUND LOT: $1 million.

MODE OF ISSUANCE: Physical and wireable:
Physical = > 7.50 < 12.49 } as of 1/89
Wireable = < 7.49 > 12.50

LAST CERTIFICATE ISSUED: Still issued.

CERTIFICATE AVAILABILITY: Still available in physical range. Available in wireable range if requested.

FACTOR PUBLICATION DATES: **Twice monthly**—6th and 12th of the month.

SOURCES OF FACTOR INFORMATION: Tape, diskette, or hardcopy by *The Bond Buyer.*

SPECIAL ASSIGNMENT RESTRICTIONS: Cannot split a tail for a face quantity of less than $5,000.

METHOD(S) OF CLEARANCE: Wireable and physical.

CLEARANCE SIZE: $50 million maximum per piece.

TRF AGENT: Chemical Bank.

TRF FEE: Normal—$10 per certificate.
Rush (24 Hours)—$20 per certificate + $5 per pool.

PRODUCT: GNMA GPM II, CUSTOM

ISSUER: FHA approved mortgage lender (e.g., commercial bank). **Single issuers. Constructed of pools from specific geographic areas. Payments increase annually for either 5 or 10 years.**
GUARANTOR: Government National Mortgage Association (GNMA).
INTEREST RATE: **Rates may vary within 1% range.**
ISSUE DATE: First day of the month (e.g., 10/1/1987).
DAYS TO FIRST PAYMENT: **50-day delay.**
PAYABLE DATE: **Twentieth** of the month (e.g., 11/20/1987).
PAYMENT FREQUENCY: Monthly.
PAYMENT AGENT: **Issuers send checks to Chemical Bank,** which pays the investor one combined check for all outstanding issues owned.
RECORD DATE: Last business day of the month.
MATURITY: **30 years** (e.g., 10/15/2017).
PREPAID LIFE: **12 years** (e.g., 10/15/1999).
CREDIT RISK: None. Government guaranteed.
LIQUIDITY: **Fair secondary market.**
MINIMUM PURCHASE: $25,000.
DENOMINATION: Increments of $5,000.
QUOTED: In increments of 1/32 of 1% of par.
ROUND LOT: $1 million.
MODE OF ISSUANCE: Physical and wireable:
Physical = > 7.50 < 12.49 ⎫ as of 1/89
Wireable = < 7.49 > 12.50 ⎭
LAST CERTIFICATE ISSUED: Still issued.
CERTIFICATE AVAILABILITY: Still available in physical range. Available in wireable range if requested.
FACTOR PUBLICATION DATES: **Twice monthly**—6th and 12th of the month. Included on GNMA II tape.
SOURCES OF FACTOR INFORMATION: Tape, diskette, or hardcopy by *The Bond Buyer.*
SPECIAL ASSIGNMENT RESTRICTIONS: Cannot split a tail for a face quantity of less than $5,000 **on a physical security.**
METHOD(S) OF CLEARANCE: Wireable and physical.
CLEARANCE SIZE: $50 million maximum per piece **for wireables.**
TRF AGENT: Chemical Bank.
TRF FEE: Normal—$10 per certificate.
Rush (24 Hours)—$20 per certificate + $5 per pool.

PRODUCT: GNMA II, CUSTOM 30 YEAR

ISSUER: FHA approved mortgage lender (e.g., commercial bank). **Single issuers. Constructed of pools from specific geographic areas.**
GUARANTOR: Government National Mortgage Association (GNMA).
POOL ASSIGNED RANGE: **0001 to 1800.**
INTEREST RATE: **Rates may vary within 1% range.**
ISSUE DATE: First day of month (e.g., 10/1/1987).
DAYS TO FIRST PAYMENT: **50-day delay.**
PAYABLE DATE: **Twentieth** of the month (e.g., 11/20/1987).
PAYMENT FREQUENCY: Monthly.
PAYMENT AGENT: **Issuers send checks to Chemical Bank,** which pays the investor one combined check for all outstanding issues owned.
RECORD DATE: Last business day of the month.
MATURITY: **30 years** (e.g., 10/15/2017).
PREPAID LIFE: **12 years** (e.g., 10/15/1999).
CREDIT RISK: None. Government guaranteed.
LIQUIDITY: **Fair secondary market.**
MINIMUM PURCHASE: $25,000.
DENOMINATION: Increments of $5,000.
QUOTED: In increments of 1/32 of 1% of par.
ROUND LOT: $1 million.
MODE OF ISSUANCE: Physical and wireable:
Physical = > 7.50 < 12.49 ⎫
Wireable = < 7.49 > 12.50 ⎭ as of 1/89
LAST CERTIFICATE ISSUED: Still issued.
CERTIFICATE AVAILABILITY: Still available in physical range. Available in wireable range if requested.
FACTOR PUBLICATION DATES: **Twice monthly**—6th and 12th of the month.
SOURCES OF FACTOR INFORMATION: Tape, diskette, or hardcopy by *The Bond Buyer.*
SPECIAL ASSIGNMENT RESTRICTIONS: Cannot split a tail for a face quantity of less than $5,000 **on a physical security.**
METHOD(S) OF CLEARANCE: Wireable and physical.
CLEARANCE SIZE: $50 million maximum per piece **for wireables.**
TRF AGENT: Chemical Bank.
TRF FEE: Normal—$10 per certificate.
Rush (24 Hours)—$20 per certificate + $5 per pool.

PRODUCT: GNMA GROWTH EQUITY MORTGAGES (GEMs)

ISSUER: FHA approved mortgage lender (e.g., commercial bank). **Single issuer. Secured by single-family mortgages with annual increases in monthly payments of either 4% per year over the life of the loan or any rate per year for any number of years.**

GUARANTOR: Government National Mortgage Association (GNMA).

INTEREST RATE: **Mortgages must have the same rate.**

ISSUE DATE: First day of month (e.g., 10/1/1987).

DAYS TO FIRST PAYMENT: **45-day delay.**

PAYABLE DATE: **Fifteenth** of the month (e.g., 11/15/1987).

PAYMENT FREQUENCY: Monthly.

PAYMENT AGENT: Individual issuers send checks to investors.

RECORD DATE: Last business day of the month.

MATURITY: **30 years** (e.g., 10/15/2017).

PREPAID LIFE: **12 years** (e.g., 10/15/1999).

CREDIT RISK: None. Government guaranteed.

LIQUIDITY: **Poor secondary market.**

MINIMUM PURCHASE: $25,000.

DENOMINATION: Increments of $5,000.

QUOTED: In increments of 1/32 of 1% of par.

ROUND LOT: $1 million.

MODE OF ISSUANCE: Physical and wireable:
Physical = > 7.50 < 12.49 ⎫ as of 1/89
Wireable = < 7.49 > 12.50 ⎭

LAST CERTIFICATE ISSUED: Still issued.

CERTIFICATE AVAILABILITY: Still available in physical range. Available in wireable range if requested.

FACTOR PUBLICATION DATES: Twice monthly—6th and 12th of the month.

SOURCES OF FACTOR INFORMATION: Tape, diskette, or hardcopy by *The Bond Buyer.*

SPECIAL ASSIGNMENT RESTRICTIONS: Cannot split a tail for a face quantity of less than $5,000 *on a physical security.*

METHOD(S) OF CLEARANCE: Wireable and physical.

CLEARANCE SIZE: $50 million maximum per piece **for wireables.**

TRF AGENT: Chemical Bank.

TRF FEE: Normal—$10 per certificate.
Rush (24 Hours)—$20 per certificate + $5 per pool.

PRODUCT: GNMA (GPM)

ISSUER: FHA approved mortgage lender (e.g., commercial bank). **Single issuer. Secured by mortgage on which monthly payments increase annually for either 5 years (GP program) or 10 years (GT program).**
GUARANTOR: Government National Mortgage Association (GNMA).
INTEREST RATE: **Mortgages must have the same rate.**
ISSUE DATE: First day of month (e.g., 10/1/1987).
DAYS TO FIRST PAYMENT: **45-day delay.**
PAYABLE DATE: **Fifteenth** of the month (e.g., 11/15/1987).
PAYMENT FREQUENCY: Monthly.
PAYMENT AGENT: Individual issuers send checks to investors.
RECORD DATE: Last business day of the month.
MATURITY: **30 years** (e.g., 10/15/2017).
PREPAID LIFE: **12 years** (e.g., 10/15/1999).
CREDIT RISK: None. Government guaranteed.
LIQUIDITY: **Fair secondary market.**
MINIMUM PURCHASE: $25,000.
DENOMINATION: Increments of $5,000.
QUOTED: In increments of 1/32 of 1% of par.
ROUND LOT: $1 million.
MODE OF ISSUANCE: Physical and wireable:
Physical = > 7.50 < 12.49 $\left.\right\}$ as of 1/89
Wireable = < 7.49 > 12.50
LAST CERTIFICATE ISSUED: Still issued.
CERTIFICATE AVAILABILITY: Still available in physical range. Available in wireable range if requested.
FACTOR PUBLICATION DATES: **Thrice monthly**—6th, 12th, and 19th of the month. Included on GNMA I tape.
SOURCES OF FACTOR INFORMATION: Tape, diskette, or hardcopy by *The Bond Buyer.*
SPECIAL ASSIGNMENT RESTRICTIONS: Cannot split a tail for a face quantity of less than $5,000 **on a physical security.**
METHOD(S) OF CLEARANCE: Wireable and physical.
CLEARANCE SIZE: 50 million maximum per piece **for wireables.**
TRF AGENT: Chemical Bank.
TRF FEE: Normal—$10 per certificate.
Rush (24 Hours)—$20 per certificate + $5 per pool.

PRODUCT: GNMA GPM II, JUMBO

ISSUER: FHA approved mortgage lender (e.g., commercial bank). **Multiple issuers. Constructed of large pools that provide investors with geographic diversity. Monthly payments increase annually for either 5 or 10 years.**

GUARANTOR: Government National Mortgage Association (GNMA).

INTEREST RATE: **Rates may vary within 1% range.**

ISSUE DATE: First day of month (e.g., 10/1/1987).

DAYS TO FIRST PAYMENT: **50-day delay.**

PAYABLE DATE: **Twentieth** of the month (e.g., 11/20/1987).

PAYMENT FREQUENCY: Monthly.

PAYMENT AGENT: **Issuers send checks to Chemical Bank,** which pays the investor one combined check for all outstanding issues owned.

RECORD DATE: Last business day of the month.

MATURITY: **30 years** (e.g., 10/15/2017).

PREPAID LIFE: **12 years** (e.g., 10/15/1999).

CREDIT RISK: None. Government guaranteed.

LIQUIDITY: **Fair secondary market.**

MINIMUM PURCHASE: $25,000.

DENOMINATION: Increments of $5,000.

QUOTED: In increments of 1/32 of 1% of par.

ROUND LOT: $1 million.

MODE OF ISSUANCE: Physical and wireable:
Physical = > 7.50 < 12.49 $\left.\right\}$ as of 1/89
Wireable = < 7.49 > 12.50

LAST CERTIFICATE ISSUED: Still issued.

CERTIFICATE AVAILABILITY: Still available in physical range. Available in wireable range if requested.

FACTOR PUBLICATION DATES: **Twice monthly**—6th and 12th of the month. Included on GNMA II tape.

SOURCES OF FACTOR INFORMATION: Tape, diskette, or hardcopy by *The Bond Buyer.*

SPECIAL ASSIGNMENT RESTRICTIONS: Cannot split a tail for a face quantity of less than $5,000 **on a physical security.**

METHOD(S) OF CLEARANCE: Wireable and physical.

CLEARANCE SIZE: $50 million maximum per piece **for wireables.**

TRF AGENT: Chemical Bank.

TRF FEE: Normal—$10 per certificate.
Rush (24 Hours)—$20 per certificate + $5 per pool.

PRODUCT: GNMA II JUMBO, 15 YEAR

ISSUER: FHA approved mortgage lender (e.g., commercial bank). **Multiple issuers. Constructed of large pools that provide geographic diversity.**

GUARANTOR: Government National Mortgage Association (GNMA).

INTEREST RATE: **Rates may vary within 1% range.**

ISSUE DATE: First day of month (e.g., 10/1/1987).

DAYS TO FIRST PAYMENT: **50-day delay.**

PAYABLE DATE: **Twentieth** of the month (e.g., 11/20/1987).

PAYMENT FREQUENCY: Monthly.

PAYMENT AGENT: Individual issuers send checks to investors.

RECORD DATE: Last business day of the month.

MATURITY: **15 years** (e.g., 10/15/2002).

PREPAID LIFE: **7 years** (e.g., 10/15/1994).

CREDIT RISK: None. Government guaranteed.

LIQUIDITY: **Fair secondary market.**

MINIMUM PURCHASE: $25,000.

DENOMINATION: Increments of $5,000.

QUOTED: In increments of 1/32 of 1% of par.

ROUND LOT: $1 million.

MODE OF ISSUANCE: Physical and wireable:
Physical = > 7.50 < 12.49 ⎫
Wireable = < 7.49 > 12.50 ⎬ as of 1/89

LAST CERTIFICATE ISSUED: Still issued.

CERTIFICATE AVAILABILITY: Still available in physical range. Available in wireable range if requested.

FACTOR PUBLICATION DATES: Twice monthly—6th and 12th of the month. Included on the GNMA II tape.

SOURCES OF FACTOR INFORMATION: Tape, diskette, or hardcopy by *The Bond Buyer*.

SPECIAL ASSIGNMENT RESTRICTIONS: Cannot split a tail for a face quantity of less than $5,000 **on a physical security.**

METHOD(S) OF CLEARANCE: Wireable and physical.

CLEARANCE SIZE: $50 million maximum per piece **for wireables.**

TRF AGENT: Chemical Bank.

TRF FEE: Normal—$10 per certificate.
Rush (24 Hours)—$20 per certificate + $5 per pool.

PRODUCT: GNMA II JUMBO, 30 YEAR

ISSUER: FHA approved mortgage lender (e.g., commercial bank). **Multiple issuers.** Constructed of large pools that provide investors with geographic diversity.

GUARANTOR: Government National Mortgage Association (GNMA).

INTEREST RATE: **Rates may vary within 1% range.**

ISSUE DATE: First day of month (e.g., 10/1/1987).

DAYS TO FIRST PAYMENT: 50-day delay.

PAYABLE DATE: **Twentieth** of the month (e.g., 11/20/1987).

PAYMENT FREQUENCY: Monthly.

PAYMENT AGENT: **Issuers send checks to Chemical Bank,** which pays the investor one combined check for all outstanding issues owned.

RECORD DATE: Last business day of the month.

MATURITY: **30 years** (e.g., 10/15/2017).

PREPAID LIFE: **12 years** (e.g., 10/15/1999).

CREDIT RISK: None. Government guaranteed.

LIQUIDITY: **Fair secondary market.**

MINIMUM PURCHASE: $25,000.

DENOMINATION: Increments of $5,000.

QUOTED: In increments of 1/32 of 1% of par.

ROUND LOT: $1 million.

MODE OF ISSUANCE: Physical and wireable:
Physical = > 7.50 < 12.49 ⎫
Wireable = < 7.49 > 12.50 ⎭ as of 1/89

LAST CERTIFICATE ISSUED: Still issued.

CERTIFICATE AVAILABILITY: Still available in physical range. Available in wireable range if requested.

FACTOR PUBLICATION DATES: **Twice monthly**—6th and 12th of the month. Included on GNMA II tape.

SOURCES OF FACTOR INFORMATION: Tape, diskette, or hardcopy by *The Bond Buyer.*

SPECIAL ASSIGNMENT RESTRICTIONS: Cannot split a tail for a face quantity of less than $5,000 **on a physical security.**

METHOD(S) OF CLEARANCE: Wireable and physical.

CLEARANCE SIZE: $50 million maximum per piece **for wireables.**

TRF AGENT: Chemical Bank.

TRF FEE: Normal—$10 per certificate.
Rush (24 Hours)—$20 per certificate + $5 per pool.

PRODUCT: GNMA MOBILE HOME A THROUGH D

ISSUER: FHA approved mortgage lender (e.g., commercial bank). **Secured by mobile homes or by combination of mobile homes and developed lots.**
GUARANTOR: Government National Mortgage Association (GNMA).
INTEREST RATE: **Mortgages must have the same rate.**
ISSUE DATE: First day of month (e.g., 10/1/1987).
DAYS TO FIRST PAYMENT: 45-day delay.
PAYABLE DATE: **Fifteenth** of the month (e.g., 11/15/1987).
PAYMENT FREQUENCY: Monthly.
PAYMENT AGENT: Individual issuers send checks to investors.
RECORD DATE: Last business day of the month.
MATURITY: **Up to 20 years** (e.g., 10/05/2017).
PREPAID LIFE: **15 to 7 years** (e.g., 10/12/1998).
CREDIT RISK: None. Government guaranteed.
LIQUIDITY: **Fair secondary market.**
MINIMUM PURCHASE: $25,000.
DENOMINATION: Increments of $5,000.
QUOTED: In increments of 1/32 of 1% of par.
ROUND LOT: $1 million.
MODE OF ISSUANCE: Physical and wireable:
Physical = > 7.50 < 12.49 $\left.\right\}$ as of 1/89
Wireable = < 7.49 > 12.50
LAST CERTIFICATE ISSUED: Still issued.
CERTIFICATE AVAILABILITY: Still available in physical range. Available in wireable range if requested.
FACTOR PUBLICATION DATES: Twice monthly—6th and 12th of the month.
SOURCES OF FACTOR INFORMATION: Tape, diskette, or hardcopy by *The Bond Buyer*.
SPECIAL ASSIGNMENT RESTRICTIONS: Cannot split a tail for a face quantity of less than $5,000.
METHOD(S) OF CLEARANCE: Wireable and physical.
CLEARANCE SIZE: $50 million maximum per piece.
TRF AGENT: Chemical Bank.
TRF FEE: Normal—$10 per certificate.
Rush (24 Hours)—$20 per certificate + $5 per pool.

PRODUCT: GNMA PROJECT LOAN (PL)

ISSUER: FHA approved mortgage lender (e.g., commercial bank). **Secured by one mortgage representing a single loan on a completed project.**

GUARANTOR: Government National Mortgage Association (GNMA).

INTEREST RATE: **Mortgages must have the same rate.**

ISSUE DATE: First day of month (e.g., 10/1/1987).

DAYS TO FIRST PAYMENT: **45-day delay.**

PAYABLE DATE: **Fifteenth** of the month (e.g., 11/15/1987).

PAYMENT FREQUENCY: Monthly.

PAYMENT AGENT: Individual issuers send checks to investors.

RECORD DATE: Last business day of the month.

MATURITY: **No restrictions. Normally 40 years** (e.g., 10/25/2017).

PREPAID LIFE: **Normally 20 years** (e.g., 10/05/1999).

CREDIT RISK: None. Government guaranteed.

LIQUIDITY: **Poor secondary market.**

MINIMUM PURCHASE: $25,000.

DENOMINATION: Increments of $5,000.

QUOTED: In increments of 1/32 of 1% of par.

ROUND LOT: $1 million.

MODE OF ISSUANCE: Physical and wireable:
Physical = > 7.50 < 12.49 ⎫
Wireable = < 7.49 > 12.50 ⎭ as of 1/89

LAST CERTIFICATE ISSUED: Still issued.

CERTIFICATE AVAILABILITY: Still available in physical range. Available in wireable range if requested.

FACTOR PUBLICATION DATES: **Twice monthly—6th and 12th of** the month.

SOURCES OF FACTOR INFORMATION: Tape, diskette, or hardcopy by *The Bond Buyer.*

SPECIAL ASSIGNMENT RESTRICTIONS: Cannot split a tail for a face quantity of less than $5,000.

METHOD(S) OF CLEARANCE: Wireable and physical.

CLEARANCE SIZE: $50 million maximum per piece.

TRF AGENT: Chemical Bank.

TRF FEE: Normal—$10 per certificate.
Rush (24 Hours)—$20 per certificate + $5 per pool.

PRODUCT: GNMA I, PUERTO RICO 30 YEAR

ISSUER: FHA approved mortgage lender (e.g., commercial bank). **Single issuer.**

GUARANTOR: Government National Mortgage Association (GNMA) **in conjunction with Puerto Rico.**

INTEREST RATE: **Mortgages must have the same rate.**

ISSUE DATE: First day of month (e.g., 10/1/1987).

DAYS TO FIRST PAYMENT: **45-day delay.**

PAYABLE DATE: **Fifteenth** of the month (e.g., 11/15/1987).

PAYMENT FREQUENCY: Monthly.

PAYMENT AGENT: Individual issuers send checks to investors.

RECORD DATE: Last business day of the month.

MATURITY: **30 years** (e.g., 10/15/2017).

PREPAID LIFE: **12 years** (e.g., 10/15/1999).

CREDIT RISK: None. Government guaranteed.

LIQUIDITY: **Poor secondary market.**

MINIMUM PURCHASE: $25,000.

DENOMINATION: Increments of $5,000.

QUOTED: In increments of 1/32 of 1% of par.

ROUND LOT: $1 million.

MODE OF ISSUANCE: Physical and wireable:
Physical = > 7.50 < 12.49 ⎫ as of 1/89
Wireable = < 7.49 > 12.50 ⎭

LAST CERTIFICATE ISSUED: Still issued.

CERTIFICATE AVAILABILITY: Still available in physical range. Available in wireable range if requested.

FACTOR PUBLICATION DATES: Twice monthly—6th and 12th of the month. Included on GNMA I tape.

SOURCES OF FACTOR INFORMATION: Tape, diskette, or hardcopy by *The Bond Buyer.*

SPECIAL ASSIGNMENT RESTRICTIONS: Cannot split a tail for a face quantity of less than $5,000 **on a physical security.**

METHOD(S) OF CLEARANCE: Wireable and physical.

CLEARANCE SIZE: $50 million maximum per piece **for wireables.**

TRF AGENT: Chemical Bank.

TRF FEE: Normal—$10 per certificate.
Rush (24 Hours)—$20 per certificate + $5 per pool.

SPECIAL TAX ADVANTAGE: Exempt from Puerto Rican Income Tax if owner is domiciled in Puerto Rico.

PRODUCT: GNMA II, PUERTO RICO 30 YEAR

ISSUER: FHA approved mortgage lender (e.g., commercial bank). **Single and multiple issuers. Constructed of pools from specific geographic areas.**

GUARANTOR: Government National Mortgage Association (GNMA) **in conjunction with Puerto Rico.**

INTEREST RATE: **Rates may vary within 1% range.**

ISSUE DATE: First day of month (e.g., 10/1/1987).

DAYS TO FIRST PAYMENT: **50-day delay.**

PAYABLE DATE: **Twentieth** of the month (e.g., 11/20/1987).

PAYMENT FREQUENCY: Monthly.

PAYMENT AGENT: **Issuers send checks to Chemical Bank,** which pays the investor one combined check for all outstanding issues owned.

RECORD DATE: Last business day of the month.

MATURITY: **30 years** (e.g., 10/15/2017).

PREPAID LIFE: **12 years** (e.g., 10/15/1999).

CREDIT RISK: None. Government guaranteed.

LIQUIDITY: **Fair secondary market.**

MINIMUM PURCHASE: $25,000.

DENOMINATION: Increments of $5,000.

QUOTED: In increments of 1/32 of 1% of par.

ROUND LOT: $1 million.

MODE OF ISSUANCE: Physical and wireable:
Physical = > 7.50 < 12.49 ⎱
Wireable = < 7.49 > 12.50 ⎰ as of 1/89

LAST CERTIFICATE ISSUED: Still issued.

CERTIFICATE AVAILABILITY: Still available in physical range. Available in wireable range if requested.

FACTOR PUBLICATION DATES: Twice monthly—6th and 12th of the month. Included on GNMA II tape.

SOURCES OF FACTOR INFORMATION: Tape, diskette, or hardcopy by *The Bond Buyer*.

SPECIAL ASSIGNMENT RESTRICTIONS: Cannot split a tail for a face quantity of less than $5,000 **on a physical security.**

METHOD(S) OF CLEARANCE: Wireable and physical.

CLEARANCE SIZE: $50 million maximum per piece **for wireables.**

TRF AGENT: Chemical Bank.

TRF FEE: Normal—$10 per certificate.
Rush (24 Hours)—$20 per certificate + $5 per pool.

SPECIAL TAX ADVANTAGE: Exempt from Puerto Rican Income Tax if owner is domiciled in Puerto Rico.

FEDERAL HOME LOAN MORTGAGES (FHLMC)

PC Pool Prefix	Program
14	FHA/VA 30-Year Guarantor
15	FHA/VA 30-Year Cash
16-17	30-Year Cash
18, 25	30-Year Guarantor
27-30, 53	30-Year Guarantor
20	15-Year Cash (Gnome)
21, 50	15-Year Guarantor (Non-Gnome)
22	Multifamily 15-Year Balloon Cash
23	Multifamily Fully Amortizing Guarantor
24	Multifamily Amortizing Balloon and Interest Only Balloon Guarantor
26	30-Year Scheduled Payment of Principal Guarantor
31	Multifamily 30-Year Variable Interest Rate Guarantor
32	15-Year Scheduled Payment of Principal Guarantor
33	FHA/VA 30-Year Scheduled Payment of Principal Guarantor
34	Single Family 40-Year Variable Interest Rate Guarantor
35	2% Annual Capped Treasury ARM Cash
36	30-Year Cash (Pools formed after 6/1/87)
38	15-Year Cash (Pools formed after 6/1/87)
39	Cost-of-Funds ARM Guarantor
40	2% Annual Capped Convertible Treasury ARM Guarantor
42	Cost-of-Funds Scheduled Payment of Principal ARM Guarantor
43	30-Year Mini-250K Guarantor
44	15-Year Mini-250K Guarantor
45	FHA/VA 30-Year Mini-250K Guarantor
46	30-Year Scheduled Payment of Principal Mini-250K Guarantor
47	15-Year Scheduled Payment of Principal Mini-250K Guarantor
48	FHA/VA 30-Year Scheduled Payment of Principal Mini-250K Guarantor
49	Multifamily 10-Year Balloon Cash
60	2% Annual Capped Treasury ARM Guarantor
63	1% Annual Capped Convertible Treasury ARM Guarantor
64	1% Annual Capped Treasury ARM Guarantor
68	Convertible Fixed-Rate Guarantor
71	2% Annual Capped Convertible Treasury ARM Cash
72	1% Annual Capped Convertible Treasury ARM Cash
76	5-Year Treasury ARM Guarantor
77	Cost-of-Funds Rate Capped ARM Guarantor
78	3/1 and 5/1 Treasury ARM Guarantor
79	Cost-of-Funds Multifamily ARM Guarantor
80	30-Year Principal Only Strip Guarantor
82	15-Year Principal Only Strip Guarantor
86	3-Year Treasury ARM Guarantor
90	30-Year Interest Only Strip Guarantor
92	15-Year Interest Only Strip Guarantor

PRODUCT: FHLMC 15-YEAR GUARANTOR PROGRAM

ISSUER: FHLMC approved mortgage lender (e.g., commercial bank **cash market**). Participation certificates (PC) and pass-throughs (PT) are secured by mortgages on one- to four- family homes.

GUARANTOR: Federal Home Loan Mortgage Association (FHLMC) owned by the 12 Federal Home Loan Banks.

POOL ASSIGNED RANGE: 210000 and 500000 Series.

INTEREST RATE: Rates may vary within a 2% range.

ISSUE DATE: First day of month (e.g., 10/1/1987).

DAYS TO FIRST PAYMENT: **75-day delay.**

PAYABLE DATE: **Fifteenth** of the month (e.g., 11/15/1987).

PAYMENT FREQUENCY: Monthly.

PAYMENT AGENT: Individual issuers send checks to investors.

RECORD DATE: Last business day of the month.

MATURITY: **15 years** (e.g., 10/15/2002).

PREPAID LIFE: **7 years** (e.g., 10/15/1994).

CREDIT RISK: Not directly government guaranteed.

LIQUIDITY: **Good secondary market.**

MINIMUM PURCHASE: $25,000.

DENOMINATION: Any.

QUOTED: In increments of 1/32 of 1% of par.

ROUND LOT: $1 million.

MODE OF ISSUANCE: Wireable.

LAST CERTIFICATE ISSUED: January 1, 1985.

CERTIFICATE AVAILABILITY: Available if requested.

FACTOR PUBLICATION DATES: Once monthly—1st of the month.

SOURCES OF FACTOR INFORMATION: Tape, diskette, or hardcopy by *The Bond Buyer.*

SPECIAL ASSIGNMENT RESTRICTIONS: **Series 210000 and 500000 only.**

METHOD(S) OF CLEARANCE: Wireable.

CLEARANCE SIZE: $50 million maximum per piece.

TRF AGENT: Federal Reserve Bank of NY.

PRODUCT: FHLMC 30-YEAR GUARANTOR
AND CASH PROGRAMS

ISSUER: FHLMC approved mortgage lender (e.g., commercial bank). Participation certificate (PC) and pass-throughs (PT) are secured by conventional mortgages on one- to four-family houses.

GUARANTOR: Federal Home Loan Mortgage Association (FHLMC) owned by the 12 Federal Home Loan Banks.

POOL ASSIGNED RANGE: Guarantor Series: 180000, 250000, 270000, 280000, 290000, 300000; Cash Series: 160000, 170000, 360000.

INTEREST RATE: Rates may vary within a 2% range.

ISSUE DATE: First day of month (e.g., 10/1/1987).

DAYS TO FIRST PAYMENT: **75-day delay.**

PAYABLE DATE: **Fifteenth** of the month (e.g., 11/15/1987).

PAYMENT FREQUENCY: Monthly.

PAYMENT AGENT: Individual issuers send checks to investors.

RECORD DATE: Last business day of the month.

MATURITY: **30 years** (e.g., 10/15/2017).

PREPAID LIFE: **12 years** (e.g., 10/15/1999).

CREDIT RISK: Not directly government guaranteed.

LIQUIDITY: **Good secondary market.**

MINIMUM PURCHASE: $25,000.

DENOMINATION: Any.

QUOTED: In increments of 1/32 of 1% of par.

ROUND LOT: $1 million.

MODE OF ISSUANCE: Wireable.

LAST CERTIFICATE ISSUED: January 1, 1985.

CERTIFICATE AVAILABILITY: Available if requested.

FACTOR PUBLICATION DATES: Once monthly—1st of the month.

SOURCES OF FACTOR INFORMATION: Tape, diskette, or hardcopy by *The Bond Buyer.*

SPECIAL ASSIGNMENT RESTRICTIONS: **430000 and 440000 Series not good delivery for generic assignment.**

METHOD(S) OF CLEARANCE: Wireable.

CLEARANCE SIZE: $50 million maximum per piece.

TRF AGENT: Federal Reserve of Bank of NY.

PRODUCT: FHLMC ADJUSTABLE RATE MORTGAGES (ARMs)

ISSUER: FHLMC approved mortgage lender (e.g., commercial bank). Participation certificate (PC) and pass-throughs (PT) are secured by conventional mortgages on one- to four-family houses.

GUARANTOR: Federal Home Loan Mortgage Association (FHLMC) owned by the 12 Federal Home Loan Banks.

POOL ASSIGNED RANGE: Series 350000.

INTEREST RATE: Rates may vary on a monthly basis.

ISSUE DATE: First day of month (e.g., 10/1/1987).

DAYS TO FIRST PAYMENT: **75-day delay.**

PAYABLE DATE: **Fifteenth** of the month (e.g., 11/15/1987).

PAYMENT FREQUENCY: Monthly.

PAYMENT AGENT: Individual issuers send checks to investors.

RECORD DATE: Last business day of the month.

MATURITY: **30 years** (e.g., 10/15/2017).

PREPAID LIFE: **12 years** (e.g., 10/15/1999).

CREDIT RISK: Not directly government guaranteed.

LIQUIDITY: **Fair secondary market.**

MINIMUM PURCHASE: $25,000.

DENOMINATION: Any.

QUOTED: In increments of 1/32 of 1% of par.

ROUND LOT: $1 million.

MODE OF ISSUANCE: Wireable.

LAST CERTIFICATE ISSUED: January 1, 1985.

CERTIFICATE AVAILABILITY: Available if requested.

FACTOR PUBLICATION DATES: Once monthly—1st of the month.

SOURCES OF FACTOR INFORMATION: Tape, diskette, or hardcopy by *The Bond Buyer.*

SPECIAL ASSIGNMENT RESTRICTIONS: None.

METHOD(S) OF CLEARANCE: Wireable.

CLEARANCE SIZE: $50 million maximum per piece.

TRF AGENT: Federal Reserve Bank of NY.

PRODUCT: FHLMC GNOME, 15-YEAR CASH PROGRAM

ISSUER: FHLMC approved mortgage lender (e.g., commercial bank). **Auction bonds or noncash. Trade at a premium over regular 15-year FHLMCs.** Participation certificates (PC) and pass-throughs (PT) are secured by mortgages on one- to four- family homes.

GUARANTOR: Federal Home Loan Mortgage Association (FHLMC) owned by the 12 Federal Home Loan Banks.

POOL ASSIGNED RANGE: **Series 20 and 38.**

INTEREST RATE: Rates may vary within a 2% range.

ISSUE DATE: First day of month (e.g., 10/1/1987).

DAYS TO FIRST PAYMENT: **75-day delay.**

PAYABLE DATE: **Fifteenth** of the month (e.g., 11/15/1987).

PAYMENT FREQUENCY: Monthly.

PAYMENT AGENT: Individual issuers send checks to investors.

RECORD DATE: Last business day of the month.

MATURITY: **15 years** (e.g., 10/15/2002).

PREPAID LIFE: **7 years** (e.g., 10/15/1994).

CREDIT RISK: Not directly government guaranteed.

LIQUIDITY: **Good secondary market.**

MINIMUM PURCHASE: **$50,000.**

DENOMINATION: Any.

QUOTED: In increments of 1/32 of 1% of par.

ROUND LOT: $1 million.

MODE OF ISSUANCE: Wireable.

LAST CERTIFICATE ISSUED: January 1, 1985.

CERTIFICATE AVAILABILITY: Available if requested.

FACTOR PUBLICATION DATES: Once monthly—1st of the month.

SOURCES OF FACTOR INFORMATION: Tape, diskette, or hardcopy by *The Bond Buyer*.

SPECIAL ASSIGNMENT RESTRICTIONS: **200000 and 380000 Series only.**

METHOD(S) OF CLEARANCE: Wireable.

CLEARANCE SIZE: $50 million maximum per piece.

TRF AGENT: Federal Reserve Bank of NY.

FEDERAL NATIONAL MORTGAGE ASSOCIATION (FNMA)

PRODUCT: FNMA ADJUSTABLE RATE MORTGAGES (ARMs)

ISSUER: FNMA approved mortgage lender (e.g., commercial bank). Participation certificate (PC) and pass-throughs (PT) are secured by conventional mortgages on one- to four-family homes.
GUARANTOR: Federal National Mortgage Association (FNMA). Privately owned. Government sponsored.
POOL ASSIGNED RANGE: AS prefix followed by 6-digit pool number.
INTEREST RATE: Rates may vary on a monthly basis.
ISSUE DATE: First day of month (e.g., 10/1/1987).
DAYS TO FIRST PAYMENT: **54-day delay.**
PAYABLE DATE: **25th** of the month (e.g., 11/25/1987).
PAYMENT FREQUENCY: Monthly.
PAYMENT AGENT: Individual issuers send checks to investors.
RECORD DATE: Last business day of the month.
MATURITY: **30 years** (e.g., 10/15/2017).
PREPAID LIFE: **12 years** (e.g., 10/15/1999).
CREDIT RISK: Not directly government guaranteed.
LIQUIDITY: **Fair secondary market.**
MINIMUM PURCHASE: $25,000.
DENOMINATION: Any.
QUOTED: In increments of 1/32 of 1% of par.
ROUND LOT: $1 million.
MODE OF ISSUANCE: Wireable.
LAST CERTIFICATE ISSUED: January 1, 1985.
CERTIFICATE AVAILABILITY: Available if requested.
FACTOR PUBLICATION DATES: Once monthly—5th of the month.
SOURCES OF FACTOR INFORMATION: Tape, diskette, or hardcopy by *The Bond Buyer.*
SPECIAL ASSIGNMENT RESTRICTIONS: None.
METHOD(S) OF CLEARANCE: Wireable.
CLEARANCE SIZE: $50 million maximum **per piece.**
TRF AGENT: Federal Reserve Bank of NY.

PRODUCT: FNMA CONSTRUCTION LOAN, 15 YEAR

ISSUER: FNMA approved mortgage lender (e.g., commercial bank). Secured by one mortgage representing a single loan on a project under construction.

GUARANTOR: Federal National Mortgage Association (FNMA).

POOL ASSIGNED RANGE: CI or CS prefix followed by 6-digit pool number.

INTEREST RATE: Rate may vary within a 2% range.

ISSUE DATE: First day of month (e.g., 10/1/1987).

DAYS TO FIRST PAYMENT: **54-day delay.**

PAYABLE DATE: **24th** of the month (e.g., 11/25/1987).

PAYMENT FREQUENCY: Monthly.

PAYMENT AGENT: Individual issuers send checks to investors.

RECORD DATE: Last business day of the month.

MATURITY: **15 years** (e.g., 10/15/2002).

PREPAID LIFE: **7 years** (e.g., 10/15/1994).

CREDIT RISK: None. Government guaranteed.

LIQUIDITY: **Poor secondary market.**

MINIMUM PURCHASE: $25,000.

DENOMINATION: Any.

QUOTED: In increments of 1/32 of 1% of par.

ROUND LOT: $1 million.

MODE OF ISSUANCE: Wireable.

LAST CERTIFICATE ISSUED: January 1, 1985.

CERTIFICATE AVAILABILITY: Available if requested.

FACTOR PUBLICATION DATES: Once monthly—5th of the month.

SOURCES OF FACTOR INFORMATION: Tape, diskette, or hardcopy by *The Bond Buyer.*

SPECIAL ASSIGNMENT RESTRICTIONS: None.

METHOD(S) OF CLEARANCE: Wireable.

CLEARANCE SIZE: $50 million maximum **per piece.**

TRF AGENT: Federal Reserve Bank of NY.

PRODUCT: FNMA CONSTRUCTION LOAN (CL), 30 YEAR

ISSUER: FNMA approved mortgage lender (e.g., commercial bank). Secured by one mortgage representing a single loan on a project under construction.

GUARANTOR: Federal National Mortgage Association (FNMA). Privately owned. Government sponsored.

POOL ASSIGNED RANGE: CL prefix followed by 6-digit pool number.

INTEREST RATE: Rates may vary within a 2% range.

ISSUE DATE: First day of month (e.g., 10/1/1987).

DAYS TO FIRST PAYMENT: **54-day delay.**

PAYABLE DATE: **25th** of the month (e.g., 11/25/1987).

PAYMENT FREQUENCY: Monthly.

PAYMENT AGENT: Individual issuers send check to investors.

RECORD DATE: Last business day of the month.

MATURITY: **30 years** (e.g., 10/15/2017).

PREPAID LIFE: **12 years** (e.g., 10/15/1999).

CREDIT RISK: Not directly government guaranteed.

LIQUIDITY: Poor secondary market.

MINIMUM PURCHASE: $25,000.

DENOMINATION: Any.

QUOTED: In increments of 1/32 of 1% of par.

ROUND LOT: $1 million.

MODE OF ISSUANCE: Wireable.

LAST CERTIFICATE ISSUED: January 1, 1985.

CERTIFICATE AVAILABILITY: Available if requested.

FACTOR PUBLICATION DATES: Once monthly—5th of the month.

SOURCES OF FACTOR INFORMATION: Tape, diskette, or hardcopy by *The Bond Buyer.*

SPECIAL ASSIGNMENT RESTRICTIONS: None.

METHOD(S) OF CLEARANCE: Wireable.

CLEARANCE SIZE: $50 million maximum **per piece.**

TRF AGENT: Federal Reserve Bank of NY.

PRODUCT: FNMA GENERAL LOAN (GL), 15 YEAR

ISSUER: FNMA approved mortgage lender (e.g., commercial bank). Secured by mortgages on single-, two-, or four-family homes.
GUARANTOR: Federal National Mortgage Association (FNMA).
POOL ASSIGNED RANGE: CI prefix followed by 6-digit pool number.
INTEREST RATE: Rate may vary within a 2% range.
ISSUE DATE: First day of month (e.g., 10/1/1987).
DAYS TO FIRST PAYMENT: **54-day delay.**
PAYABLE DATE: **25th** of the month (e.g., 11/25/1987).
PAYMENT FREQUENCY: Monthly.
PAYMENT AGENT: Individual issuers send checks to investors.
RECORD DATE: Last business day of the month.
MATURITY: **15 years** (e.g., 10/15/2002).
PREPAID LIFE: **7 years** (e.g., 10/15/1994).
CREDIT RISK: Loans are FHA/VA guaranteed.
LIQUIDITY: Fair secondary market.
MINIMUM PURCHASE: $25,000.
DENOMINATION: Any.
QUOTED: In increments of 1/32 of 1% of par.
ROUND LOT: $1 million.
MODE OF ISSUANCE: Wireable.
LAST CERTIFICATE ISSUED: January 1, 1985.
CERTIFICATE AVAILABILITY: Available if requested.
FACTOR PUBLICATION DATES: Once monthly—5th of the month.
SOURCES OF FACTOR INFORMATION: Tape, diskette, or hardcopy by *The Bond Buyer.*
SPECIAL ASSIGNMENT RESTRICTIONS: None.
METHOD(S) OF CLEARANCE: Wireable.
CLEARANCE SIZE: $50 million maximum **per piece.**
TRF AGENT: Federal Reserve Bank of NY.

PRODUCT: FNMA GENERAL LOAN (GL), 30 YEAR

ISSUER: FNMA approved mortgage lender (e.g., commercial bank). Participation certificate (PC) and pass-throughs (PT) are secured by conventional mortgages on one-, two-, or four-family homes.

GUARANTOR: Federal National Mortgage Association (FNMA). Privately owned. Government sponsored.

POOL ASSIGNED RANGE: GL prefix followed by 6-digit pool number.

INTEREST RATE: Rates may vary within a 2% range.

ISSUE DATE: First day of month (e.g., 10/1/1987).

DAYS TO FIRST PAYMENT: **54-day delay.**

PAYABLE DATE: **25th** of the month (e.g., 11/25/1987).

PAYMENT FREQUENCY: Monthly.

PAYMENT AGENT: Individual issuers send check to investors.

RECORD DATE: Last business day of the month.

MATURITY: **30 years** (e.g., 10/15/2017).

PREPAID LIFE: **12 years** (e.g., 10/15/1999).

CREDIT RISK: Loans are FHA/VA guaranteed.

LIQUIDITY: **Good secondary market.**

MINIMUM PURCHASE: $25,000.

DENOMINATION: Any.

QUOTED: In increments of 1/32 of 1% of par.

ROUND LOT: $1 million.

MODE OF ISSUANCE: Wireable.

LAST CERTIFICATE ISSUED: January 1, 1985.

CERTIFICATE AVAILABILITY: Available if requested.

FACTOR PUBLICATION DATES: Once monthly—5th of the month.

SOURCES OF FACTOR INFORMATION: Tape, diskette, or hardcopy by *The Bond Buyer.*

SPECIAL ASSIGNMENT RESTRICTIONS: None.

METHOD(S) OF CLEARANCE: Wireable.

CLEARANCE SIZE: $50 million maximum **per piece.**

TRF AGENT: Federal Reserve Bank of NY.

PRODUCT: FNMA GROWTH EQUITY MORTGAGES (GEMs)

ISSUER: FNMA approved mortgage lender (e.g., commercial bank). **Single issuer.** Secured by single-family mortgages with annual increases in monthly payments of either 4%/year over the life of the loan or any rate/year for any number of years.
GUARANTOR: Federal National Mortgage Association (FNMA).
POOL ASSIGNED RANGE: C3, C4, and C5 prefixes followed by 6-digit pool number.
INTEREST RATE: Rates may vary within a 2% range.
ISSUE DATE: First day of month (e.g., 10/1/1987).
DAYS TO FIRST PAYMENT: **54-day delay.**
PAYABLE DATE: **25th** of the month (e.g., 11/25/1987).
PAYMENT FREQUENCY: Monthly.
PAYMENT AGENT: Individual issuers send checks to investors.
RECORD DATE: Last business day of the month.
MATURITY: **30 years** (e.g., 10/15/2017).
PREPAID LIFE: **12 years** (e.g., 10/15/1999).
CREDIT RISK: None. Government guaranteed.
LIQUIDITY: Poor secondary market.
MINIMUM PURCHASE: $25,000.
DENOMINATION: Any.
QUOTED: In increments of 1/32 of 1% of par.
ROUND LOT: $1 million.
MODE OF ISSUANCE: Wireable.
LAST CERTIFICATE ISSUED: January 1, 1985.
CERTIFICATE AVAILABILITY: Available if requested.
FACTOR PUBLICATION DATES: Once monthly—5th of the month.
SOURCES OF FACTOR INFORMATION: Tape, diskette, or hardcopy by *The Bond Buyer.*
SPECIAL ASSIGNMENT RESTRICTIONS: None.
METHOD(S) OF CLEARANCE: Wireable.
CLEARANCE SIZE: $50 million maximum **per piece.**

MISCELLANEOUS

PRODUCT: INTEREST ONLY/PRINCIPAL ONLY STRIPS (IO/PO)

ISSUER: FHA, FHLMC, or FNMA approved mortgage lender (e.g., commercial bank). **Single or multiple issuer.** Offshoot derivative product of pools. First introduced by FNMA and Goldman Sachs in July, 1986.
GUARANTOR: Issuing party.
POOL ASSIGNED RANGE: None. Each principal or interest strip is assigned its own CUSIP. A pool does exist for the underlying mortgage.
INTEREST RATE: Mortgages must have the same rate.
ISSUE DATE: First day of month (e.g., 10/1/1987).
DAYS TO FIRST PAYMENT: **Contingent upon the underlying pool.**
PAYABLE DATE: Contingent upon the underlying pool.
PAYMENT FREQUENCY: Monthly. Principal to the holder of the P/O; interest to the holder of the I/O. Interest is paid on the "notional" face value or the current outstanding balance of the underlying pool.
PAYMENT AGENT: Individual issuers send checks to trustees of issue.
RECORD DATE: Last business day of the month normally.
MATURITY: **Contingent upon the underlying pool. Normally 15 or 30 years.**
PREPAID LIFE: **Contingent upon the underlying pool.** Normally 7 or 12 years. Average life for I/Os = sum of interest payments/total interest received.
CREDIT RISK: Great potential risk for holders in volatile interest rate markets.
LIQUIDITY: No secondary market.
MINIMUM PURCHASE: Normally $25,000.
DENOMINATION: Increments of $5,000 for GNMAs.
QUOTED: P/Os in increments of 1/32 of 1% of par. I/Os in a percentage of the notional face value of the underlying pool.
ROUND LOT: $1 million.
MODE OF ISSUANCE: Physical and wireable:
Physical (GNMA = > 7.49 < 12.50)
Wireable FNMA, FHLMC (GNMA = < 7.50 and > 12.49)
LAST CERTIFICATE ISSUED: Still issued.
CERTIFICATE AVAILABILITY: Still available in physical range. Available in wireable range if requested.
FACTOR PUBLICATION DATES: Based upon the monthly tapes received for the underlying pool (product).
SOURCES OF FACTOR INFORMATION: Tape, diskette, or hardcopy by *The Bond Buyer*.
SPECIAL ASSIGNMENT RESTRICTIONS:
METHOD(S) OF CLEARANCE: Wireable and physical.
CLEARANCE SIZE: $50 million maximum per piece for **wireables.**

PRODUCT: COLLATERALIZED MORTGAGE OBLIGATION (CMO)

ISSUER: Government agency (i.e., FHLMC) or a nonagency (i.e., Norwest Mortgages Inc.) or an approved mortgage lender (e.g., commercial bank). A bond backed by mortgages. Organized in series (i.e., Series D) and tranches or classes within the series (i.e., Class D–1, Class D–2, Class D–3). All classes have different maturities and coupons. First introduced in February, 1984, by GNMA Mortgage-Backed Securities Trust, Inc.

GUARANTOR: The issuer only.

POOL ASSIGNED RANGE: None. Each class is assigned its own CUSIP.

INTEREST RATE: All classes have different coupons.

ISSUE DATE: First day of month (e.g., 10/1/1987).

DAYS TO FIRST PAYMENT: **6-month delay.**

PAYABLE DATE: **Fifteenth of the sixth month** (e.g., 11/15/1987).

PAYMENT FREQUENCY: Prioritized principal and interest payments. Principal is paid to fully retire the first class before the second class receives any principal payments, and so on. Interest is paid semiannually to all classes. "Accrual class" bonds do not receive P&I until all classes above it are paid down. (Interest on the accrued principal and interest is added onto the final payment.) "Z" bond series trade at a discount with no interest payments.

PAYMENT AGENT: Individual issuers send checks to investors.

RECORD DATE: Can be different for each class.

MATURITY: Varies per class. FHLMC-backed CMOs have 5-, 12.5-, and 30-year maturities.

PREPAID LIFE: Varies according to the maturity of the class.

CREDIT RISK: Some. May not be government guaranteed.

LIQUIDITY: Poor secondary market.

MINIMUM PURCHASE: $25,000.

DENOMINATION: Increments of $5,000.

QUOTED: In increments of 1/32 of 1% of par or dollar discount price on zero coupon tranche.

ROUND LOT: $1 million.

MODE OF ISSUANCE: Physical and wireable:
Physical (GNMA = > 7.49 < 12.50)
Wireable FNMA, FHLMC (GNMA = < 7.50 and > 12.49).

LAST CERTIFICATE ISSUED: Still issued.

CERTIFICATE AVAILABILITY: Still available in physical range. Available in wireable range if requested.

FACTOR PUBLICATION DATES: Once monthly—12th or 15th of the month.

SOURCES OF FACTOR INFORMATION: Tape, diskette, or hardcopy by *The Bond Buyer.*

SPECIAL ASSIGNMENT RESTRICTIONS: No TBAs. Bond form only.

METHOD(S) OF CLEARANCE: Wireable, physical, or DTC eligible.

CLEARANCE SIZE: $50 million maximum per piece **for wireables.**

Mortgage-Backed Securities Product Characteristics

	Federal Housing Administration (FHA)	Government National Mortgage Association Series I (GNMAX)	Government National Mortgage Association Series II Customer Pool (GNMAC)	Government National Mortgage Association Series II Multi-issuer "Jumbo" (GNMAM)	Federal Home Loan Mortgage Association "Freddie Mac" (FHLMC)	Federal National Mortgage Association "Fannie Mae" (FNMA)
Issue Date	1st/month	1st/month	1st/month	1st/month	1st/month	1st/month
First Coupon	55 days/issue	45 days/issue	50 days/issue	50 days/issue	75 days/issue	55 days/issue
Maturity Date	25th of month	15th of month	20th of month	20th of month	15th of month	25th of month
Interest Payment	25th of month	15th of month	20th of month	20th of month	15th of month	25th of month
Interest Frequency	monthly	monthly	monthly	monthly	monthly	monthly
Principal Frequency	monthly	monthly	monthly	monthly	monthly	monthly
Record Date	last business day/month	30th	30th	30th	last business day/month	last business day/month
Calc. Type	30/360	30/360	30/360	30/360	30/360	30/360

Mortgage-Backed Security Product Matrix

Instrument	Collateral	Maturity	Denomination	Interest	Principal	Prepayments
GNMA Single Family	Each pool must have at least 12 fixed-payment residential loans, none of which can be greater than 10% of original principal of the pool. Original principal must be at least $1 million.	Minimum of 90% of mortgages must be greater than 20 years. Average life is 12 years.	$25,000 minimum. $5,000 increments thereafter. One certificate can be for an amount not a multiple of $5,000 and greater than $25,000.	Monthly payment by issuer whether or not collected.	Monthly payment by issuer whether or not collected.	Passed through when collected.
GNMA Mobile Home	Loans secured by mobile homes or by combination mobile homes and developed lots. Original principal must be at least $500,000.	Minimum of 90% of mortgages must be greater than 20 years. Average life is 12 years.	$25,000 minimum. $5,000 increments thereafter. One certificate can be for an amount not a multiple of $5,000 and greater than $25,000.	Monthly payment by issuer whether or not collected.	Monthly payment by issuer whether or not collected.	Passed through when collected.
GNMA Graduated Payment Mortgage (GPM)	Loans secured by mortgages on which monthly payments increase annually for either 5 years (GP program) or 10 years (GT program). Aggregate original principal must be at least $500,000. Must have at least 12 loans, none of which can be greater than 10% of original principal of pool.	Minimum of 90% of mortgages must be greater than 20 years. Average life is 12 years.	$25,000 minimum. $5,000 increments thereafter. One certificate can be for an amount not a multiple of $5,000 and greater than $25,000.	Monthly payment by issuer whether or not collected.	Monthly payment by issuer whether or not collected. Monthly payments in the first years may not cover full amount of interest or any principal. The unpaid interest is added to the outstanding principal balance.	Passed through when collected.

53

Mortgage-Backed Security Product Matrix (cont'd.)

Instrument	Collateral	Maturity	Denomination	Interest	Principal	Prepayments
GNMA Growing Equity Mortgage	Single-family mortgages with annual increase in monthly payments of either (1) 4% /year over life or (2) any rate /year for any number of years. Original principal of $50,000. Not required to pay equal monthly installments.	Minimum of 90% of mortgages must be greater than 20 years. Average life is 12 years.	$25,000 minimum. $5,000 increments thereafter. One certificate can be for an amount not a multiple of $5,000 and greater than $25,000.	Monthly payment by issuer whether or not collected.	Monthly payment by issuer whether or not collected.	Passed through when collected.
GNMA Buydown	Level-payment home mortgages where funds have been provided to reduce borrowers' monthly payments in the first years. Aggregate principal at issuance must be at least $500,000. Pool must have minimum of 12 loans with none greater than 10% of the original principal.	Minimum of 90% of mortgages must be greater than 20 years. Average life is 12 years.	$25,000 minimum. $5,000 increments thereafter. One certificate can be for an amount not a multiple of $5,000 and greater than $25,000.	Monthly payment by issuer whether or not collected.	Monthly payment by issuer whether or not collected.	Passed through when collected.

54

Mortgage-Backed Security Product Matrix (cont'd.)

Instrument	Collateral	Maturity	Denomination	Interest	Principal	Prepayments
Mortgage-Backed Serial Notes	Single-family mortgages combined to form a pool of at least $5 million original principal. Used as collateral for 200 consecutively numbered notes.	Minimum of 90% of mortgages must be greater than 20 years. Average life is 12 years.	$25,000 minimum. $5,000 increments thereafter. One certificate can be for an amount not a multiple of $5,000 and greater than $25,000.	Monthly payment by issuer whether or not collected	Scheduled payment whether or not collected. Used to retire notes in sequence.	Used to retire notes in sequence when collected.
GNMA Project Loans	One mortgage representing a single loan on a completed project. (Can be more than one loan if purchased under GNMA Tandem Mortgage disposition program.) At issue, principal balance must be at least $500,000.	No restriction. 40-year original maturity is common with 20-year average life.	$25,000 minimum. $5,000 increments thereafter. One certificate can be for an amount not a multiple of $5,000 and greater than $25,000.	Monthly payment by issuer whether or not collected.	Monthly payment by issuer whether or not collected.	Passed through when collected.
GNMA Construction Loans	One mortgage representing a single loan on a project under construction. At issue, principal balance must be at least $500,000. Provides for conversion to project loan at maturity.	150% of length of construction period. (It may be increased.)	$25,000 minimum. $5,000 increments thereafter. One certificate can be for an amount not a multiple of $5,000 and greater than $25,000.	Monthly payment by issuer whether or not collected.	Usually matures upon and is redeemed by issuance of project loan. Purchasers agree to accept such a redemption. If liquidated or if no project loan is issued, the holder receives cash.	

Mortgage-Backed Security Product Matrix (cont'd.)

Instrument	Collateral	Maturity	Denomination	Interest	Principal	Prepayments
GNMA II—Fully Modified Pass-Through	Large, multi-issuer pools. Interest rates within a pool can vary within a 1% limit. Central paying agent. GNMA I pools can be converted to GNMA II.	Minimum of 90% of mortgage must be greater than 20 years. Average life is 12 years.	$25,000 minimum. $5,000 increments thereafter. One certificate can be for an amount not a multiple of $5,000 and greater than $25,000.	Monthly payment by central paying agent whether or not collected.	Monthly payment by central paying agent whether or not collected.	Passed through when collected.
—Single Family						
—Graduated Payment Mortgage						
—Manufactured Housing Loans						
GNMA Participation Certificates	Issued against assembled loan assets of several government agencies whose management and liquidation functions were taken over by GNMA.		$5,000 or $10,000 minimum depending on the issue.	Monthly	Monthly	Fifteen issues outstanding. None issued since 1978. Not traded.*

*From *The Money Market: Myth, Reality, and Practice* by Marcia Stigum.

Mortgage-Backed Security Product Matrix (cont'd.)

Instrument	Collateral	Maturity	Denomination	Interest	Principal	Prepayments
FHLMC Participation Certificates	Undivided interest in a group of first-lien, fixed-rate conventional mortgages on one- to four-family houses. FHLMC may purchase an entire loan or a participation of 50% to 95% of the loan's principal amount Original principal of the pool is $100 to $300 million.	30 years maximum life. Average life of 12 years.	$25,000; $100,000; $200,000; $500,000; $1,000,000; $5,000,000.	Monthly (timely payment guaranteed).	Monthly; passed through as collected. Full repayment is guaranteed no later than 1 year after it becomes due.	Passed through as collected.
			Regardless of the number of PCs owned, the investor will receive a single check each month from FHLMC.			
FHLMC Participation Certificates. Guarantor Program	Mortgage lenders sell whole loans or participations in groups of conventional mortgages to FHLMC at par in return for PCs representing an undivided interest in that pool of loans. New loans and seasoned mortgages may be swapped. Auctions daily with minimum pool size of $1,000,000. In addition to conventional 30-year mortgages, FHLMC can swap 15-year, fixed-rate conventional mortgages as well as FHA/VA mortgages.	30 years or 15 years.	$25,000; $100,000; $200,000; $500,000; $1,000,000; $5,000,000.	Monthly (timely payment guaranteed).	Monthly passed through as collected. Full repayment is guranteed no later than 1 year after it becomes due.	Passed through as collected.

Mortgage-Backed Security Product Matrix (cont'd.)

Instrument	Collateral	Maturity	Denomination	Interest	Principal	Prepayments
FHLMC Guaranteed Mortgage Certificate	Loans backing GMC are similar to those used in the PC program.	30 years maximum life. Average life of 12 years. Holders of GMCs may require FHLMC to repurchase the GMC 15, 20, or 25 years after issuance at par.	$100,000; $500,000; $1,000,000.	Paid semi-annually.	Paid annually in guaranteed minimum amounts.	If principal received by FHLMC exceeds minimum for year, excess is passed through to GMC holders.
FNMA Pass-Throughs	Level payment mortgages on single-family or 2- to 4-family residential property. May be conventional mortgages or FHA/VA mortgages and either new or seasoned loans. May also be growing equity mortgages, minimum pool size of $1,000,000.	30-year mortgages with 12-year assumed life. Also can have pools with 15-year mortgages.	$25,000 minimum.	Monthly payment by central paying agent (Chemical Bank) whether or not collected.	Monthly payment by central paying agent (Chemical Bank) whether or not collected.	Passed through as collected.
FNMA Pass-Through WAM	Level-payment mortgages on single-family or 2- to 4-family residential property. May be conventional mortgages or FHA/VA mortgages and either new or seasoned loans. May also be growing equity mortgages, minimum pool size of $1,000,000.	Difference between a WAM and a regular FNMA pass-through is that the weighted average maturity of the pool is significantly shorter than the 30-year original term. This fact affects the pricing of the security.	$25,000 minimum.	Monthly payment by central paying agent (Chemical Bank) whether or not collected.	Monthly payment by central paying agent (Chemical Bank) whether or not collected.	Passed through as collected.

58

Mortgage-Backed Security Product Matrix (cont'd.)

Instrument	Collateral	Maturity	Denomination	Interest	Principal	Prepayment
Connie Mac	Major commercial banks, thrift institutions, and mortgage bankers who originate conventional mortgages, create pools, and issue pass-through securities backed by those mortgages.	30 years maximum life with 12-year assumed life.				
GNMA Mortgage-Backed Bonds	Bonds issued by FHLMC and FNMA. Principal and interest payments guaranteed by GNMA.	From 12 to 25 years.	$25,000 minimum.	Paid semi-annually.	Full repayment of principal at maturity.	No such bonds have been issued since the early 1970s.

4

The Broker-Dealers

Terminology can be confusing especially since designations such as broker, dealer, and broker-dealer are often used incorrectly. When you refer to an organization by one of these three terms, you are describing distinctly different functions provided by securities firms.

THE BROKER

The clientele of a broker is normally the retail segment of the investment community, individuals like yourself. However, some brokers also handle institutional accounts, such as those of large investment portfolios and money managers. As a broker, a firm acts as an agent (or finder) to locate a contra-party to a customer's order. For example, a customer of a firm acting as a broker places an order to buy a particular security. The brokerage firm, through its telecommunications links with the various stock exchanges and over-the-counter marketmakers, finds a party who wants to sell the security that its customer wishes to purchase. It then buys the security from the seller for the account and risk of its customer. Although it is a fact that the security is being sold to the purchaser's broker, at no time is it actually owned directly (beneficially) by the broker. The broker is merely responding to its customer's purchase order and is acting as the customer's agent. The purchased securities are bought for the account and risk of the customer who placed the order. For this order execution service, the firm charges a fee (commission). There is no markup of the purchase price when a firm acts as a broker. The internal records of the brokerage firm and the customer's trade confirmation will both reflect the fact that the firm acted on an agency basis when it bought the securities.

THE DEALER

Generally, a dealer is a securities firm that provides an active marketplace for those investment products not traded on listed security exchanges. A dealer is a marketmaker and, as such, has responsibilities similar to those of a specialist on the floor of the New York Stock Exchange (NYSE). A dealer must be able and willing, at all times and at a reasonable price relative to current market conditions, to buy and sell the securities for which it has been designated as a marketmaker.

A firm must file for dealer status and meet and maintain regulatory and capital requirements. It must be willing and able to maintain an active and stable marketplace in the securities it trades. It must continually file to the appropriate regulatory bodies reports concerning its trading activities and its trading account positions. Government securities, government agencies, municipal bonds and notes, and mortgage-backed securities are some types of securities traded over the counter with registered dealers.

When a customer executes an order directly with a dealer firm, the dealer is the seller, or contra-party, to the order. The agency relationship previously described for a brokerage firm does not exist for a dealer firm. To trade as a dealer, a firm must maintain a broad-based inventory in the products its customers wish to trade. An employee of the firm known as a *trader* purchases securities for the account and risk of the dealer organization for which he or she works. Purchases are booked into the firm's trading account(s), which are referred to as the firm's inventory accounts. The dealer firm must pay for these purchases with its own capital, which puts that organization's capital at risk to the extent of the overall value of its inventory. As long as there is a position in the firm's trading account, it is the dealer who is the beneficial owner of the securities. When securities are sold out of the trading accounts to a customer, the firm acts as a *principal* in the transaction.

A broker's profits are generated from commissions. Because a dealer is a principal to the transactions it executes with its customers, commissions cannot be charged. Revenues are derived from inventory markups. As is true with all investments, however, a dealer's inventory is affected by industry and general economic factors. Adverse news and conditions will force a dealer to mark down inventory and sustain a loss on sales. A typical problem faced by mortgage-backed traders is fluctuations in interest rates. As with all debt securities, MBS prices rise when general interest rates decrease and fall when they increase. If the trading account is long and rates decrease, the firm will realize a substantial increase in the value of its inventory. If the firm has a short position, it could incur a substantial loss. As long as the inventory remains unsold, gains and/or losses resulting from these value fluctuations are known as *unrealized P&L*. There is no realized P&L until the time of execution on the trade date of sale.

THE BROKER-DEALER

The broker-dealer is an organization that provides both of the services previously described. It is usually a highly capitalized firm with an extensive network of regionally located branch offices. These branches, for the most part, represent the retail division, or consumer's market side, of the broker-dealer's business.

Broker-dealers also have a second group of branch offices, frequently referred to as the capital markets division. Although there may be regional offices associated with the capital markets side, these are usually confined to major financial centers and are therefore far fewer in number. Investment banking and dealer trading are the two main services of the capital markets division.

THE BROKER'S BROKER

Numerous firms actively trade securities. Presently there are more than 40 primary government dealers (who are authorized to deal in primary issues of U.S. government securities). Each of them has the same goal: earn trading profits. Naturally, this puts them in competition with one another. A dealer does not want to lose its competitive edge by disclosing to another dealer that it is an active buyer or an active seller of a particular security.

Think of this situation in the context of economic supply and demand. An owner of inventory that is in high demand is in a position to raise the price charged for that inventory. The owner's profits will be higher because the demand is great, whereas the purchaser's profit margin will be narrowed as a result of the high cost of materials. This principle also applies to the securities market. If there is an active demand for an issue, sellers will raise their asking price. If there is a preponderance of sellers, the buyers will lower their bids (offerings).

It is important that a dealer not disclose to the competition that he or she is an active buyer or seller, thereby causing an adverse impact on the bid or asked price. But how can a dealer execute orders without disclosing current strategy? Through the use of a broker's broker! A broker's broker serves as a finder, a noninterested intermediary, that specializes in providing electronic quotation and execution systems that it markets to the entire dealer community. Subscribing dealers enter their quotes into the system of a broker's broker, and other dealers execute their orders against the quotes on their screens. Although the quotes do not originate from the broker's broker, trades are executed as if they do. This provides the desired anonymity. Quotes are displayed to all subscribers. A dealer executes against a specific quote in the central system. The system captures and reports the execution. Because it is the system of an uninvolved third party, neither the buyer nor the seller knows the other's identity at the time of execution. The identity of the dealer is disclosed for comparison and clearance purposes at a later date when there is little, if any, market advantage. The broker's broker receives a fee for each trade it executes. At no point does it have a beneficial interest in the trade. Some of the familiar broker's broker systems used in the mortgage-backed market are the Cantor, Garban, JPC (a division of FBI), and RMJ trading systems.

DEALERS AND THE MBS MARKET

The elements that affect the profitability of mortgage-backed securities are broader in scope than for other security products. An MBS dealer maintains two distinct, yet related, markets. There is the "to be announced" (TBA) market, which consists of "forward" generic transactions, and there is the secondary market in specific outstanding securities. Chapter 2 discussed the dealer's role in the issuance of MBS. Dealers in MBS maintain relationships with the external organizations and firms, such as mortgage bankers, that issue securities. Dealers make commitments to purchase pools, pass-through certificates, PCs, and so on before the fact and realize income from the fees these commitments generate. Commitments play an important role in the decisions dealers must make concerning their TBA trading positions since those commitments will provide a partial source of the securities needed to fulfill open TBA contracts. All open TBA trading positions due for settlement must be allocated actual securities for delivery against the terms of the contract. Decisions can be made during this pool assignment, or allocation process, that can substantially affect the profitability of the original TBA trade.

Each of the profitability factors will be disscussed at length in later chapters. The point to realize here is that, in addition to the P&L associated with the trading of specified issues in the secondary marketplace, MBS dealers must synchronize and maintain a tight control over many different functions in order to produce a profit for the firm.

5

Overview of the Operations Processing Cycle

The challenges presented to systems and operational professionals who are actively involved in processing mortgage-backed securities can be the source of great personal satisfaction. The basic product is more complex than most. Today, the industry is marketing some sophisticated derivatives of the original pass-through certificates, such as real estate mortgage investment conduits (REMICs), convertible and inverse rate floaters, and asset-backed issues.

If you are new to the MBS industry, you have no doubt talked with people who have been quite outspoken about the problems associated with MBS. Well, there *are* quite a few problems, but the problems are the challenges that can bring enormous satisfaction when you find solutions. Having read the preceding chapters should have clarified many basic industry concepts for you. You are on the road to understanding mortgage-backeds; that alone has to be rewarding. Once you understand the basic concepts underlying the product, you will be able to perform your job well—so well that within a short time you too will realize processing mortgage-backeds is, as stated in the introduction, a controllable process. The satisfaction of knowing that you have done a good job with a difficult product is well worth the effort you put into understanding this text.

The purpose of this chapter is to provide a capsulized view of the operations cycle. At this stage it is not important to be concerned with details. Do not be concerned just now with understanding the "hows." Better than half the battle is won by understanding the general concepts. To help in that understanding, Figure 5–1 addresses "what happens" and the text will explain "why."

Figure 5–1 depicts a sequential processing chain that includes the following steps.

❑ Order origination.

❑ Order execution.

❑ Trade processing.

❑ Trade confirmation and comparison.

❑ When-issued processing.

❑ TBA allocation processing.

❑ Trade file storage and analysis.

❑ Clearance, or settlement, processing.

❑ Money settlement and financing.

❑ Control of fails.

❑ Collection and disbursement of P&I payments.

ORDER ORIGINATION

There are three main sources of orders:

1. Retail.
2. Institutional.
3. Interdealer.

Retail Orders

Retail customers contact their account executive who immediately enters the order into the cycle by writing an order ticket for subsequent entry into the firm's system or by keying it directly into the system. In the scenario depicted in Figure 5–1, the order goes to a trading group that has been established for

FIGURE 5–1. Sequential Processing Chain

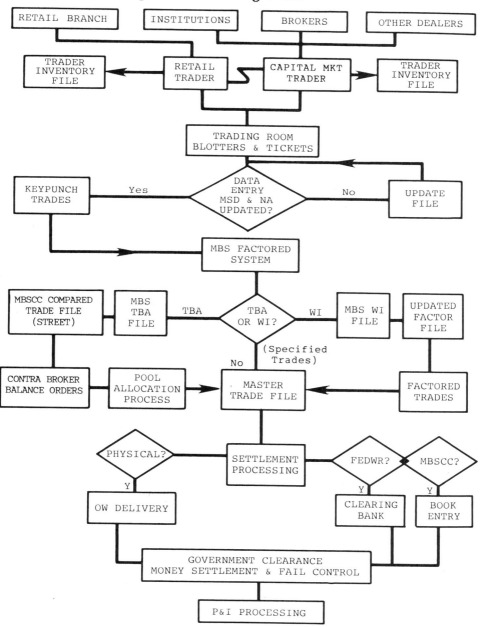

handling the firm's retail orders. That group is linked with the capital market's traders of the firm with whom they execute their larger trades. If the firm involved has no trading room, the order is forwarded to the order room where the firm's traders, through phone and electronic links with other dealers and brokers, execute the order as a broker on the client's behalf. Orders coming from this segment of the market consist mainly of orders for specific or secondary issues although a fairly large number of orders are taken for TBAs.

Retail orders are handled separately for several reasons. The size of the orders is small relative to the market, and therefore there are odd lot pricing considerations and the effect of breaking round lots, which are by far more marketable, into odd lots. The control of this problem is one of the reasons for creating a self-contained retail trading unit. The retail traders are more familiar with the problems and costs associated with this type of business and are therefore in a better position to mark up odd lot prices effectively. The costs involved include the cost of financing unsold odd lot inventory and the extra operational processing required. Retail customers make cash payments for their trades and in most cases must leave their securities deposited in their account to be serviced by the broker. The costs of administering monthly P&I payments plus fees for inventory maintenance and associated insurance have to be factored into the pricing of the securities. And a retail trader becomes more involved with details because, particularly in the case of mortgage-backeds, the average retail customer is less familiar with the product than the institutional accounts and there are frequent questions to be answered.

Institutional Orders

Institutional accounts are customers who are professional money managers. In this category are large corporate portfolios, banks, investment trusts, and investment advisory organizations acting on behalf of their customers. These types of accounts frequently employ their own traders who interface directly with the capital market traders of a dealer firm. The orders generated from these accounts frequently have a "high ticket value," which means that they are high quantity (block) orders. There is a heavy participation in the primary (TBA) market by institutional accounts.

Interdealer Orders

A great deal of trading activity occurs in the interdealer market. Brokers, acting as the agent for the customers of their firms, execute trades with the capital markets traders (dealers). Other dealers, either on behalf of their customers or on behalf of their firm's trading account, execute large amounts of orders in TBA and secondary issues as well as repos, reverse repos, and rollovers, each of which is discussed in a later chapter.

ORDER EXECUTION

In a dealer organization, it is the trader who executes an order. The trader must be considered a marketmaker in an over-the-counter securities market. Executed orders are done for the account and risk of the firm and are bought into or sold out of the firm's own inventory accounts. These accounts represent the capital of the firm, and the effective trading of this inventory is what makes a dealer profitable. In the context of order execution, the most important point of discussion is control.

Every trader has an inventory file that must be maintained on a real-time basis. That means that the information concerning every executed order must be added (buy side) or subtracted (sell side) to the opening inventory. Some dealers handle this recordkeeping manually through trader-originated updates to the opening figures recorded on sheets of paper referred to as *slates*. Each trader has his or her own slate of securities to trade. Some dealers record their daily executions using microcomputers and others through real-time, on-line mainframe system applications. The latter method is preferable because it affords the head traders and managing directors of the firm an opportunity to monitor the firm's capital exposure on broad and real-time bases. It also permits a continuous accounting stream that cannot get out of synch with subsidiary files. Because order executions are entered at the point of execution, there is no need for any additional entries after that. File integrity is preserved.

Another major consideration is the speed at which an order gets executed. In the bond market, which is what we are talking about when discussing mortgage-backeds, prices move swiftly and sometimes violently up and down. To facilitate the prompt execution of a trade, an abbreviated form of the order sometimes referred to as a *skeletal trade*, is transmitted to the traders for execution. (Skeletal orders are discussed in more detail in Chapter 6.) This order contains the minimum information required for a proper execution. It will be expanded later with all the specific detail required for internal and external processing. To include all this information in the original transmission of the order would result in unnecessary and potentially costly delays. The skeletal trade bears a unique identification number plus the time and date of entry. Order executions are recorded on the skeletal trade, which must subsequently be matched to the completed order. These matches must occur because customers have the legal right to have their orders executed at the time they are placed. In terms of execution, an order received at 10:00 A.M. must receive execution priority over an identical order received at 10:05 A.M.

TRADE PROCESSING

It is difficult to be definitive about a trade processing group because its duties can vary radically from firm to firm. Some of the responsibilities discussed in this section may apply to a different group in your firm. In referencing Figure 5–1, the areas of reference are the data entry decision, the blotter and ticket process, and the MBS factored system process.

Trade processing is responsible for the following functions:

❑ Maintenance of the customer's name and address file.

❑ Maintenance of the security master file.

❑ Coding transactions and trade entry.

❑ Confirmation and comparison processing.

❑ Balancing trade blotters.

❑ Balancing trading positions.

❑ Trade cancellation and correction processing.

❑ Updating factor files.

To process an order, two data elements that must be available are the customer's account number and the security number used to identify the full description of the issue being traded. Trade processing updates these files. The master file of names and addresses must be updated whenever a new account is introduced to the firm. An order cannot be processed under that customer's name unless an account number has been assigned to the client and the client's account information has been added to the file. Updates must also be made to reflect such things as address or delivery instructions for existing accounts. Daily updates are required to the security master file for two reasons. First, many firms do not keep a master file of every issued mortgage-backed security. If one of the missing issues is traded for the first time, the files must be updated before any orders can be entered into the record stream. Second, the mortgage-backed marketplace is constantly issuing new pools, pass-throughs, and other MBS types. These must be added to a firm's security master file.

Many firms process orders through the creation of a hand-written order ticket that contains only the basic information required by the trader. Trade processing adds the additional information needed to process the trade and also adds codes used to identify general and specific accounting and processing cycles associated with every trade. An example is a code that triggers or routes reports and blotters to a specific person or area to facilitate the settlement of the trade in the future. This is an important trade processing function because it sets the direction for the future processing of the transaction. Once the order ticket, with the trade input information, is properly coded, the actual keyentry processing of the order is completed. The importance of this function cannot be overemphasized because it is this process that creates all the firm's internal records associated with each trade. There is no other area in which the old cliché "Garbage in, garbage out!" is more applicable.

TRADE CONFIRMATION AND COMPARISON

The order entry process results in two outputs: (1) the confirmation of the transaction for the customer and (2) the comparison for the dealer (or streetside). Both documents contain all the details of a trade executed with the parties to whom the confirmation and comparison are addressed. All customers' trades must be confirmed. Unless clients advise to the contrary, it is assumed that the details of trades are correct and that the customers

FIGURE 5–2. A Confirmation for a Mortgage-Backed Security

CUSTOMER COPY

Securities Corporation
MEMBER NEW YORK STOCK EXCHANGE INC

NEW YORK, N.Y. 10005

TELEPHONE

5 3 4 3 5

ACTING AS **PRINCIPAL**   WE CONFIRM HAVING   **SOLD TO**

Originating No.	Representative	Account Number	Trans. No.
	07	13 19Ø	F Ø5

CODES

	Fed	Tr.	Cap.	Sett.
	1	7		

	Trade Date	Settlement Date	As-Of Date
YOU:	11/11/88	11/18/88	

CONTRA PARTY

XY ZEE MBS FUND, INC.

DELIVERY INSTRUCTIONS

BANK OF NEW YORK

ABA #Ø21ØØØØ18
BK OF NYC/

. . . .
BT #14

We	Quantity/Par	Cusip	Security Description	Internal Use ONLY
SLD	1,ØØØM	WHØØØ111T	GNMA Pool 123456 SF LEVEL PAY	T86-11

FIXED RATE 10% DUE Ø8-15-2Ø11

CURRENT FACTOR .87654321

VERSUS FED FUNDS RECEIVE FROM
SECURITY PACIFIC
127 JOHN STREET 23RD FLOOR
NEW YORK, N.Y. 1ØØ38

Basis Price	Coupon	Maturity Date	Dated Date	Accrued Interest From

Dollar Price	Principal	Interest/Discount	Misc.	**NET AMOUNT DUE**
99 1/8	$ 868,873.46	$ 4,139.23		$ 873,012.69

WE CONFIRM THE ABOVE TRADE(S), SUBJECT TO TERMS AND CONDITIONS ON REVERSE SIDE will settle their trades as confirmed. Figure 5–2 is an example of a typical trade confirmation for a mortgage-backed issue.

The confirmation process is automatic and mechanical and involves only the firm. The comparison process is far more involved. The basic accounting concept that every debit must have an offsetting credit applies to every trade execution made by a securities firm. For every buyer (the debit side of a trade execution), there must be a seller (the offsetting credit side of a trade execution). This relationship must exist and must be entered on the books of the firm. When we talk about the trade processing group balancing the blotters, we are referring to the daily task of balancing debits to credits. The group is making sure that the offsetting side of every transaction has been recorded.

Aside from the mandates of accounting, why is balancing necessary? Envision yourself as Broker A who has just bought a $25,000 mortgage-backed security for a customer. You forwarded that order to your trader who contacted Broker B who sold the issue to him. The next step is to receive the securities you bought on behalf of your customer, and to deliver them. Unless you book a receivable (the sale by Broker B), your operations staff will see only your customer's purchase and will have no idea of where to obtain the securities to deliver to that client. To ensure that the required information is available, trade processing balances the daily trade blotters to make sure that the debits equal the credits. In other words, they make sure an offsetting transaction has been posted for every purchase and sale. Voilà, the P&S Department! Furthermore, Broker A must ensure that the details of the trade as booked on the firm's internal records are the same as the details of the trade as booked on the records of Broker B to preclude any problems when it comes time for the brokers to settle (clear) the trade. The manner in which streetside transactions are compared is discussed in length later; for now, the summary in Table 5–1 will suffice.

In addition to balancing and comparing the trade blotters, trade processing also balances the inventory or trading account balances each day. This is a requirement for every dealer that does not have a fully integrated system. If the traders' real-time inventory is maintained manually or on a microcomputer or by any other system not directly linked to the official accounting system

TABLE 5–1. The Confirmation and Comparison Process

Contra-Party Type	Method of Confirmation or Comparison
The Primary or TBA Market	
Retail customer	Written confirmation; margin required.
Institutional customers	Commitment letter signed & returned.
Brokers	Acknowledged comparison *or* automated comparison through MBSCC Clearing Division.
Dealers	Automated comparsion, MBSCC Clearing Division.
Broker's brokers	Give up comparison through the MBSCC Clearing Division.
The Secondary, or Specified, Pool Market	
Retail customer	Written confirmation; no affirmation.
Institutional customers	Written confirmation; no affirmation.
Brokers	Written comparison signed & returned.
Dealers	Written comparison signed & returned.
Broker's brokers	Not applicable.

of the firm, it is necessary to balance—that is, to ensure that the two records contain the identical inventory information.

Inventories of the firm's trading positions are controlled through a series of trading accounts. These accounts are similar to an account that would be used to identify a transaction done with another broker or dealer. But these accounts are used solely to record (book) trades that have been executed by a dealer as principal to a trade. The activity that is reflected by the entries in the account represents the contra-side of a trade that the dealer's trader has executed on behalf of the firm. When talking about *buys* and *sells*, people at a dealer organization are referring to the side of the trade in which the firm has an interest. So when a trader refers to a buy done with a customer, the trader is referring to a trade in which the customer sold and the trading account bought. Many dealer firms confirm their trades from the standpoint of the trading account. This can be confusing for the person who is doing internal research for the first time. Carefully note the wording on your internal records. Copies of customer's confirmations that state "We have BOUGHT this day as principal" are records of sales from the customer's perspective, and they are records of buys from the dealer's perspective.

A firm normally maintains multiple trading accounts for each desk. *Desk* is the term used to refer to the traders responsible for buying and selling a particular product (e.g., the mortgage-backed desk). There may be several, even dozens, of trading accounts being used by an MBS dealer. Minimally, there is a trading account for the forward (or TBA) trading activity and another account for secondary market trades in previously issued pools, PCs, and so on. Typically, separate accounts are used for trading the current or active TBA coupon, with one or more accounts for the inactive coupons. Because there is no specific pool or group number available when a trade is executed as a TBA, all TBAs are traded on a coupon basis. For trades in the secondary market, the trading desk is subdivided by individual issuer such as GNMA, FNMA, or FHLMC. There is a separate trading account for each issuer, or perhaps a separate trading account for each individual trader. It is important to know how your particular firm has structured its trading desks.

Each trading account in the firm should be balanced daily, no later than 8:00 A.M. on the following business day. This is an extremely critical control measure. Unless a firm is certain that its opening trading positions are correct, there is a strong danger of trading a position that does not exist. History has repeated itself many times over in this respect, and the actual and potential losses of selling the wrong inventory are significant.

Processing trade cancellations and corrections is another function of trade processing. It too is a vital function of the group. The word *vital* should be emphasized. All processing activities that take place after execution are dependent on correct trade information. MBS trading is a high-volume and complex environment in which some mistakes will always occur. What is critical is to correct those mistakes immediately on discovery and to triple-check the corrected information so that there is no need to correct a correction. Multiple corrections are not good for customer relations and inevitably lead to further processing problems and actual revenue losses downstream in the processing cycle. Procedures must be in place that control this function. The manager of the trade processing group should have access to information that reflects all open trade problems at the end of each business day. Both the customer and streetside of a firm's trading activity market must be considered. In addition to the details of problem trades, management reports should include information concerning potential exposure resulting from all unresolved problem trades and a date-sorted pending report to prevent a backlog in the correction process.

Monitoring Factor Information

If a trade processing area finds itself bored with nothing to do, it can always fall back on its role in monitoring factor information. Factors are unique to securities that amortize (pay down) their orginal principal amount. Each time a mortgage payment is made, the outstanding principal amount of the loan is reduced (amortized) by the amount of principal repayment that was included in the total payment. A separate factor is available for every outstanding mortgage-backed issue. It represents the percentage of the original face value of the security presently outstanding and is expressed as an eight-decimal-place integer. These factors are updated monthly through the facilities of a service organization such as *The Bond Buyer* or *Trepp Information Services* which provide tapes of the updated factors. The service bureaus receive their information from the original issuers (the mortgage bankers and the like) that are servicing the individual mortgages that collateralize each pool. Table 5–2 illustrates a factor and how it is used.

MBS firms update their internal systems using factor tapes from the service bureaus. However, whether the fault of the MBS issuer in transmitting incorrect information to the service agency or the fault of the agency itself in the creation of its files, there are times when the factor for an issue is incorrect. When this type of error is discovered, two steps must be taken by trade processing. First, the factor file must be adjusted to reflect the corrected information. Second, all trades that have been processed with the incorrect factor must be cancelled and corrected. As Table 5–2 demonstrates, the factor application produces the principal amount of a trade transaction. If the factor used in this calculation is incorrect, then all associated trade calculations will be incorrect and must be reprocessed.

TABLE 5–2. A Factor and Its Application

Security description	MBS SFMtg Pool #654321 10.50% due 8/15/2019
Original principal amount of pool	$1,503,023.82
Current factor	0.87654321
Application	Original × factor = amortized principal amount (face)
	$1,503,023.82 × 0.87654321 = $1,317,465.32
Outstanding principal	$1,317,465.32

WHEN-ISSUED PROCESSING

The term *when issued* (WI) refers to the execution of a secondary market trade in a specific pool for which the current factor is not available. The only major issuers of MBS that issue their factor information on the first of the month are FHLMC and FNMA. GNMA factors are available on approximately the sixth business day each month; private issuers vary. Most firms process their trades using the original face amount, which is then multiplied by the current factor to produce the current principal value of a trade. If the current factor is not available, then the trade cannot be calculated correctly. In this case, it is processed as when issued. Then when the current month's factor is published, the trade will be (re)calculated to reflect its true value.

The use of the term *when issued* in the MBS market has nothing to do with the pending issuance of a security. No "pool-specific" trade should have to be processed "when issued" after the eighth business day of the month provided the settlement date of the trade occurs in the same month. Previously executed WIs should be cleared from WI status by that time.

TBA ALLOCATION PROCESSING

The dealer market in the primary, or to-be-announced (TBA) marketplace, is extremely active. When an MBS is traded on a TBA basis, the specific pool that will be ultimately received or delivered is not known. The information that is known and that cannot change, unless both parties to the trade agree, is the following:

- ❑ The guarantor of the issue (GNMA, FHLMC, FNMA, etc.).
- ❑ The type of collateral underlying the MBS (single family, for example).
- ❑ The coupon rate (the interest rate).
- ❑ The maturity range, not date, of the issue (15 or 30 years).
- ❑ An approximate principal value (can vary 2.499999% plus or minus).
- ❑ The price.
- ❑ The settlement date of the pool to be announced.

All TBA trades represent forward transactions in a generic MBS security and, depending on the identity of the guarantor, settle on a specific date once each month. There are presently five different monthly settlement dates for TBA transactions. Anyone who has an open TBA position five days before the assigned settlement date for the underlying pools is obligated to settle the transaction through the delivery of an actual pool, which gets assigned to the TBA. This assignment process is called *the TBA allocation process.* Every seller must advise the buyer, no later than two days before the settlement date, of the specific pool it intends to deliver in settlement of the TBA contract.

The allocation process is governed by the Uniform Practices Committee of the Public Securities Association (PSA), which is a user-directed, self-regulatory body. One of its functions is the formation of the rules and practices that govern the mortgage-backed industry. Allocation rules permit a variance between the face amount sold under a TBA contract and the actual amortized quantity deliverable under that contract. If the rules of allocations are properly and carefully administered, P&L can be realized over and above the original TBA trade P&L. This variance is not an arbitrary decision designed for the benefit of the MBS dealers. Allocation is a difficult process to control and can result in revenue losses as well as gains, but it is a necessary component of the MBS market. Recall for a moment the mortgage bankers who pool their mortgage loans with an issuer for the purpose of receiving a guaranteed MBS. In the pooling process, each issuer has its own specifications that must be met in order to obtain an MBS. The size of the individual loans and the overall size of the pool are defined. Details such as the date of issuance of the loan, the term of the loan, the coupon rate, insurance or the lack of it, and the loan-to-value ratio are details that must be the same or similiar. There must be some marketplace to be able to establish some method of pricing the MBS.

Therefore, the proper mortgages have to be bundled to fit within these parameters. After the mortgage banker pools the loans, a document review process takes place to ensure that all the loans meet the required specifications of the program. During this review period, the mortgages continue to pay down. There is no set time allowed for the review, and there is no way to predetermine the amount of principal that will be paid down during the review process. Because mortgage loans vary in amount and because they will have been partially paid down before the actual issuance of the MBS, it is impossible to accurately predetermine the face value of an MBS on issuance date. But because there are fixed parameters within which all eligible loans must adhere, the face value of new mortgage issues can be reasonably predicted. Based on the facts that come into play during the creation and lifecycle of mortgage-backed issues, the industry has established its standard permissible variance. Using this variance, anyone who has purchased a $1 million face value TBA contract can expect delivery from the seller of an amortized amount ranging from $975,000.01 to $1,024,999.99. It is during the allocation process that the sellers decide the pools and the amounts they will deliver in settlement of their TBA sales.

TRADE FILE STORAGE AND ANALYSIS

We have covered up to this point everything that transpires before the settlement (clearance) of mortgage-backed trades.

Every execution adds an entry to some trade file: the TBA file, the when-issued file, the compared trade file, or the uncompared trade file. Before securities and money can change hands during the settlement cycle, however, processing must be completed on each of the entries contained in all these files. Once satisfactorily processed, they all become part of the master trade, or pending, file.

Every entry in the master trade file should be a valid contract, each balanced, confirmed, or compared. For a moment, assume that all functions have been completed and all discrepancies resolved on a timely basis (no later than settlement date minus two). Assume also that the master trade file contains all the information needed by a firm to clear (i.e., receive the purchases and/or deliver the sales). At this time, a presettlement analysis of the contents of the file should be made. The goal of this analysis is to ensure that every sale made by the firm is delivered on the settlement date of the trade and no later. Let's quickly review why this is the paramount objective of all clearance operations.

On the settlement date of a trade, all benefits associated with the ownership of a security now accrue to the purchaser. The important consideration here is the right to any accrued interest and principal payments on mortgage-backed issues. Up to but not including the settlement date of the sale, the seller has been receiving the benefit of the interest accruing on the issue. On the settlement date, that benefit passes to the purchaser. If the securities that were sold are not delivered on the settlement date, the selling broker does not receive the cash value of the trade. The seller at this point is receiving no income and does not have the proceeds of the sale to reinvest in some other income-producing security. Failing to deliver a security on the settlement date of the trade is a real loss to the seller. The amount of that loss is at least the value of the current rate of interest multiplied by the value of the proceeds of the sale.

The point of this discussion is to highlight the reason for performing a presettlement analysis of the master trade file. It identifies for the clearance operation of a firm every sale that has to be delivered. Furthermore, it identifies the source of the inventory to be used in the clearance of the settling sales. Sources can include securities currently in inventory or purchases made for the same settlement date. Whatever the source, the goal of the analysis is twofold as follows:

1. Identify delivery requirements.
2. Identify situations that might preclude the possibility of making a delivery on the settlement date of a sale.

Once a firm has identified its potential problems, steps can be taken beforehand to rectify the situation. The purpose of the analysis is to improve the cash flow of a firm.

CLEARANCE OR SETTLEMENT PROCESSING

The terms *clearance, settlement,* and *receive and deliver* (R&D) are used interchangeably. They refer to the process by which purchased securities are received and paid for, and sold securities are delivered and cash received. This process takes place in the cashier's department of a brokerage firm.

The cashiering department of a brokerage firm has direct control over the custody and movement of the assets of both the firm and its customers. Therefore, tight security controls are imperative, and no securities may be received or delivered without the proper authorization. Although the trade processing department is not usually thought of as being a source of authorization for the cashier's department, effectively it is. An R&D department depends on the information contained in the trade master file. This file is the end product of all the processing discussed in connection with a trade processing group. If the information passed on by this group is incorrect or out of balance, then the R&D activities of the firm will contain errors and be out of balance.

There are several ways to clear a security. It may be accomplished by an over-the-window (OW) delivery. A physical certificate, also called a definitive certificate, is delivered by a messenger to the office or representative of the purchaser. Either a check or a bank money wire is received in payment of the delivered issue. Clearance may also be effected physically through the facilities of a registered clearing corporation. A registered clearing corporation serves as a central drop-off and pick-up point for securities traded between its members. A third way to settle is through the facilities of the Federal Reserve wire system, which is an electronic method of processing security receipts and deliveries in a nondefinitive (book-entry-only) format. Finally, clearance may be done through the facilities of a securities depository, which serves as a custodian for all the physical certificates held by its members. Receipts and deliveries made through a securities depository are accomplished through book-entry movements into and out of the accounts of each of the members of the depository. Presently, at the beginning of the first quarter of 1989, all of the foregoing settlement methods must be used. It is expected, however, that the mortgage-backed depository, Participants Trust Company (PTC), formerly MBSCC & Co., Depository Division, will be fully functional in 1989. Then the need, indeed the ability, to deliver all but a few MBS physically will be eliminated.

The kind of security dictates the method of clearance that must be used. The following chart identifies current clearance requirements.

TABLE 5–3. Clearance Requirements

Type of Security	Method of Clearance
FNMA and FHLMC issues*	Federal Reserve Wire System
GNMA current coupon issues	Physical
GNMA noncurrent coupons	Participants Trust Company
Private issuers/CMOs/REMICs	Physical and Depository Trust Company

* Exclusive of zero tranche CMOs/REMICs and ARM issues.

MONEY SETTLEMENT

Both money settlement and financing are the responsibility of the cashier's department. Money settlement is the process of collecting or paying the funds associated with the daily R&D activity. There are several ways of accomplishing this, as follows:

❑ Individual check payments or money wires.

❑ Net end-of-day settlement through a clearing corporation and/or a depository.

❑ Bulk money movements at the end of a day reflecting the consolidated R&D activity as transacted through the Fedwire system.

Individual checks and money wires are used when a delivery is made over the window. An OW delivery is the physical delivery of certificates to the purchaser. When this method of delivery is used, the buyer is expected to have a check ready for the seller's messenger when he returns to the firm later that same day. Because most deliveries of MBS must be settled in federal funds, most payments for OW deliveries are made through the money wire system of the Federal Reserve. Although it is possible to have a Fed check drawn, the process must be done through a reserve member bank. It is a time-consuming process, so the wire system is used in almost all cases.

Payment for deliveries made through either a clearing corporation or a depository is accomplished via a single, netted money settlement. Each is a centralized location through which its members receive and deliver their purchases and sales. Each entity debits the accounts of its members for the value of the securities received by them and credits the same account for the value of the securities delivered by the member. At the end of each day, the accounts of members whose receipts exceeded the value of its deliveries have a net debit. The accounts of those members whose deliveries exceeded the value of its receipts have a net credit. The clearing corporation or depository becomes a conduit for all net balances at the end of each business day. Members with net debits make a single payment to the clearing agency, and the agency pays each member with a credit balance.

The third method—bulk money movements—could almost be considered a hybrid of the first and second inasmuch as there is a one-on-one relationship between delivery and payment and the delivery is made by book entry. The important difference is that when eligible securities are delivered through the Fed, there is a simultaneous book-entry transfer of both securities and money. The funds representing the proceeds of a delivered sale are immediately available to the delivering party. There is no end-of-day net settlement. The bulk money movement is a reference to the process of moving excess funds in one bank to cover the end-of-day and/or an intra-day shortage of funds at another.

FINANCING

Financing has the same meaning to brokers and dealers that it does to you as an individual. It is the process of securing cash loans for the purpose of paying for purchased merchandise. Brokers have to pay for the securities they buy on behalf of their customers. Dealers have the same requirement plus the need to finance their trading inventory. The value of inventory in the largest of the dealers often exceeds $1 billion.

When you made your first mortgage payment, did the amount of interest you paid for a single month amaze you? Shock is probably a better word. Think of what it costs to finance $1 billion! Assuming a noncompounded interest rate of 7.50% per annum, interest on $1 billion is $75 million a year. That's an enormous sum of money, and it's a straight expense, a cost of doing business, which reduces the P&L of the dealer involved.

The obvious goal of a financing area is to keep interest costs to the lowest possible level. There are numerous ways of doing this. The key word is *control*. Control of cash flow, control of fails, and, to the extent possible, control of interest costs. Cash flow is associated with the income on investments and inventory. Monthly principal and interest payments and redemptions of maturing securities fall into this category. If these kinds of payments are received on the due date and used immediately, they are under control. Fails increase financing costs when securities that have been sold cannot be delivered on the settlement date of the trade. The cash proceeds of the sale will not be received, and the firm must borrow the money it did not collect. Analyzing delivery requirements before settlement and taking all steps possible to avoid a fail equates with control of fails. An effective use of long- and short-term loans, repos, letters of credit, substitutions, and dollar rolls result in controlled financing.

CONTROL OF FAILS

A fail is a trade that is not cleared on settlement date. Broker A buys $1,000,000.00 MBS Pool 654321 from Broker B; the trade settled yesterday and no delivery/payment was made. Broker A's records reflect a fail to receive from Broker B, and Broker B's records reflect a fail to deliver.

The first aspect of the control of fails is prevention. By doing a presettlement review of the master trade file, the clearance department of any broker or dealer will be able to determine which of their sales may result in a fail. For example, securities may have been sold on behalf of a customer. A review of the customer's account reveals that the securities are not positioned; the assumption has to be that the customer will mail them to the firm. Depending on the dollar value of the sale, it may be prudent to contact the client before settlement to ensure that timely receipt of the securities will be accomplished. This is preventive control.

Volume and inevitable problems join forces and result in sizeable amounts of both fails to receive and fails to deliver on the books of any large broker or dealer. Procedures must be in place to enable a firm to carefully examine each of the trades that have failed. The purpose of this review process is to determine the actual cause of the fail. Once the cause is determined, steps can then be taken to rectify the situation. Fails will always occur; the firm that clears them quickly, "cleans them up" in street parlance, is the firm that is under control.

6

Data Entry and Trade Processing

The function of the order room and trading desk is the execution of buy and/or sell orders for both the firm and its customers. Ensuring the proper processing of the executed trades is the function of the data entry department. The importance of the data entry area cannot be stressed enough. Its personnel are responsible for the origination of the official books and records of the firm. Their work creates the records that feed a firm's accounting systems and back office operations.

Data entry is usually a subdivision of a department known as the trade processing department. This department has multiple functions, as follows:

❑ Maintenance of the customer's name and address file.

❑ Maintenance of the security master file.

❑ Coding transactions and trade entry.

❑ Confirmation processing and verification.

❑ Trade comparison and trade blotter balancing.

❑ Balancing trading positions.

❑ Updating factor files.

❑ Processing trade cancellations and corrections.

Before any processing can take place, two files must be available: the name and address master file and the security master file. These files must be kept current. They contain the individualized numbers assigned to each customer and to each security. They provide the source of information that systems require to interpret account and security numbers into names and security descriptions. They also contain instructions and regulatory and trading information used throughout the execution, processing, and custodial cycles. These files are considered by many persons to be the cornerstones required to build and maintain efficient trade execution, processing, and clearance support for a firm.

THE NAME AND ADDRESS MASTER FILE (NAMSTR)

First, let's examine the uses of the name and address master file. It provides the following information:

- ❑ Account number for every individual and firm account.
- ❑ Basic customer information (address, tax ID, etc.).
- ❑ Account classification for regulatory compliance.
- ❑ Authorized trading levels and/or restrictions.
- ❑ Identity of the assigned account executive.
- ❑ Status concerning the receipt of required documents.
- ❑ Names and addresses of authorized interested parties (duplicates).
- ❑ Trade clearance (R&D) instructions.
- ❑ Custody, registration, check payment, and P&I instructions.
- ❑ Linkages to external interfaces (clearing banks, depositories).

The use of the file is broad in scope. Most firms have a single NAMSTR file. Therefore, the information required to process any type of product, be it an equity, corporate bond, or whatever, must be incorporated into this single file.

Orders cannot be processed without an account number. But in terms of the NAMSTR file, initially an account number is all that is required. So a major concern has to be the timely addition of new account information into the file. Order execution is of paramount importance for any securities firm. It takes time to add all the information required by a record layout in order to have a complete record on the NAMSTR file. If all that work were always done before order execution, many orders and accounts would be lost to competition. To facilitate timely execution of orders, new customers are frequently assigned an account number from an available range of unused numbers. This number is entered onto an order that is then immediately processed as a "no name" order. Later in the day the account executive gathers the information required and transmits it to trade processing for updating. If trade processing is unable to complete the updates by the time the files have to be closed for the night's processing, then "no name" confirmations are produced. These are held by trade processing until the NAMSTR file is updated the following day, at which time correct confirmations are generated and mailed to the clients involved.

Correcting the information on old records is just as important as adding new records. Never make the mistake of thinking that because an account is already opened on a file, account changes do not need to receive priority attention. Nothing could be further from the truth. Remember that the information in this file feeds many different links. Trade processing is one of the first links in a long chain. If the first link is weak, incorrect, or missing, then the entire chain is weak and the operations cycle for that trade will fall apart. Timely updating of all changes to the NAMSTR file is imperative.

The individual fields in each record (i.e., the contents of the NAMSTR file) must contain certain basic information that rarely changes from firm to firm. However, additional information is desirable for a variety of reasons.

THE SECURITY MASTER FILE (SECMST)

The security master file is the second file to receive the "cornerstone" label. It contains the descriptive information of every security a firm trades and contains the following information:

❑ Full description of every security.
❑ Short name of each security to facilitate certain reporting.

❑ CUSIP number of each issue (should be expanded to ISN number).

❑ In-house security number of each issue.

❑ Routing of orders for execution.

❑ Factor tables required to calculate amortized amounts.

❑ Formula to be used in the calculation of accrued interest.

❑ Routing of information for comparison and confirmation purposes.

❑ Pricing history of each security.

❑ In-house generic routing information for clearance and custody.

❑ Type of funds associated with the security.

The problems associated with maintaining this file are, in certain respects, more critical than those involved with the NAMSTR. First, there is no such thing as processing a "no name" or "no number" security. To get an order onto the books of a firm, a security number must be available. Therefore, the need for timely updating of missing issues is critical. This means that all orders should be processed promptly so that if the order is for an issue not on file, the SECMST can be updated immediately.

Second, a serious problem being experienced by all firms today is the proliferation of derivatives. These are securities that have common generic features but that incorporate one or more unusual features in their structure that are designed to make them more marketable to a particular segment of the investment community. An example of this was the introduction of principal only (P/O) and interest only (I/O) strips created by separating the cash flow derived from a regular MBS. The unusual characteristics affect the way the issues are traded, the way they are calculated, the way they are cleared. They change from issue to issue so an operations staff can no longer depend on generic consistencies to determine how a product should be handled. And not only do they change from issue to issue but also from issuer to issuer. Similar derivatives will be originated by various banks, brokers, or agencies, and each program will have its own variation on a common theme. Most security master files were created before the derivatives were envisioned, and therefore they employ a logic that depends on consistency throughout a product line. Collateralized mortgage obligations (CMOs) provide an example of what can happen. Some CMOs accrue interest on a 360-day basis, others on a 365-day basis. Some settle in Fed funds, and some settle in clearinghouse funds. Some systems categorize all CMOs as corporate issues. Therefore, the CMOs are calculated on a 30/360-day basis and routed to the corporate desk in the cashier's department for clearance. Either or both could be incorrect, and as a result significant delays and losses can be sustained.

In the near term, the people who are responsible for maintaining the SECMST file should have a broad knowledge of products and an excellent knowledge of their components. In the long term, the industry must change the logic it has depended on, rightfully and successfully so, for decades. The types of processes alluded to in the CMO example must be triggered by specific codes assigned on a security-by-security basis rather than by a generic security type.

Another concern pertaining to both of the files just discussed must be addressed: maintaining dual NAMSTR and SECMST files for two independent, interfaced systems. Some firms purchase or lease a secondary system designed to process its mortgage-backed orders. They then feed the information from this system into the main primary system, which produces the official books and records of the firm. This arrangement is necessary when the primary system is not "pool-driven" and is designed neither to calculate amortized amounts nor to carry security positions requiring decimals or pennies. When these secondary independent systems are used, they require their own master files and generate their own record files.

In this scenario, there are two security master files, and each must contain a complete description of all securities traded by the firm. Before entering an update into the SECMST of the secondary system, always make sure that the CUSIP number being added does not already exist in the primary file. This could result in records that contain the same CUSIP in both systems but different descriptive information. It is possible for an update to be accepted in the secondary system but rejected in the primary system; monitor your reject reports daily. Remember, under these circumstances, the secondary trade file will contain the order but the primary system will not. Communicate this information to the appropriate people in the firm. The same situation can occur with the NAMSTR file. An update could be accepted by the secondary file but rejected in the primary file. The trade will be processed in the primary system as a "no name" account. The position files will remain in synch. However, the primary NAMSTR must be updated immediately.

Before leaving the discussion of the NAMSTR and SECMST files, it would be a useful exercise for you to review the recap at the beginning of this chapter that highlights the uses of each. The purpose of this exercise is to help you focus on the long-range direction of this industry. Keep in mind the operational cycle explained in Chapter 5. As automated processing becomes more sophisticated, the NAMSTR and SECMST files become more important. This is best exemplified by looking at where automation has already taken us in terms of processing most equities and corporate bonds. In a fully automated, real-time, on-line environment, trades in these issues are entered once into a trading system at the point of origin: the account executive's desk. Under certain circumstances there is *no need for any additional manual intervention*. The order can be automatically routed (by SECMST) to the floor of the exchange. It can be programmatically executed through an automated specialists' book and compared. If the order is executed for an institutional client, it is automatically confirmed; once confirmed, it is automatically delivered (NAMSTR). If the order is for a retail customer, the system generates transfer instructions (provided there are no debits in the account) that are forwarded programmatically through a depository to the transfer agent, which mails registered securities to the purchasing customer and provides automated entries to update the records of the originating broker. The age of totally automated execution, comparison, and clearance is here, and it will continue to expand. The firms that are able to take full advantage of this automation are the firms that fully understand the design concepts and the maintenance requirements of the name and address master file and the security master file.

CODING TRANSACTIONS AND TRADE ENTRY

For the purpose of this discussion, we make the hypothetical assumption that the processes described are those required by a firm whose traders record executions on a manual order ticket that is passed to a central data input unit. The same information and considerations must be incorporated into the design of any on-line processing system.

Coding orders is a fine-tuning process by which additional information and/or codes are added to a basic order entry ticket. Codes are numeric or alpha characters, each serving as an identifier that triggers one or more processes and/or reports. Codes assist in routing information to the proper areas within a firm.

There are two facets to the coding process, the first of which is generic to all firms and which will be referred to as *basic coding*. A trader needs to be able to enter an order into a firm's computer system quickly and easily. Orders need only contain what some firms refer to as skeletal information, the bare bones data required for execution. To expedite the trading process, traders in many firms enter skeletal trades that contain quantity bought or sold (expressed as a face amount), price, a short security identifier (e.g., a pool number or an abbreviated TBA description), a customer short name, and an original trade date if the order is being executed "as of."

Trade processing takes the skeletal orders and expands them so that they include all the information needed. If any information is missing or illegible, the problem is referred to the traders or their assistants for immediate resolution. Trade and settlement dates, security numbers, customer account numbers, and sales credit information are added. A trade number is assigned to each order and becomes the trade's unique ID number to be used for referencing and future processing. Codes that identify the trading account and trade classification (TBA, secondary market, and when issued) must be assigned. These codes must be accurate because they determine which inventory account will be updated and they trigger future systems cycles. Trade corrections should contain a reference to the original transaction and an explanation of the change.

Trade numbers preserve the identity of an order and have multiple uses. Consider an order that originates from a regional branch office of a large broker-dealer. To expedite execution, the minimal information needed (skeletal trade) is transmitted to the trading desk of the firm. The order may be fulfilled through one execution versus the firm inventory account, or there may be several executions with other broker-dealers. The trade number enables a firm to properly assign multiple executions to the proper order. This is necessary in a situation where there are multiple orders for the same issue. Later in the day, the branch that originated the skeletal order transmits an order message containing additional information. An order message must be matched to the proper skeletal trade through the use of the trade number. Trade numbers are also useful in situations requiring tracking executions related to a particular order.

The extent to which a firm uses processing codes depends on its size and product diversity. Envision the operations group of a large firm; it could be a dozen different departments containing hundreds, perhaps thousands, of people. In such an organization, each person has a specific function similar to industrial assembly line processing. Each time one of these individuals performs his or her function, an accounting entry will probably be necessary. Depending on the type and nature of a transaction, accounting entries are made by various people throughout the firm. However, a firm's accounting records are singular in nature—that is, there is a single stock and bond record and a single trial balance that must be balanced daily. Balancing these records would be an impossible task if there were no way to segment the work done by individual groups. Each processing unit within a firm must balance its own daily entries. If the individual units are balanced, then the official firm records will be in balance. For a processing unit to balance within itself, it must be able to obtain extracts of the work for which it is responsible. This is where coding comes in. Codes are assigned on the basis of product and/or transaction type. They are the indicators that cause records within a file to be sorted into the sequence required by the individual processing units of the firm. It is necessary to understand the internal structure of the firm for which you work in order to be able to establish a proper coding structure. In a simplistic example for the MBS industry, individual codes might be applied to trades in FHLMC and FNMA wireables, FHLMC and FNMA nonwireables, GNMA book-entry eligibles, GNMA physicals, and the MBS of other issuers. These must then be subdivided into transactions executed with customers, brokers and dealers, and broker's brokers. The product type code facilitates internal reporting and balancing. The contra-party codes facilitate the creation of ancillary files required for trade comparison through the MBSCC Clearing Division. There are many other uses of these codes; each firm is different. Familiarize yourself with the coding structure established within your own organization and use them even if they are nonmandatory, as is the case in the preparation of certain journal entries. Proper use can save hours, possibly days, of work.

CONFIRMATION PROCESSING AND VERIFICATION

There are two terms that are sometimes mistakenly used interchangeably: confirmation and comparison. The confirmation process refers to the written notification given to a customer concerning the details of an executed order. Unlike a comparison, a confirmation is a one-way communication between a broker or dealer and its customer. It serves as the legal notification of the trade contract and provides the customer with all the details of the trade, as illustrated in Figure 6–1.

Customer confirmations are produced from the information entered into the system by an account executive or the data entry section of the trade processing group. Most systems in use today store the orders and trade executions of the day on separate intra-day files that are used at the end of the day for a batch-mode update of the main files. This provides an opportunity that should be used. All trade input should be verified on the same day before the batch updating, which will produce client confirmations. The original source documents, be they skeletal trades, order blotters, or customer order tickets, should be compared to the hard-copy facsimile of the trade confirmation that gets produced, or to the information that appears on the operator's screen after the data have been processed. If errors are not caught immediately, actual losses in revenue will occur and some may be significant as reflected in Table 6–1.

TABLE 6–1. Results of Erroneous Trade Input

Result	Cost to Firm
1. Incorrect confirms	Material, personnel and system time to process a cancel and correct; approximately $63.00 per order.
2. Incorrect positions	As above *plus* potential for trading losses and P&I losses.
3. Strained relations	Loss of revenue from reduction of business, or complete loss of account.

FIGURE 6-1. A Confirmation for a Purchase by a Customer

PaineWebber GOVERNMENT SECURITIES COMMERCIAL PAPER CONFIRMATION

GOVERNMENT SECURITIES DEPARTMENT
120 BROADWAY, NEW YORK, N.Y. 10271
TELEPHONE (212) 437 2121

TO BE DELIVERED

XY ZEE MBS FUND INC
ONE FINANCIAL PLAZA
JERSEY CITY, NJ

AS PRINCIPAL WE HEREBY CONFIRM

OUR SALE TO

AGAINST PAYMENT OF FEDERAL
FUNDS UNLESS OTHERWISE NOTED.

YOU TODAY OF THE FOLLOWING SECURITIES

CLIENT NUMBER	TRADE I.D. #	REF. #	TRADE DATE	AS OF DATE	SETTLEMENT DATE	
	F 005	602270	11/11/88		11/18/88	FACTOR .87654321

PAR VALUE	SECURITY				DISCOUNT/BASIS	PRICE
1,000,000.00	GNMA POOL 123456 SF LEVEL PAY FIXED RATE 10% DUE 08-15-2011					99 1/8

PRINCIPAL	INTEREST/DISCOUNT PERIOD	INTEREST/DISCOUNT	CHARGES	TOTAL
$ 868,873.46		$ 4,139.23		$ 873,012.69

SECURITY NO.	HOUSE ACCOUNT NO.	CUSIP NO.	
123456	ABC-13190	WH00011T	

DELIVERY INSTRUCTIONS

DVP-BANK OF NY   110 WASHINGTON
          CLEAR DIV 19th FLOOR
          AC XY ZEE MBS FUND INC
WIRE FUNDS TO: CHEM NY
ABA021000128   AC PWJC AC 0660077

GNS-1298 REV 8/87 PTG 4/88

95

The specific fields that can be verified by the input operator are as follows:

- ❏ The "buy" or "sell" and "principal" or "agency" indicators.
- ❏ Quantity and price.
- ❏ Security number (e.g., pool or CUSIP) and security description.
- ❏ Account number and/or account name.
- ❏ The trade and settlement dates.

There are several points to keep in mind during this verification process. Some firms confirm "buy" and "sell" from the standpoint of the firm, others from the standpoint of the customer. Confirms that read "we have this day sold to you—" indicate "buy" from the customer's perspective. Watch for the transposition of pool numbers, which would result in an incorrect description. Many security descriptions are similar, especially those of TBA contracts. Early FHLMCs issued under the 16 and 17 group numbers had duplicate pool numbers. When trading these issues, care must be taken not only to match the pool number but also the coupon and maturity date. If the original order was entered using a short name, there may be several account numbers on file for that name; ascertain which is the correct account.

There are other fields of information in the trade confirmation that are not verified because they are generated by the system on the basis of the other information. These are the principal money, the accrued interest, commission if applicable (agency trade only), and the final net amount of the trade. However, it is useful to understand how a trade is calculated. In the calculation of a security that amortizes (that is, periodically pays down its outstanding principal), the amount of the outstanding debt is constantly changing. Interest on debt is paid on the outstanding amount, not on the amount of the original loan. So an extra step must be taken in the calculation of a trade for an MBS that is not required in other fixed-debt instruments such as corporate, municipal, or government bonds. That extra step is the calculation of the outstanding or amortized value of the security. Every issuer of mortgage-backed securities knows the amount of the underlying mortgage loans that has been paid down during the preceding month. A record is maintained of all paydowns, and each month the percentage of the original loans, representing the current outstanding balances, is calculated and reported. This figure, expressed as an eight-integer decimal, is known as the factor.

The trade depicted in the confirmation example was an order entered by a customer on 11-11-88 to sell $1,000,000.00 of MBS Pool 123456 SF Fixed Rate Mtg 10% due 08-15-2011; the order was executed the same day (principal basis) at 99 1/8. The November factor for Pool 123456 is 0.87654321. The trade is calculated as follows:

Face amount × factor   = amortized amount (outstanding quantity)
$1,000,000.00 × 0.87654321 = $876,543.21 (note decimal in quantity field)

Face amount × factor   × price   = principal amount of trade
$1,000,000.00 × 0.87654321 × 0.99125 = $868,873.46

Principal amount + accrued interest ± commission = net amount
$868,873.46   + $4,139.23   − 0   = $873,012.69

An investor in debt securities expects to receive interest on the principal amount of his or her investment. When an issue is sold before the payment of interest due for a specified period, the seller is entitled to receive part of the future payment in an amount proportionate to the length of time during which the seller's funds were invested. Accrued interest for standard MBS issues is calculated on a 30/360 basis; interest pays monthly and accrues from the first day of the month up to, but not inclusive of, the settlement date of the trade. Interest on the trade in this example is paid monthly to the person who owns the security on the last business day of the month. This investor sold the securities for settlement on the eighteenth day and is therefore entitled to interest for the 17 days during which the funds were invested in the loan to the issuer. The 10% coupon paid by this issue is a per annum rate. A year, for this type of security, is considered to have 360 days. Hence, the value of a single day's interest is 1/360th of the yearly coupon rate times the current principal, calculated by multiplying the *original face* times the current factor. Accrued interest for this trade is calculated as follows:

Face $\times$ factor $\times$ coupon $\times$ $\dfrac{\text{no. of days}}{\text{from 1st to SD}}$ / $360 =$ accrued interest

$\dfrac{\$1}{\text{million}}$ $\times$ 0.87654321 $\times$ 0.10 $\times$ 17 / $360 =$ \$4,139.23

If commission had been applicable to this trade, the amount would have been subtracted from the gross proceeds of the sale; it is an amount that the customer must pay, so the proceeds are reduced. If a customer is purchasing a security and commission is due, then that amount is added to the purchase cost of the trade.

TRADE COMPARISON AND TRADE BLOTTER BALANCING

Unlike the one-sided communication process associated with customer confirmations, the comparison process requires that both parties to a transaction affirm the complete details of each trade with each other. In the primary, or TBA, market, the comparison process applies to all transactions in which another broker or dealer is the contra-party and to transactions involving nonmargined institutional types of accounts. In the secondary market, which deals in orders of previously issued MBS, the comparison process is confined to transactions with brokers and dealers.

If a trade is confirmed, why does it have to be compared? Protection!!! Protection of both the broker's assets and the assets of its customers. Remember that all trading must be accounted for. In any accounting function, debits always have to equal credits. A purchase is a debit; a sale is a credit. Therefore, every time a purchase is recorded on a broker's books, an offsetting sale must also be recorded. The buyer/seller relationship is inseparable. When a broker sends a customer a confirmation of purchase, no response is required. First, there is a one-on-one client/broker relationship based on trust and a knowledge of the customer's ability to pay for a trade. Second, the broker has direct control over the customer's account. Should the client fail to pay for purchased assets, the securities can be sold out to cover the debit in the customer's account. When the contra-side of a purchase made for a customer (the seller) is another broker or dealer, that one-on-one relationship does not exist, nor is there any control over unsettled assets. An active broker can deal with more than 100 brokers during the course of a day, many of whom will be trading identical or similar issues. So it is imperative that these brokers exchange information with one another to ensure that both sides agree to the terms of the transaction. A compared trade becomes a legal obligation of both parties. Should the selling broker fail to honor its commitment for any reason, the purchasing customer is still entitled to and will receive the securities bought. Unless the customer's broker has compared the trade, there will be little opportunity for recourse from the seller, and the customer's broker will be liable for losses sustained in delivering the proper securities to its customer.

The discussion of comparisons needs to be segmented into physical comparison processing and automated comparison processing. The latter, available for primary market transactions executed among banks, brokers, and dealers who are members of the MBSCC, is not considered here but will be explained in length in Chapter 8.

TBA transactions executed for the account of an institution are compared through the use of a commitment letter. This letter does not replace the confirmation; it is an additional document. An example is illustrated in Figure 6–2. Commitment letters contain all the terms of the trade and must be signed by the recipient and returned to the initiating broker. These letters are important! TBA trades are forward contracts that do not settle for a month or more following the trade date. Should there be a discrepancy in the trade, the parties involved would not become aware of it until the settlement date, which could be six months later. Signed commitment letters preclude the possibility that the institution's records differ from the broker's records in terms of the details of a trade. When you consider the volume of trading that is done, it is reasonable to expect some differences. *Procedures must be in place to follow up on commitment letters that have not been signed and returned* within a reasonable time. The further you get away from the date of an execution, the more difficult it becomes to correct differences.

Remember that institutional TBA trades are frequently for large block orders. If your firm sold a 5MM TBA contract to an institution for settlement two months in the future, think of what could happen. Assume for the moment that for some reason the trade was not entered into the records of the purchasing firm. When they received your mailed confirmation, the first-day-on-

FIGURE 6–2. Commitment Letter

Date: August 26, 1988

Upon acceptance and in consideration of our oral agreement, this letter constitutes your commitment to buy from us, an option to sell 30 Year Mortgage-Backed Securities (Modified Pass-Through Type) to be fully guaranteed as to timely payment of principal and interest by the Federal Home Loan Mortgage Corporation as described herein:

PRINCIPAL AMOUNT:	5,000,000	SETTLEMENT DATE:	1/19/89
COUPON RATE:	11.0%	STRIKE PRICE:	100
ISSUER:	TBA	COMMITMENT FEE:	$17,187.50
ISSUE DATE:	TBA	NOTIFICATION:	1/12/89
TRADE DATE:	8/26/88	LIFE CAP:	N/A
POOL NUMBER:	TBA		

In consideration of our commitment to purchase the above security at your option, a non-refundable commitment fee amounting to $17,187.50 will be paid to   by you. This fee is fully earned by us soley in consideration of the issuance of this commitment letter.

Monthly payment of principal and interest on this issue of mortgage-backed securities to commence on the 15th day of the month following settlement.

If you elect to deliver securities, you will notify us on or before notification date by 4:00 p.m. EST.

Please acknowledge your agreement to the foregoing and to the standard terms and conditions attached hereof by signing the enclosed copy of this letter and returning it together with the commitment fee to

This is a private contract between two parties herein that is not assignable, negotiable or transferable.

Accepted & Confirmed   Very truly yours,

_____
Name
                                              Mortgage-Backed Securities
_____
Date

Contract # B 8234

S/P FHLMC

the-job mail clerk misroutes the confirm to someone who has nothing to do with trading or clearance. Not knowing what the confirmation is, that person puts it in the "circular file"—a wastebasket. A month later, the trader at the institution leaves. When you call with the allocation information for settlement of the trade a month later, there is no longer anyone at the institution with knowledge of the transaction, and they refuse to accept it. If the market has dropped just a single point, your firm is now facing an unnecessary loss of $50,000.00. The potential for loss can be much larger!

Control of commitment letters, both the issuance of them and the maintenance of signed copies, should remain under the domain of the trade processing group. For quality control reasons, the function should not become the responsibility of either trading or sales, in whole or in part.

The other aspect of physical comparisons is in connection with secondary market trading with other brokers and dealers. Although no commitment letters are prepared for these trades, one of two documents should be obtained for each executed trade—either a confirm or comparison from the contra-party, or a signed comparison.

A firm that accepts the contra-party's written comparison as proof of the trade must make sure that the comparison is examined when it is received and that it agrees in every detail to the accepting firm's own trade information. Care must be taken to follow up on any trade for which a comparison or confirm has not been received.

Comparison processing and trade blotter balancing go hand in hand. The comparison process ensures that the contra-side of a trade has identical trade details. When a firm balances its trade blotters, it is ensuring that an offsetting sale has been booked for every purchase, and vice versa. The simple question "Do our debits equal our credits?" becomes a bit complicated when you consider the thousands of customers and the hundreds of traders and contra broker-dealers involved in a typical day of trading. Based on the trade codes, blotters (accounting ledgers) are produced for customer, firm, and broker trades. The following transactions were executed on the same trade date for customers, and the resulting trade blotters are shown in Table 6–2:

Firm, as agent, bought 1MM Pool #1 for Cust A @ par from Brkr X.
Firm, as agent, bought 1MM Pool #2 for Cust B @ 99 from Brkr Y.
Firm, as principal, sold 1MM Pool #3 to Cust C @ 99.5.
Firm, as principal, sold 1MM Pool #4 to Cust D @ 103.
Firm, as principal, sold 1MM Pool #5 to Cust E @ 100.

TABLE 6–2.

Customer's Trade Blotter

Customer	Bought	Description	Price	Principal Value	Interest	Commission	Net Amount
A	1MM	Pool 1	100	995,999.89	4,166.67	250.00	1,000,416.56
B	1MM	Pool 2	99	878,612.75	3,660.89	230.00	882,503.64
C	1MM	Pool 3	99.5	990,101.02	4,125.45	NA	994,226.47
D	1MM	Pool 4	103	412,024.42	2,145.96	NA	414,170.38
E	1MM	Pool 5	100	851,999.99	3,550.00	NA	855,549.99
Tot	5MM			4,128,738.07	17,648.97	480.00	4,146,867.04

Broker's Trade Blotter

Broker	Sold	Description	Price	Principal Value	Interest	Commission	Net Amount
X	1MM	Pool 1	100	995,999.89-	4,166.67-	NA	1,000,166.56-
Y	1MM	Pool 2	99	878,612.75-	3,660.89-	NA	882,273.64-
Tot	2MM			1,874,612.64-	7,827.56-	0.00	1,882,440.20-

Firm Trading Blotter

Trader	Sold	Description	Price	Principal Value	Interest	Commission	Net Amount
88	1MM	Pool 3	99.5	990,101.02-	4,125.45-	NA	994,226.47-
88	1MM	Pool 4	103	412,024.42-	2,145.96-	NA	414,170.38-
88	1MM	Pool 5	100	851,999.99-	3,550.00-	NA	855,549.99-
Tot	3MM			2,254,125.43-	9,821.41-	0.00	2,263,946.84-

Recap—Internal Balancing of Blotters

Blotter	Principal Amount	Accrued Interest	Commission	Net Amount
Cust Buys	4,128,738.07	17,648.97	480.00	4,146,867.04
Cust Sales	0.00	0.00	0.00	0.00
Broker Buys	0.00	0.00	0.00	0.00
Broker Sales	1,874,612.64-	7,827.56-	0.00	1,882,440.20-
Firm Buys	0.00	0.00	0.00	0.00
Firm Sales	2,254,125.43-	9,821.41-	0.00	2,263,946.84-
Net Comm Adj				480.00-
TOTALS	0.00	0.00	480.00	0.00

The net commission adjustment is always the total value of the commissions charged to customers. This amount is paid by a firm's clients. For balancing purposes, it becomes a credit, as the adjustment reflects, to the commission income account. Table 6–2 subdivided trading into three major categories; that number can be expanded to meet the needs of individual firms. The zero balances in the recap indicate that the P&S blotters for this day's activity are in balance; the value of the purchases equals the value of the sales recorded on the books of the firm.

This balancing process must be performed daily; separate balances must be computed for all transactions due to settle on a particular day. Differences must be journaled into a Julian-dated suspense account no later than the settlement date minus one (SD – 1) so that the cashier's department will be able to balance their work on the following day. Julian-dated accounts enable you to maintain a clear audit trail for suspense entries because a separate account is used for each new date. This precludes the possibility of having an offsetting error on a subsequent date zeroing out a suspense account balance, thus leaving everyone with the erroneous belief that the records are balanced.

BALANCING TRADING POSITIONS

Every organization that acts as a dealer in securities maintains one or more inventory trading positions. As previously mentioned, a dealer is a marketmaker who purchases securities for the account and risk of the firm and sells those securities to the public. Presumably the price of the sale is higher than the purchase price. It is this dealer's markup that provides the trading profits for dealer firms. But being a dealer does not guarantee trading profits; losses can also be sustained. A registered dealer is obligated to maintain an active marketplace in the securities it trades. In both upside and downside markets, a dealer is obligated to attempt to stabilize the market by executing against all reasonable bids and offerings.

To trade securities, a dealer must maintain a large inventory. This inventory is controlled, from an accounting standpoint, through the use of a series of inventory, or trading, accounts. Purchases and sales are booked in these accounts in the same manner in which a trade is booked into a customer's account. Every dealer satisfies its own requirements when setting up its trading accounts. Some have a separate account for each product; some have a separate account for each trader. Others separate a generic product, such as mortgage-backed issues, into a series of trading desks, each desk servicing an identifiable segment of the broad product group. A trading account is assigned to each of the desks.

The market value of the trading positions of the larger dealer organizations is in the hundreds of millions of dollars; the largest have positions in the billions. Envision actively traded accounts, dozens of different trading desks, thousands of different positions, billions of dollars worth of trades, and you will have an idea of the magnitude of the effort required to safely control this business on a day-to-day basis. Now, couple all this with the fact that many trading desks are supported during the day by their own real-time, on-line inventory trading systems—which must be synchronized with the official books of the firm—which must be synchronized with the system dedicated to mortgage-backed processing. Now you have the whole picture. Control! Control! Control! Control is the primary responsibility, the essence, of a trade processing division.

The trading inventory control process must be addressed from several angles, as follows:

- ❑ The traders' inventory system must be validated.
- ❑ The main and ancillary system positions must be validated.
- ❑ Realized and unrealized P&L must be calculated.
- ❑ Exposure must be reviewed.

Validation of Traders' Inventory Versus Official Systems Files

Traders' inventory consists of the securities they have purchased or sold short in their trading accounts; their inventory is their current positions. Trading positions change every time a trade is executed. A trader must always be able to accommodate a frequently unpredictable flow of buy and sell orders, simultaneously maintain a trading profit and a stable market, and maintain an inventory level consistent with trading requirements without creating undue market exposure. Few firms today have fully integrated computer systems capable of handling the dynamic requirements of the trading desk as well as the accounting and operational needs of the entire firm. Many firms support the trading desk with microcomputers. The micros are used by the traders to maintain inventory and execution records on a real-time basis.

Trade processing must ensure that the positions in the trading system are the same as the positions in the main computer system as well as the ancillary MBS computer system, if applicable. Both pool (secondary market) positions and TBA positions are monitored using the same methods. A position extract from the main system is compared line by line for each inventory account against a position listing generated from the traders' micro system. Differences are researched; unresolved items are referred to the traders or their assistants. In addition to this comparison, the positions in the main system are compared to the positions recorded in any ancillary system that the firm may be using. All records in all systems must be in synch. Adjustments, if not made directly by trade processing personnel, must be monitored by them. This process must be finished well before the beginning of trading each day. It is important that the traders have accurate inventory records so that they can plan trading strategies for the day and ensure they do not sell positions which they do not own. Daily validation ensures that a firm can honor its commitments, it ensures the ability to properly finance the firm's activities, and it serves as an internal audit of assets. Lack of proper inventory controls has put firms out of business and cost others millions of dollars. There is also a very positive side to this picture as well. A firm that is always in control of the flow of its inventory and other assets is the firm that can take maximum advantage of sudden, unexpected market movements. The extract from the *Wall Street Journal* shown in Figure 6–3 says it all.

FIGURE 6–3.

Timely Updating and Verification of Positions Is Imperative!!!!

"The in-house proprietary trading department of one Wall Street firm reportedly made $40 million during the week of the Oct. 19 stock market crash."

Quoted from the *Wall Street Journal*, Jan. 25, 1988

Realized and Unrealized P&L

It may seem strange to categorize what appears to be an accounting function as a responsibility of a trade processing area. There are strong arguments for doing so, however, and they will be discussed after we briefly define the process itself.

For our purpose, P&L refers to the profits and losses associated with the trading activity of a firm. It is derived by subtracting the *principal value* of a sale from the *principal value* of the original purchase. Principal value is stressed for a reason. As is true with all interest-bearing securities, MBS transactions trade with accrued interest. The interest income and interest expense associated with trading activity are accounted for separately and are not included in the calculation of trading P&L. There are several methods of accounting for P&L, the main ones being on a realized and an unrealized basis. Realized P&L means that inventory has actually been sold, enabling the firm to calculate the profit or loss associated with a transaction. Unrealized P&L is fictitious. It is a figure arrived at by comparing the current market price to the original purchase cost of unsold inventory and calculating the P&L that would be realized if a sale took place. Unrealized P&L serves as a trading barometer used by senior management to make decisions concerning the direction of their general trading activities. Furthermore, realized P&L can be looked at from several perspectives. *Realized but not settled* is the P&L on sales that have been executed, but the trades have not yet reached settlement date. *Realized and settled* P&L refers to trades that have reached the contracted due date for the exchange of cash and securities. *Realized but not cleared* is the P&L associated with trades that have reached or passed settlement date. The securities involved in the trade have not yet been received or delivered, and therefore the cash settlement value is still outstanding. From a trader's standpoint, P&L is realized at the time of execution. There is another point to keep in mind. A trader can take a short position. In this situation, the P&L is the difference between the proceeds of the sale and the cost of the purchase covering the short.

No matter what methods are used, the P&L calculation process is an accounting and systems function involving the development of an average inventory price by desk, marking prices to the market, and calculating P&L on executed trades.

Trade processing can take advantage of the P&L process to assist in controlling the inventory accounts. If the same P&L process is simultaneously applied to the dozens of trading accounts in the trading system, the main system, and the ancillary system if used, then the P&L figures in all systems should be identical. This type of verification should be coupled with the inventory verification done by the trade processing group. If there is a P&L discrepancy in the multiple records for a particular trading account, the positions in that account should be examined. Differences in prices in the various systems used by a firm can cause a serious problem for a firm in the over- or understatement of the value of its trading assets. There is a close coordination between the trading and operations staff of a firm relative to the financing of its trading inventory. Discrepancies between these groups concerning the value of assets can severely restrict the overall operations of a firm.

Exposure Review

A firm carrying an inventory position valued at $250 million would experience a $5 million decline in asset value if market prices were to drop 2 full points. This is not mere hypothesis. It is the real risk dealers face daily, an exposure that must be controlled to the extent possible. This risk can be controlled in the following ways:

❑ Limiting the size of the positions a trader or desk may take.

❑ Offsetting TBA positions with secondary market positions.

❑ Hedging positions with options, futures, or other securities such as Treasuries.

Although it is true that the primary responsibility for risk exposure lies with the head traders and managing directors of the firm, operations must play an important secondary role. In terms of the size of positions, operations should constantly monitor each trading account relative to the authorized established limits. Here is an area where the adequate design of the NAMSTR file can be effective. Limitations can be plugged directly into the record information for each trading account. The system can then perform an edit rejection any time a trade exceeds authorized limits or creates a position exceeding authorized limits. The rejection can be overridden with the proper authorization codes known only to the head trader. Reports should be issued daily on all accounts exceeding authorized limits, thus ensuring a constant monitoring of the exposure.

Position exposure in TBAs must be considered in relation to secondary market positions. There has to be a free interchange of information between the TBA traders and the secondary market traders. A large percentage of sales of TBA contracts are settled using existing secondary market inventory. TBA positions must be constantly monitored to determine the *net exposure in each TBA coupon after applying all available inventory.* Limits are established for this net exposure amount. Positions hedged with options are more difficult to control because it is necessary to model the execution of the option before you can determine the net cost and exposure to the firm. In each situation, trade processing should receive copies of exposure reports and perform their own exposure audit. This is definitely a situation where "two heads are better than one."

UPDATING FACTOR FILES

Accurate processing of MBS trades in the secondary market is impossible unless factor tables are available to calculate the principal value of the executions. A person who buys an MBS is investing in a group, or pool, of mortgages. Home loans are paid monthly by the mortgagors. These payments are the interest due on the outstanding amount of the mortgage plus a partial repayment of the original loan. When you buy an MBS, you are buying loans, and you need to know the current outstanding principal value of those loans. Factors, supplied by the issuers of every MBS, provide that information. Factors represent the percentage (expressed as an eight-decimal-place figure) of the original face amount of a mortgage-backed security that is presently outstanding. Because most MBS pay down principal and interest each month, the factors change every month. Trades must be calculated using *the factor in effect on the first of the month in which the trade settles.* Why does the settlement date, not the trade date, determine which month's factor should be used? The trade date is a contractual date; price is determined on that date because you entered into a contract (the trade) on the basis of the yields effective on that day. However, the consummation of the contract (the exchange of cash for securities) does not occur until the trade's settlement date. The purchaser does not begin to accrue interest on the investment until the settlement date of the trade. If a trade settles on the first, or later in the month following the trade date, the investor receives interest based on a principal amount reduced by the previous month's loan payments. By using the factor applicable to the settlement month, the calculated principal amount reflects the true loan amount on which the investor will accrue interest. Refer to the trade calculation routine reviewed earlier in this chapter if necessary.

Some of the issues associated with factor file updating are the following:

❑ Timeliness of the updates and processing "when-issued" trades.
❑ Updating erroneous factor information.
❑ Maintaining a factor file history.

When you consider that hundreds of thousands of MBS have been issued since 1970, you can appreciate that obtaining the factor information for every outstanding issue is difficult. Factors must originate from the issuers. In the GNMA I and II programs, the individual mortgagee institutions advise the transfer agent (Chemical Bank, New York) of the preceding month's paydowns and the current outstanding principal amount of each pool. Issuers under the FHLMC and FNMA programs advise these agencies direct. The Mortgage-Backed Securities Information Services, a division of *The Bond Buyer*, compiles all this information and supplies it to brokers, dealers, and investment companies in printed, microfiche, diskette, or tape format. Figures 6–4 and 6–5 are examples of the information that is available. It is *The Bond Buyer* tapes that most organizations use to update their internal master files. Under their program, factors are available according to the schedule given in Table 6–3.

The first observation you will probably make after you read Table 6–3 is that many factors are not available until the second week of the month. Does trading stop because a current factor has

TABLE 6–3. Factor Availability Schedule

Issuer	First NYC Availability Date	Second	Third
GNMA I	6th Business Day of month	9th BD	18th BD
GNMA II	7th Business Day of month	9th BD	18th BD
FHLMC	1st Business Day of month		
FNMA	5th Business Day of month		
FNMA ARMs	12th Business Day of month		
CMO	15th Business Day of month		
PRIVATE	Varies		

not been announced? No. When the current factor is not available, trades are executed on what is known as a when-issued basis. When issued in the MBS marketplace has a different connotation from its meaning for all other product types. It simply means that the *trade will be recalculated when the new factor is issued.* Some firms calculate these trades on the basis of the old factor and then pay or collect the differences due when the new factor is published. There are situations (a large block trade, for example) in which a firm does not want to wait for the information from *The Bond Buyer.* In such cases, trade processing personnel contact the transfer agent, or issuer, directly for the factor information and process the information manually on the basis of the unpublished information. In these cases, care should be taken to compare the official factor information when it becomes available with the prepublished factor to ensure that there is no discrepancy.

The second observation you may have made is that there are multiple iterations of the factor tables. The two reasons for this are (1) some issuers have not compiled their information on a timely basis, and (2) some of the original information was incorrect, necessitating a factor change. If the factor information is late, process your trade as a when issued. However, if subsequent factor information reflects a change in the originally published figure, a quality control procedure must be in place. Your system must identify each issue that has been changed, identify every transaction that has been processed with the original incorrect information, issue cancellations and corrections, and finally provide notification to the appropriate operations area for the collection or payment of the differences that result from the corrections. In

FIGURE 6–4. The Bond Buyer CMO Principal, Interest, and Factor Report

$MOF – PER $1000 ORIGINAL FACE AMOUNT

PAGE 6

ISSUE TYPE: C

FEB /87

ISSUE DATE: 03/24/1986

ISSUER & SERIES DESCRIPTION:
COLLATERALIZED MORTGAGE OBLIGATION TR. 1
CMO/Series 3.

RECORD DATE:	PAYMENT DATE:	S&P RATING:	DELIVERY: DTC
CURRENT 00/00/0000	CURRENT 03/25/1987	MOODYS RATING:	DEL. FUNDS: C
PREVIOUS 00/00/0000	PREVIOUS 12/25/1986		

PAYMENT FREQUENCY: Q   UNDERWRITER: SALOMON BROTHERS
DELAY DAYS: 30

INTEREST START DATE: 00/00/0000
FIRST COUPON DATE: 00/00/0000

CLASS DESCRIPTION	MARKET CODE	CUSIP # MATUR DATE	CURR/PREV PRIN. FACTOR	PAY CODE	ORIG PRIN. BAL PRIN. PAY MOF	INT. NO CALC CODE	INTEREST $MOF / INT $MOF EXTRA / INT $MOF TOTAL	RETIRE DATE NEW INT DATE	COUPON # DAYS	CHANGE TYPE
Class A		19419LAA6 09/25/2005	0.5618239 0.73457954	P	0283350000.00 0172.767149		0015.977105 0000.000000 0015.977105	00/00/0000 00/00/0000	0.73457 090-DAYS	
CALL CODE:		CALL DATE: 00/00/0000			CALL COMMENTS:					
Class B		19419LAB4 12/25/2006	1.00000000 1.00000000	I	0052000000.00 0000.000000		0022.250000 0000.000000 0022.250000	00/00/0000 00/00/0000	1.00000 090-DAYS	
CALL CODE:		CALL DATE: 00/00/0000			CALL COMMENTS:					
Class C		19419LAC2 12/25/2009	1.00000000 1.00000000	I	0126650000.00 0000.000000		0022.500000 0000.000000 0022.500000	00/00/0000 00/00/0000	1.00000 090-DAYS	
CALL CODE:		CALL DATE: 00/00/0000			CALL COMMENTS:					
Class Z		19419LAD0 03/25/2016	1.06863812 1.04525064	I	0038000000.00 0000.000000		0023.387483 0000.000000 0023.387483	00/00/0000 00/00/0000	1.04525 090-DAYS	
COMMENTS: DFINTEREST										
CALL CODE:		CALL DATE: 00/00/0000			CALL COMMENTS:					

FIGURE 6–5. GNMA Mortgage-Backed Securities—GNMA I Program

APR /86

POOL NO	FACTOR	ISSUER NO	ISSUER	POOL TYPE	ORIGINAL BALANCE	3/86 BALANCE	INTEREST RATE	ISSUE DATE	MATURITY DATE
000001X	.30312545	1595	THE LOMAS & NETTLETON COMPANY	SF	7,501,196.85	2,273,803.65	7.000	02/19/70	02/15/00
000002X	.28008913	1453	MANUFACTURERS HANOVER MORTGAGE CORPORA	SF	2,008,979.45	562,693.30	8.000	02/01/70	04/15/00
000003X	.29317934	1595	THE LOMAS & NETTLETON COMPANY	SF	5,054,613.82	1,481,908.34	7.000	03/19/70	05/15/00
000004X	.29456024	1538	FORT WORTH MORTGAGE CORPORAT	SF	5,004,121.56	1,474,015.27	8.000	03/01/71	01/15/01
000007X	.25178059	1543	CHEMICAL MORTGAGE COMPANY	SF	2,001,182.99	503,859.04	8.000	09/30/70	11/15/00
000008X	.21917042	1746	GILLDORN MORTGAGE MIDWEST CORPORATION	SF	1,948,038.32	865,293.23	7.000	12/01/70	07/15/00
000009X	.26144155	1447	CAMERON-BROWN COMPANY	SF	2,014,071.79	526,562.05	8.000	05/22/70	07/15/00
000010X	.23551502	1595	THE LOMAS & NETTLETON COMPANY	SF	5,000,708.92	1,177,742.06	8.000	06/15/70	06/15/00
000011X	.22219543	1631	MORTGAGE INVESTMENT COMPANY OF EL PASO	SF	2,003,997.53	445,279.10	8.000	12/01/70	01/15/00
000012X	.29745423	1679	RYAN MORTGAGE COMPANY	SF	2,000,355.34	514,399.94	8.000	06/01/70	06/15/00
000013X	.36990659	2241	FLEET NATIONAL BANK	SF	2,000,447.55	739,978.73	8.000	10/01/70	09/15/00
000014X	.34580465	2741	COLWELL FINANCIAL CORPORATION	SF	2,014,837.28	696,740.10	8.000	12/01/70	12/15/00
000016X	.20449969	2472	SECURITY SAVINGS MORTGAGE CORPORAT	SF	2,002,312.22	409,472.23	8.000	12/01/70	01/15/01
000017X	.24840136	1453	MANUFACTURERS HANOVER MORTGAGE CORPORA	SF	8,196,100.28	2,035,922.47	8.000	08/01/70	08/15/00
000018X	.39586331	2653	THE CHASE MANHATTAN BANK, N A	SF	2,011,613.94	796,324.16	8.000	09/30/70	11/15/00
000019X	.23590846	1595	THE LOMAS & NETTLETON COMPANY	SF	5,002,945.55	1,180,237.18	8.000	08/07/70	07/15/00
000020X	.22328581	1595	THE LOMAS & NETTLETON COMPANY	SF	5,000,584.10	1,116,559.49	8.000	09/18/70	10/15/00
000021X	.25864919	1595	THE LOMAS & NETTLETON COMPANY	SF	5,000,492.91	1,293,373.45	8.000	10/23/70	11/15/00
000022X	.22653938	1595	THE LOMAS & NETTLETON COMPANY	SF	5,000,261.99	1,132,756.23	8.000	12/01/70	01/15/00
000023X	.23177569	1595	THE LOMAS & NETTLETON COMPANY	SF	1,507,057.99	812,850.79	8.000	01/01/71	02/15/01
000024X	.29018492	1595	THE LOMAS & NETTLETON COMPANY	SF	5,007,858.28	1,453,204.95	8.000	02/01/71	02/15/00
000025X	.30171877	1595	THE LOMAS & NETTLETON COMPANY	SF	2,503,419.29	755,328.59	8.000	03/01/71	03/15/01
000026X	.25915649	1595	THE LOMAS & NETTLETON COMPANY	SF	3,756,420.09	973,500.63	8.000	05/01/71	05/15/01
000027X	.34216183	1595	THE LOMAS & NETTLETON COMPANY	SF	4,008,737.88	1,371,637.07	7.000	04/22/70	05/15/00
000028X	.31578325	2258	COMMONWEALTH SAVINGS ASSOCIAT	SF	2,002,303.57	632,293.92	8.000	11/01/70	12/15/00
000029X	.28120808	1634	MORTGAGE AND TRUST, INC	SF	4,071,725.54	1,145,002.14	8.000	11/16/70	11/15/00
000030X	.25904590	1595	THE LOMAS & NETTLETON COMPANY	SF	5,005,851.42	1,296,745.29	8.000	06/22/70	07/15/00
000031X	.32451073	1673	THE NEW YORK GUARDIAN MORTGAGE	SF	2,004,468.44	650,471.51	8.000	10/01/70	12/15/00
000032X	.35304915	1585	J I KISLAK MORTGAGE CORPORAT	SF	3,500,222.96	1,235,750.75	8.000	04/01/71	03/15/01
000034X	.20546992	1458	RAINIER FINANCIAL SERVICES COMPANY	SF	2,004,605.83	411,886.19	8.000	03/01/71	02/15/01
000035X	.28550328	1631	MORTGAGE INVESTMENT COMPANY OF EL PASO	SF	2,004,728.41	572,356.53	8.000	06/01/70	06/15/00
000037X	.39659703	1735	WACHOVIA MORTGAGE COMPANY	SF	2,025,245.30	803,206.27	8.000	11/01/70	10/15/00
000038X	.17897125	1907	MERCURY SAVINGS ASSOCIATION OF TEXAS	SF	2,000,048.48	357,951.17	8.000	12/01/70	11/15/00
000039X	.39488704	2241	FLEET NATIONAL BANK	SF	2,002,770.64	790,866.16	7.000	10/01/70	02/15/00
000040X	.19040223	1613	DOMINION BANKSHARES MORTGAGE CORPORAT	SF	2,007,885.57	382,305.89	8.000	02/01/71	02/15/01
000041X	.15597069	2758	PACIFIC FIRST FEDERAL SAVINGS BANK	SF	2,001,494.55	312,174.48	8.000	12/01/70	12/15/00
000042X	.21805699	1586	THE KISSELL COMPANY	SF	2,094,693.58	456,762.57	8.000	07/16/70	08/15/00
000043X	.22071355	1453	MANUFACTURERS HANOVER MORTGAGE CORPORA	SF	3,000,163.57	662,176.75	8.000	06/01/70	07/15/00
000044X	.23676971	1586	THE KISSELL COMPANY	SF	2,002,200.38	474,060.41	8.000	10/01/70	11/15/00
000045X	.28337226	2251	COMMONHEALTH EASTERN MORTGAGE CORPORAT	SF	1,049,519.60	297,404.74	8.000	03/01/71	03/15/01
000046X	.22028893	1405	ALLSTATE ENTERPRISES MORTGAGE	SF	2,001,502.81	440,908.91	8.000	12/01/70	12/15/00
000047X	.23837634	1463	GMAC MORTGAGE CORPORATION OF PENNSYLVA	SF	3,073,958.69	732,759.02	8.000	10/15/70	10/15/00
000048X	.23378531	1412	COMMONHEALTH WESTERN MORTGAGE CORPORAT	SF	2,084,212.41	487,258.25	8.000	11/01/70	10/15/00
000049X	.22240069	1742	HEYERHAEUSER MORTGAGE COMPANY	SF	2,002,397.09	445,494.49	8.000	12/01/70	12/15/00
000051X	.32623026	1673	THE NEW YORK GUARDIAN MORTGAGE	SF	2,004,035.39	653,793.01	8.000	10/01/71	11/15/00
000052X	.18812904	2389	METMOR FINANCIAL INC	SF	2,511,298.81	472,448.23	8.000	10/01/70	10/15/00
000053X	.24496592	2251	COMMONHEALTH EASTERN MORTGAGE CORPORAT	SF	2,006,503.32	491,524.93	8.000	08/27/70	09/15/00
000056X	.26937980	1585	J I KISLAK MORTGAGE CORPORAT	SF	3,046,791.43	744,808.08	8.000	01/01/71	03/15/01
000057X	.27125641	1463	GMAC MORTGAGE CORPORATION OF PENNSYLVA	SF	25,260,742.25	6,852,138.17	7.000	06/01/71	06/15/01
000058X	.33444652	1746	GILLDORN MORTGAGE MIDWEST CORPORATION	SF	5,263,431.69	1,760,336.43	8.000	12/01/70	12/15/00
000059X	.27472183	1746	GILLDORN MORTGAGE MIDWEST CORPORATION	SF	1,985,448.83	1,094,889.81	8.000	10/01/70	08/15/00
000060X	.24433322	1722	FIRST INTERSTATE BANK OF CALIFORNIA	SF	2,501,460.20	611,189.83	8.000	01/01/71	11/15/00
000061X	.17508203	1759	BOWEST CORPORATION	SF	2,002,057.16	350,524.23	8.000	04/01/71	02/15/01

most firms, the comparison of the updated factors to the original factors is accomplished by means of an automated exception report, but the remaining requirements demand some degree of manual control.

The last topic to be discussed concerning factors is the importance of maintaining historical data. Historical data files are used by analysts and traders to determine the current principal paydown rate of an issue. This is a very important piece of information because it assists in predicting the estimated remaining life of an issue, which must be known to establish a reasonable price relative to yield to maturity. The data are used to correct orders executed in a previous month. The information is also needed by the people responsible for collecting monthly principal and interest payments (P&I) on contracts from previous months that are open or failing.

PROCESSING TRADE CANCELLATIONS AND CORRECTIONS

Regardless of the product involved, cancellations are usually the result of an earlier problem, and care must be taken during the correction process to avoid further complications. This is especially true when processing MBS corrections. Because the outstanding principal amount of an MBS is constantly being amortized, corrections must be coordinated with the group controlling the positions file to ensure that their records properly reflect position differences resulting from interim P&I paydowns. Because MBS pay P&I monthly, the dividend department must be advised of all corrections in secondary issues that originally settled in a noncurrent month (exclude price-only corrections, which is another coding consideration). This is necessary so that the dividend department can adjust their record date positions, credit P&I to the proper accounts, and recover payments erroneously made based on the original trade information.

All when-issued trades must be cancelled and corrected when the current factors become available; this can be done programmatically. All other cancellations and corrections should be properly researched to ensure that the new information is correct. The original trade number can be used to reference the original transaction. Whenever a cancel/correct is processed, the transaction should have a clear, concise explanation of the reason for the change. If a factor has changed, indicate the value of the old and new factor. "Corrected as to price," "Corrected as to quantity," "Corrected as to description of issue" are typical examples of explanations. Each type of correction should have a unique code that can be used to interpret consistent "trailer" information on all corrections. Another advantage of coding error types is that it affords you the ability to perform a computerized analysis of the errors. The analysis will ultimately lead to better customer service and a more economically efficient operation.

7

The TBA Market

TBA ("to be announced") refers to a type of securities transaction associated solely with the mortgage-backed marketplace. A TBA trade can be considered a futures, or forward, transaction for mortgage-backed securities. There is a very important difference, however, between a futures trade and a TBA trade. When trading futures, you always know what commodity, quantity, and grade thereof that will be delivered to you at the expiration of the contract. A futures contract is definitive; the same is not true of a TBA contract.

TBAs trade on a generic basis for settlement, either in the same month or on a specific date up to six months into the future. When you purchase a TBA, you do not purchase a specific pool, participation certificate, or other specific issue. What you buy is *a commitment for a face amount* (not a designated amortized amount) of an MBS *issued under a specific program that will yield a specified coupon.* It is important to understand that TBA purchases, unless closed out through a sale before settlement date, will become a purchase order for one or more specific mortgage-backed securities. Moreover, the specific MBS that will be allocated (that is, assigned) to the TBA may be a new issue or it may be a previously issued MBS that has been trading for a number of years. This allocation is done by and at the option of the seller. Pur-

FIGURE 7–1. Typical TBA Order and Confirm

	A.E. NO.	RISK	NON-RISK
BUY TRADE DATE 8/26	COUPON 11 7. PRICE 100	SETTLE 1/19/89	TRADING ACCOUNT
CURRENT BALANCE 5000 MM	CUSTOMER NAME 1st International		
POOL NUMBER	ACCOUNT NUMBER 280510		
ORIGINAL FACE	SECURITY NAME - CIRCLE TWO OR MORE GNMA (FHLMC) FNMA		
FACTOR:	30 YEAR 15 YEAR GNOME		
SPECIAL INSTRUCTIONS:	OTHER: Put option No tsfication date 1/12/89 A 8234 FEE: 11/32 $ 19,187.50		

RECORD COPY

TRADE NO. B8234

TRADE DATE 8/26/88   SETTLEMENT DATE 1/19/89

WE CONFIRM BUY FROM   YOU TODAY

FACE VALUE	SECURITY DESCRIPTION		PRICE	AMOUNT	
5,000,000.00	YIELD MAINTENANCE CALL FHLMC TBA BUYER	90111010 JAN 11.0	100 SM	PRINCIPAL INTEREST	5,000,000.00 .00

AMORTIZED VALUE	COUPON	MATURITY	ISSUED	FACTOR	TOTAL	
5,000,000.00	11.000	T.B.A.	T.B.A.	1.00000000		5,000,000.00

INTEREST FROM: TO: DELIVERY INSTRUCTIONS

80230510 FIRST INTERNATL. CORP.
BD –
.
:
8/26/88

SECURITY NYC/SPOS/FICAL

ABA 026085885   BBM

0017

DELIVERY   NOT DATE – 1/12/89

SUBJECT TO PSA UNIFORM PRACTICES FOR THE CLEARANCE AND SETTLEMENT OF MORTGAGE-BACKED SECURITIES.

chasers cannot designate the issue they wish to receive. The only guarantee implied when you purchase a TBA is that the securities ultimately assigned and delivered in settlement of the TBA commitment will conform to the generic terms of the TBA contract. The assignment must be made in conformity with the Uniform Practices of the Public Securities Association.

Figure 7–1 is an example of a typical TBA order and confirm.

At the time of execution of the order shown in Figure 7–1, the information that is given in Table 7–1 is known and cannot change.

TABLE 7–1.

Issuer or guarantor	(GNMA)
Mortgage type[a]	(Single-family level payment)
Coupon rate	(10.50%)
Maturity range[b]	(30 years)
Face amount	(1MM, or $1,000,000.00)
Price	(Par, or 100)
Approximate principal amount	(Face × price, or $1,000,000.00)
Trade date	(11-04-88)
Settlement date[c]	(01-23-89)

[a] Because there is no description of the kind of MBS written on this order, it is assumed that this TBA is for a single-family level payment pool. This is common street practice.

[b] It is common street practice to assume that a TBA trade is for pools having a 30-year maturity unless otherwise indicated on the original order.

[c] This is the settlement date for the actual pool that will be allocated to this TBA trade. If the firm with whom the TBA was executed requires a good faith deposit, that amount is due no later than five business days after the TBA trade date.

Not known at the time of execution of the TBA and maybe not known as late as two days prior to the settlement date are the following:

❑ Pool number(s) of the GNMA that will be delivered.

❑ Amortized amount(s) of the pool(s).

❑ Principal amount (may vary as much as ± 2.499999% of the approximate principal).

❑ Accrued interest.

❑ Net amount of funds due in payment of purchase.

ISSUER/GUARANTOR

The issuer/guarantor is the entity under whose program the MBS has or will be issued. This entity will generally be one of the following:

❑ Government National Mortgage Association (GNMA).
❑ Federal Home Loan Mortgage Corporation (FHLMC).
❑ Federal National Mortgage Association (FNMA).

KIND OF MORTGAGE

Kind of mortgage refers to the nature of the mortgaged property represented in the mortgage loans collateralizing a particular MBS. There is no specific type indicated in the example, so single-family level payment mortgages are assumed. The various types of TBAs that are traded include the following:

❑ Single-family (SF) level payment mortgages.
❑ Adjustable rate mortgages (ARMs) (a subdivision of SF mortgages).
❑ Graduated payment mortgages (a subdivision of SF mortgages).
❑ Mobile homes (must be classified by type A, B, C, or D).
❑ Construction loans (multifamily mortgages).
❑ Project loans (multifamily mortgages).
❑ Buydown loans.
❑ Growing equity mortgages.
❑ Reverse annuity mortgages.
❑ Pledged account mortgages.

COUPON RATE AND MATURITY RANGE

The coupon rate being paid on the MBS that are ultimately delivered in connection with a TBA contract must be identical to the rate recorded on the original TBA. In the case of a TBA for an ARM, the rate in effect at the time of settlement must be the rate indicated on the TBA. At one time, it was permissible to assign any coupon that would satisfy the yield stipulated in the TBA contract. This was known as a *firm yield maintenance contract*. Today coupons, not yields, must be identical to the original recorded rate.

The maturity range on a TBA trade refers to the length, or *term*, of the loans used to collateralize an MBS. When you buy a 30-year TBA, you may receive an MBS that is due to mature 30 years from the settlement date of the trade. But you could also receive several different MBS due to mature in 15, 20, or 25 years. As long as the aggregate amortized value(s) of the MBS that are assigned fulfill the parameters of the TBA, the purchaser must accept the securities assigned by the seller. When you buy a 30-year TBA, you may or may not ultimately receive an MBS maturing 30 years from the settlement date of purchase. You will definitely receive one that is collateralized by loans that terminate approximately 30 years from the original date of issuance of the MBS.

FACE AMOUNT

To understand the significance of the face amount of a TBA trade, you must understand the differences between that value and (1) the original face amount of a mortgage-backed security, and (2) the current amortized amount of a mortgage-backed security.

The *original face amount* refers to the principal value of the underlying mortgage loans on the date of issuance of an MBS. This is the amount of money that must be repaid on the outstanding loans as of the date of original issuance of the MBS. If a single certificate was issued for an entire pool, the principal amount is the amount that appears on the face of the certificate. Regardless of the amount of principal that is paid down during the life of the issue, the value imprinted on the certificate will not change even if it is reregistered into other names every time a principal payment is made. Multiple certificates are usually issued, and each certificate indicates the original principal amount that particular certificate represents. Information concerning the original aggregate principal amount of the MBS is also available.

When you amortize a loan, you reduce it through a series of periodic payments. The *current amortized amount* of an MBS is the present-day outstanding principal (loan) value of all the loans collateralizing an issue. It is the amount of the mortgage loans that has not been repaid.

Both terms—original face amount and current amortized amount—relate to MBS that are issued and outstanding. When you buy a TBA contract, you do not know the specific issue you are buying. Therefore it is impossible to associate a true amortized value with a TBA trade. The face amount of a TBA trade is an *approximated* amortized amount. It represents a commitment to buy or sell an amortized amount equal to, but in no case greater than or less than 2.499999% of the amount that has been recorded as the face value of the trade.

Normally, a TBA round lot is a transaction for a face amount of $1 million or a multiple thereof. TBAs can be traded in odd lots having a minimum value of $25,000.00 which may be incremented in lots of $5,000.00.

PRICE AND APPROXIMATED PRINCIPAL VALUE

The price that is recorded on a TBA order will not change. The price reflects the relationship between the coupon being traded and the current interest rate market. It is usually quoted on a yield-to-average life basis, and whole dollars are incremented in 32nds. A trade for 1MM at 99 31/32 would have a gross principal value of $999,687.50. Chapter 1 discusses the inverse relationship between bond prices and current interest rates. When you review that material, keep in mind that the formula given is merely a rule of thumb. An MBS collateralized with 30-year loans has an average life of 12 years. The fact that most or all principal will be repaid to the investor within 12 years plays an important part in actual pricing. Actual pricing formulas differ, are very complicated, and are not addressed in this book.

In calculating any trade, the quantity is multiplied by the price to produce the gross principal value of the transaction. Because the face amount of a TBA order is an approximate value, the gross principal calculation produces an estimated net value per trade. This figure will change depending on the true amortized value plus (buy-side) or minus (sell-side) the accrued interest due on the securities assigned to the TBA.

TABLE 7–2. MBS Settlement Cycle

Class A	Monday before the third Wednesday of each month.
	Freddie Mac securities below 10% with the exception of multi-family, ARMs, and VRMs.
	Fannie Mae securities below 10% with the exception of multi-family, ARMs, and VRMs.
Class B	Tuesday before the third Wednesday of each month.
	Ginnie Mae securities below 10% with the exception of multi-family, ARMs, and VRMs, and those listed in Class D.
Class C	Third Wednesday of the month.
	All Freddie Mac securities 10% and above with the exception of multifamily, ARMs, and VRMs.
	All Fannie Mae securities 10% and above with the exception of multifamily, ARMs, and VRMs.
Class D	Thursday following the third Wednesday.
	All Ginnie Mae GPMs. All Ginnie Mae Mobile Homes. All Ginnie Mae IIs. All Ginnie Mae, Fannie Mae, and Freddie Mac 15-year securities.
Class E	Monday following third Wednesday of each month.
	Ginnie Mae securities—all coupons 10% and above except those Ginnie Mae securities noted in Class D.
	All Ginnie Mae, Fannie Mae, and Freddie Mac ARMs. All Ginnie Mae, Fannie Mae, and Freddie Mac VRMs.
	All multifamily Freddie Mac, Ginnie Mae, and Fannie Mae securities.

TRADE DATE AND SETTLEMENT DATE

The trade date for a TBA trade is the date on which the order is executed. The settlement date for a TBA is the date on which the actual delivery and payment for the assigned MBS must take place. Unlike corporate or municipal bonds, which settle five business days after trade date, or government bonds, which normally settle the next business day, TBAs are traded for settlement during a particular month. Most TBAs trade for settlement during the current or following month although some are traded for settlement six months into the future. Trades extending beyond six months are extremely rare.

As you have seen, there are various MBS programs and within these programs, various types of collateral secure specific issues. Settlement date is determined by both program and type. Currently, there is a five-tiered settlement cycle each month that is updated periodically through the Public Securities Association (PSA). Table 7–2 defines the securities associated with each of the five classes (tiers) and identifies the settlement day for each class.

The TBA market is extremely active and provides a source of supply and demand for mortgages that have just been issued and not yet pooled. The marketplace ensures that new capital will flow back into the housing industry. It also provides an opportunity to trade on interest rate fluctuations in the housing market by margining TBA positions. The actual capital outlay for margined positions is much lower than for an outright purchase of a pool. Positions can be hedged through the use of standby and options agreements. Positions can be closed out to realize P&L before the actual settlement of the TBA contract, which is evident in the extremely heavy interdealer trading of these positions.

8

The TBA Comparison and Netting Process for Dealer Transactions

Dealer-to-dealer TBA contracts are usually high-value contracts. Formal acknowledgment of the pending contract by means of a comparison process is a necessary precaution for every firm. Several factors (the length of time between the TBA trade date and pool settlement date, the capital and interest rate risks faced by both sides of the TBA until it is settled, and the risk that the contra-broker in a trade could experience a business failure) combine to create extraordinary capital exposure for a firm that does not compare its trades. Before discussing the dealer comparison process, let's quickly review how a firm protects its interests when it executes a TBA with either a retail account or an institutional account.

Retail trades do not go through a formal comparison process. A one-way communication of the details of the trade are forwarded to each customer in the form of a confirmation. Protection is realized by requiring the customer to notify the broker if there is a discrepancy in the confirmation and by requiring a good-faith deposit (i.e., margin) on TBA transactions. Because MBS are not a federally regulated instrument from a credit standpoint, margin requirements for TBAs differ from firm to firm, ranging from 5% to 25% of the face value of the TBA contract. Each customer is obliged to immediately deposit the requested margin in the form of cash or marketable securities with a loan value equivalent to the amount of the margin call. If a customer purchases a $100,000.00 TBA from a firm requiring 10% margin, the customer must immediately deposit $10,000.00 if the deposit is in cash. If the customer chooses to deposit listed common stock as margin, that stock must be worth a minimum of $20,000.00 in the current market in order to satisfy the margin requirement. This margin is used to protect and cover any losses the broker may sustain should the customer fail or be unable to honor the TBA commitment when it is allocated and settles. The TBA comparison process for institutional transactions consists of mailing confirmations plus multipart commitment letters that contain the terms of each TBA contract. An authorized representative of the institution is expected to sign this letter and return a copy to the originating broker, thereby acknowledging the contract according to the terms of the letter. The timely receipt of these signed contracts must be carefully monitored; more than one firm has experienced substantial losses as a result of their failure to control the commitment letter cycle. A copy of a commitment letter plus additional details on the subject are in Chapter 6.

THE MBS CLEARING CORPORATION (MBSCC)

The MBSCC is a wholly owned subsidiary of the Midwest Stock Exchange. The MBSCC was created in 1979 to provide automated trade comparison and recording, margin protection, and settlement netting services to the brokers and dealers and other institutions who trade GNMA, FHLMC, and FNMA mortgage-backed issues. Since it began its operations, the MBSCC has compared over $1 trillion worth of TBA and specified pools trades. In addition to eliminating the time-consuming and costly manual comparison process, the system has also eliminated DKs ("don't know") of system-compared trades at allocation time. It fully protects its membership from losses incurred as a result of the failure of a member by requiring participants to make a basic deposit as well as subsequent margin deposits. The funds are deposited into a special escrow account used to secure the entire participant base. Furthermore, the MBSCC nets most compared trades. Clearance costs, fails, and operating expenses are reduced through the use of this additional service, which is called the Settlement Balance Order Settlement System (SBO). The board of directors of the MBSCC, which consists largely of industry representatives, establishes the rules and policies governing the participants in coordination with both the Risk Management and Operations Advisory Committees of the MBSCC. The committees are comprised of representatives from the participant firms.

Because some readers are involved with this aspect of MBS processing, it is important to mention that certain terminology used by the MBSCC has a connotation different from what is recognized by many persons. There are two divisions of the MBSCC. The one we are now discussing is the Clearing Division. The Clearing Division does not provide R&D (clearance) facilities; it provides trade comparison/recording, netting, and risk management services. The MBSCC uses the term *dealer* to encompass a broad range of more than 300 participants, including government brokers, commercial banks, thrifts, and mortgage bankers. The term *broker* refers to the broker's brokers acting as intermediaries in the transactions between dealers. The term *settlement processing* refers to the payment or collection of the net cash debit or credit resulting from trade netting and from issuing the corresponding balance order; it has nothing to do with the actual receipt or delivery of securities.

AUTOMATED TRADE COMPARISON

The first service provided to its members by the MBSCC Clearing Division is automated comparison of TBA trades executed for settlement in either the current or a future month. The MBSCC accepts information transmitted by many media, including manual blotters, tapes, and direct terminal linkage. There are two programs under which you can input trade information. The *two-sided trade comparison program* compares trades between two principals, such as a trade executed between two participating dealers. The *broker give-up program* compares trades executed by a broker's broker on behalf of two participating dealers. Within these programs, there are two settlement options. Under the *settlement balance order* (SBO) option, the compared purchases and sales of each participant are netted. Settlement instructions (i.e., SBOs) are generated representing the remaining netted balance in each participant's account for each TBA class. A specific issue will eventually be assigned or allocated to each SBO for actual delivery on settlement date. Under the *trade-for-trade* (T/T) option the compared trades are *not* netted after comparison. Each trade retains its original identity and must be cleared or settled between the original executing firms. Participants can establish their accounts on either an SBO or a T/T basis; a participant who has elected the SBO option may submit any individual trade on a T/T basis.

The concept of automated comparison is simple; it is based on the fact that for every buy trade there is an offsetting sell trade. Both the buying and selling dealers, or their broker's broker, submit trade details to a centralized clearing corporation, the MBSCC on T + 1. All the submitted trades are sorted by issue, trade date, price, quantity, settlement class, and contra-party. If both the buyer and seller have submitted identical data, the trade is compared and acknowledged by the MBSCC to each party. If they both submit data but there is some discrepancy (a price difference, for example), the trade is uncompared, and both the buyer and seller are advised by the MBSCC of the details provided by their contra-side. It is then up to the personnel of the trade processing department of each firm to resolve the difference and to submit the correction to the MBSCC. A trade that remains uncompared on settlement date cannot be cleared. A trade that has been compared through the MBSCC is considered an authorized legal and binding contract.

The following conditions must be met before a trade can be submitted to the MBSCC:

❑ Both the buyer and seller must be MBSCC members.

❑ The trade must be a future for an eligible security type.

❑ Quantity must be divisible by 1MM (except T/T program).

❑ Both sides must agree and submit T/T or SBO settlement instructions.

❑ Trade date must be equal to or less than cutoff date.

Eligibility is determined in view of the settlement option which has been chosen. Under the SBO Option TBA trades for the following security types are eligible:

❑ GNMA I Single Family, all 30-year and 15-year maturities.

- ❑ FNMA Single Family, all 30-year and 15-year maturities.
- ❑ FHLMC Single Family, all 30-year and 15-year maturities.
- ❑ GNMA GPMs.

Note: GNMA Jumbo and Custom programs are *not SBO eligible.*

TBA trades must meet additional criteria in order to be included in the SBO program:

- ❑ Must be a round lot trade [i.e., divisible by $1 million (1MM)].
- ❑ Both buyer and seller have elected to settle via SBO.
- ❑ The settlement date occurs on the class date posted by the PSA.
- ❑ TBA coupons must be multiples of 1/4.

Ineligible types of securities are compared using the trade-for-trade (T/T) settlement option as well as the following:

- ❑ All odd lot (trades or the parts of trades not evenly divisible by 1MM).
- ❑ Buyer and seller have either elected or agreed (on an individual trade basis) to settle trade-for-trade.
- ❑ Trades are executed on or after the input/correction cutoff date for SBO trades.
- ❑ The settlement date differs from the date established by the PSA.
- ❑ Put and call option contracts (recorded in special options account).

Trade data submitted to the MBSCC must be in the format depicted in Figure 8–1.

Trades are submitted to the MBSCC on T + 1. On the morning of T + 2, you will receive several reports, as follows:

- ❑ Purchase and Sales (P&S) Report.

FIGURE 8-1. MBS Clearing Corporation Trade Input

ENTRY DATE __4/24/86__ (1)
CONTACT __John Smith__ (2)
TELEPHONE, __(212) 555-2300__ (3)
SUBMITTING FIRM SYMBOL __MBXX__ (4)

(5) BUY B SELL S	(6) CONTRA SIDE	(7) UNITS	(8) CLASS	(9) TRD TYP T or O	(10) PRICE	(11) TRADE DATE	(12) SETTLEMENT DATE TRD TYP T ONLY
B	MB ZZ	4000	B180NC1	O	98 3/32	04/23/86	
S	MB ZZ	750	B172FA1	T	100	04/23/86	05/2086
	MB						
	MB						
	MB						
	MB						
	MB						
	MB						
	MB						
	MB						
	MB						
	MB						

2 MO REV 12/84   DATA INPUT

128

FIGURE 8–1 (cont'd).

Trade Input Form Preparation

The following information must be entered correctly on the MBSCC Trade Input Form. All trade terms, as submitted by both the buyer and seller, must agree before trade comparison can occur. Both SBO Destined and Trade-For-Trade transactions can be entered on the same Trade Input Form.

1   ENTRY DATE – Date trade is being submitted to MBSCC.
2   CONTACT – Name of person completing the form.
3   TELEPHONE NUMBER – Telephone number of person completing the form.
4   SUBMITTING FIRM SYMBOL – Four character MBSCC Participant symbol.
5   BUY/SELL CODE – Corresponding to the submitting firm.

    <u>B</u> = BUY   <u>S</u> = SELL

6   CONTRA-SIDE – Four character MBSCC symbol.
7   UNITS – The face value of the trade (hundred's place is omitted).

         500 = $ 500,000
       1,000 = $ 1,000,000
       5,000 = $ 5,000,000

    The System does not compare combined trades (e.g., you enter 1 × $5,000,000 trade and the contra-side enters 5 × $1,000,000).

    SBO Participants should segregate "mixed lot" trades into round and odd lots to derive maximum benefits from the SBO Settlement System. A trade of $1,500,000.00 which is eligible for SBO netting should be entered $1,000,000.00 SBO Destined and $500,000.00 Trade-For-Trade.

8   CLASS – Code denoting the settlement month, coupon rate and security type, arrived at using the configuration on page 130.
9   TRADE TYPE – Settlement Option

         O = SBO Destined   T = Trade-For-Trade

10 PRICE – Contract price in whole dollar and fraction, if any, in multiples of 1/8. (16ths, 32nds, 64ths, 128ths....)
11 TRADE DATE – Must be entered in six digit *month, day , year* format (MMDDYY).
12 SETTLEMENT DATE – Should only be used when entering trade type "T" (Trade-For-Trade). This is a six digit *month, day, year* format (MMDDYY). The settlement date for SBO Destined transactions is assumed to be the PSA established settlement date and should not be entered.

FIGURE 8–1 (cont'd).

MBSCC Class Codes

A. **Settlement Month**

The first character of the symbol designates the month of settlement as follows:

JAN	=	J	JUL	=	E
FEB	=	F	AUG	=	H
MAR	=	M	SEP	=	S
APR	=	A	OCT	=	Y
MAY	=	B	NOV	=	N
JUN	=	C	DEC	=	D

B. **Coupon Rate**

The second, third and fourth characters designate the coupon rate. The whole dollar portion of the rate occupies the second and third spaces in the class code. For example:

12%	=	12
9%	=	09

The fractional portion of the rate occupies the fourth space in the class code. The fraction should be written in quarter increments as follows:

1/4%	=	1
1/2%	=	2
3/4%	=	3

C. **Security Type**

The fifth and sixth characters represent the security types as follows:

GNMA I	=	N
GNMA II	=	H
FNMA	=	F
FHLMC	=	R

Subdivisions

A	=	15 Yr. Regular Coupon (rates higher than 10%)
B	=	15 Yr. Discount Coupon (rates equal to or less than 10%)
C	=	30 Yr. Regular Coupon
D	=	30 Yr. Discount Coupon
E	=	GPM 30 Yr. Regular Coupon
G	=	GPM 30 Yr. Discount Coupon
I	=	FHLMC 30 Yr. Specified 18/25 Series Regular Coupon
J	=	FHLMC 30 Yr. Specified 18/25 Series Discount Coupon
K	=	FHLMC 15 Yr. Specified 18/25 Series Regular Coupon
L	=	FHLMC 15 Yr. Specified 18/25 Series Discount Coupon

D. **Trade Type**

The seventh character represents the type of transaction as follows:

1	=	Guaranteed Rate
7	=	Put Option
8	=	Call Option

Examples:

B092ND1	=	MAY 9 1/2% GNMA 1 30 Yr. Disc. G/R
C150RI1	=	JUNE 15% GHLMC 30 Yr. Spec. 18/25 Ser. G/R
Y133NC7	=	OCT 13 3/4% GNMA 1 30 Yr. Put
H092RD1	=	AUG 9 1/2% FHLMC 30 Yr. Disc. G/R

❑ Open Commitment Report.
❑ Uncompared and Advisory Report.
❑ Market Margin Differential Report.

The Purchase and Sales (P&S) Report

It is the first three reports that are needed to complete the comparison process. The P&S report, which has been approved by the PSA as a formal confirmation and comparison, reflects all trades submitted and compared on the previous day. In other words, if both you and the contra-side of your trade submitted *identical* trade details to the MBSCC concerning a trade you executed the previous day, that trade will appear on the P&S report. This report is noncumulative, so trade details will appear once on a single day's report. The report is issued even if there is no activity for the day. Internally, you must ascertain that the totals contained on this report, after adjustments, reflect the trading activity of the firm. Figure 8–2 is an example of an MBSCC P&S report.

The Open Commitment Report

An open commitment report is a cumulative report of all compared trades. On any day, the trades that hit the P&S report will simultaneously update the commitment report. Trades will remain as open items on this report until the MBSCC receives notification of settlement.

As you have seen, TBA trading for a particular settlement period can be going on for several months. The commitment report is critical in controlling these executed but unsettled commitments. Eligible trading activity that is routed by your system to the MBSCC must be continually balanced. The MBSCC is an external accounting system that governs and triggers your clearance processing cycles. If there are trades recorded in the MBSCC that are not in agreement with your firm's records, you must take action to reconcile your records with those of the MBSCC. If you fail to do that and the trade reaches the settlement cycle, your firm will be forced to honor the commitment.

Each day, the summary totals contained in your commitment reports plus the summary totals contained in your unconfirmed

FIGURE 8–2. MBSCC P&S Report

```
MBXXLF                                    MBS CLEARING CORPORATION              REPORT NO. GPO50
                                     DAILY PURCHASE AND SALE REPORT
                                            DATE OF REPORT                      PAGE    1    370

(1) MBXXLF   MBSCC TEST ACCOUNT
             INTERNAL ACCT        IL 60603
        (2)  MBSCC DEPT

SECURITY SYMBOL  B 1BONC1  CUSIP NUMBER  0518ONC10     SECURITY DESCRIPTION   MAY 18 % GNMA I 30YR
                                              (3)                             (4)

TRADE    BUYER/     UNITS     UNITS              TRADED
NUMBER   SELLER     BOUGHT    SOLD     PRICE     YIELD    CONTRACT VALUE  A/C  T/C  TRADE DATE  SETTL DATE  ENTRY DATE
                                                                                   (14)        (15)        (16)
                  (7) 4,000  (8)    (9) 98 3/32 (10)  (11) 3,923,750.00       (12) (13) 04/23/86            04/24/86
(5) 355681  MBZZLI (6)
(17) *BUY TOTALS*    1 ITEMS           4.000 UNITS          3,923,750.00 VALUE
(18) *SELL TOTALS*     ITEMS                 UNITS                   .00 VALUE
(19) *NET TOTALS*    1 ITEMS           4.000 UNITS          3,923,750.00 VALUE
(20) **FINAL BUY TOTALS**  1 ITEMS     4.000 UNITS          3,923,750.00 VALUE
(21) **FINAL SELL TOTALS** ITEMS             UNITS                   .00 VALUE
(22) **FINAL NET TOTALS**  1 ITEMS     4.000 UNITS          3,923,750.00 VALUE
```

FIGURE 8–2 (cont'd).

Purchase and Sale Report

The Purchase and Sale Report serves as **formal trade confirmation and comparison** eliminating the need for Participants to exchange Commitment Letters. **All compared trades are reflected** on the Purchase and Sale Report on the business day following trade input submission. The Purchase and Sale Report is **noncumulative, listing only the previous day's compared trades.**

MBSCC generates a daily Purchase and Sale Report for each Participant. If no trades have compared, the phrase "NO ACTIVITY TODAY" prints on the report. The following information is listed on the Purchase and Sale Report:

1. Participant NAME, ADDRESS and SYMBOL
2. SECURITY SYMBOL – Class Code **denoting settlement month, coupon rate, security type and trade type.**
3. CUSIP NUMBER – Security ID number assigned by MBSCC denoting settlement month, coupon rate, security type and trade type.
4. SECURITY DESCRIPTION
5. TRADE NUMBER – Assigned by MBSCC upon comparison.
6. BUYER/SELLER – Contra-Side Participant Symbol or one character Broker Code if Give-Up Trade entered by broker. (See Broker Give-Up Input/Output Cycle.)
7. UNITS BOUGHT – Face value of the trade, hundred's place is omitted.
8. UNITS SOLD – Face value of the trade, hundred's place is omitted.
9. PRICE – Original contract price is listed in whole dollar and fraction format. Contract price of MBSCC generated SBO trades is in whole dollar and decimal format.
10. TRADED YIELD – Reserved for yield maintenance trading.
11. CONTRACT VALUE – Contract price multiplied by the face value.
12. ADD/CANCEL – Blank = Add   C = Cancellation
13. T/C – Trade Category

    OTC = SBO Destined
    T   = Trade-for-Trade
    SBO = MBSCC Generated SBO Trade

14. TRADE DATE
15. SETTLEMENT DATE – Listed for SBO and T/T transactions only.
16. ENTRY DATE
17. BUYS TOTALS – Number of buys with corresponding dollar values per class.
18. SELLS TOTALS – Number of sells with corresponding dollar values per class.
19. NET TOTALS – The sum of the buys and sells with corresponding dollar values per class.
20. FINAL BUYS TOTALS – Total number of buys with corresponding dollar values for all classes.
21. FINAL SELLS TOTALS – Total number of sells with corresponding dollar values for all classes.
22. FINAL NET TOTALS – The sum of the final buys and sells with corresponding dollar values.

reports must be equal to the overall trading activity reflected on the accounting records of your firm. This balancing is facilitated through the use of an internal omnibus account.

The Uncompared and Advisory Report

The uncompared and advisory report contains the details of trades that can be categorized as unresolved problems. *Uncompared trades* are transactions your firm submitted to the MBSCC for which the contra-party failed to submit a trade with identical terms. *Advisory trades* are transactions submitted to MBSCC by another firm for which your firm failed to submit a trade with the identical details. Both are problems because any trade on either report could represent a valid execution. It is the reponsibility of all firms to make sure that these open items are properly resolved and updated so that timely settlement will be ensured. These differences must be resolved within five business days or the trade will be deleted from the report. It is important to understand that *your firm's uncompared trade is always the contra-party's advisory trade.* When both sides submit the same trade but one side or both have an error, related advisories result.

Give immediate attention to your uncompared trades, researching all possibilities. First, examine all internal processing to determine if the error was caused within your own operation. Examine the original order ticket if possible to make sure that the information forwarded to MBSCC is identical to the original execution details. If you discover an error, correct the trade. If the original input appears to be correct, supply the contra-party's trade processing group with any additional information that could assist them in reconciling the difference. Date and time of execution and, if known, the names of the traders who executed the trade are useful pieces of information. If the contra-party continues to insist that they do not know the trade as you have reported it, the transaction must be referred to the trader or a trader's assistant for further review. Whenever an uncompared problem has to be forwarded to the trading desk, relay accurate information. If you have reported a sale at 100 31/32 and the contra-side states they know the price to be 100 29/32, relate those specifics to the trader. Do not simply indicate that the contra-party has DKed the trade because of price. Control the aged unresolved uncompared trades carefully. Remember that they will be dropped from the MBSCC listing on the sixth day after original entry; unless you record such a drop, balancing will become a nightmare.

What about advisories? Since no internal trade was processed, should they simply be ignored? No! First, check trades that are being processed on an "as-of " basis—that is, they are being booked after the original trade execution date. Second, refer the trade to the people who are responsible for balancing the trading account positions. They might have a discrepancy that relates to the advisory. If neither of these inquiries proves positive, provide the traders with complete details of the advisory. There is always the possibility that a trade did take place but was never booked.

Once the reason for an uncompared or advisory trade is discovered, it can be compared by processing an advisory notice reentry blotter with the MBSCC. When both parties to a trade have an advisory notice on the same trade, the firms involved must communicate with each other to decide which of them will respond to the advisory. If both were to submit an advisory notice reentry blotter, duplicate trades would result. Figures 8–3, 8–4 and 8–5 are examples of an open commitment blotter, an uncompared and advisory report, and an advisory notice reentry blotter.

Market Margin Differential Report

At any time, a dealer participant may have billions of dollars of positions compared and pending in the MBSCC system. Until settlement date arrives and the actual receipt or delivery versus payment is accomplished, there is potential exposure associated with the failure of one or more of the participants being unable to meet its obligations. To protect its members, the MBSCC has established a participants' fund secured by letters of credit, cash, and qualified security deposits that are required of each participant. Two types of deposits to the participants' fund are required from each member: (1) the basic deposit, and (2) the market margin differential deposit.

The *basic deposit* of a minimum of $10,000 cash is required for each account maintained by participants. The *market margin differential* (MMD) deposit is required whenever there is a potential

FIGURE 8-3. Open Commitment Blotter

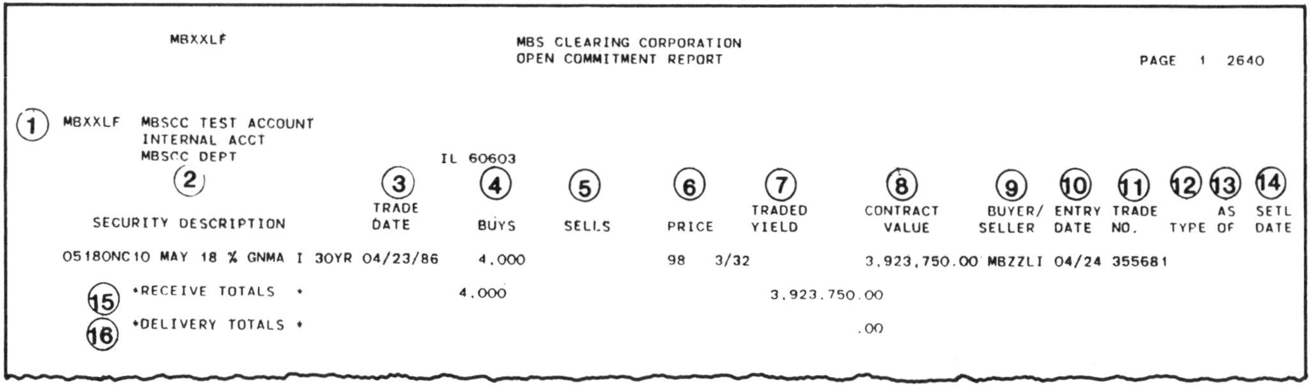

```
MBXXLF                          MBS CLEARING CORPORATION                      PAGE   1    2640
                                OPEN COMMITMENT REPORT

(1) MBXXLF  MBSCC TEST ACCOUNT
            INTERNAL ACCT
            MBSCC DEPT           IL 60603
                            (3)  (4)    (5)    (6)    (7)    (8)       (9)      (10)  (11)  (12)(13)(14)
                            TRADE BUYS  SELLS  PRICE  TRADED CONTRACT  BUYER/   ENTRY TRADE      AS  SETL
     SECURITY DESCRIPTION   DATE                      YIELD  VALUE     SELLER   DATE  NO.  TYPE  OF  DATE
(2)
   0518ONC10 MAY 18 % GNMA I 30YR 04/23/86  4.000     98 3/32       3,923,750.00 MBZZLI 04/24 355681

(15) *RECEIVE TOTALS  *            4.000                            3,923,750.00
(16) *DELIVERY TOTALS *                                                      .00
```

FIGURE 8–3 (cont'd).

Open Commitment Report

Simultaneous with being listed on the Purchase and Sale Report, all compared trades are also listed on the Open Commitment Report. The Open Commitment Report is a **cumulative** report which lists all compared trades until MBSCC receives notification of settlement. The following information is listed on the Open Commitment Report:

1 Participant NAME, ADDRESS and SYMBOL

2 SECURITY DESCRIPTION

3 TRADE DATE

4 BUYS

5 SELLS

6 PRICE – Original contract price is listed in whole dollar and fraction format. Contract price of MBSCC generated SBO trades is in whole dollar and decimal format.

7 TRADED YIELD – Reserved for yield maintenance trading.

8 CONTRACT VALUE – Contract price multiplied by the face value.

9 BUYER/SELLER – Contra-Side Participant Symbol or one character Broker Code if Give-Up Trade entered by broker. (See Broker Give-Up Input/Output Cycle.)

10 ENTRY DATE

11 TRADE NUMBER – Assigned by MBSCC upon comparison.

12 TYPE – Trade type

Blank	=	SBO Destined
T/T	=	Trade-for-Trade
SBO	=	MBSCC Generated SBO Trade

13 AS OF – This field is always blank.

14 SETTLEMENT DATE – Listed for SBO and T/T transactions only.

15 RECEIVE TOTALS – Total number of buys with corresponding dollar values.

16 DELIVERY TOTALS – Total number of sells with corresponding dollar values.

FIGURE 8-4. Uncompared and Advisory Report

MBXXLF

MBS CLEARING CORPORATION
UNCOMPARED AND ADVISORY LIST
DATE OF REPORT

REPORT NO GMO11-248
PAGE 00001

(1) MBXXLF MBSCC TEST ACCOUNT
INTERNAL ACCT
MBSCC DEPT (2) IL 60603 (3)

SECURITY MAY 17 1/2 % FNMA 15 CLASS B172FA1

(4) CONTRA SIDE (5)	BUYS (6)	SELLS (7)	PRICE (8)	CONTRACT VALUE (9)	TRADE DATE (10)	ENTRY DATE (11)	ADVISORY NO (12)	TRD TYP (13)	SETL DATE (14)	TRD NUM
MBZZLI	750	100		750,000.00	04/23/86	04/24/86		T/T	05/20/86	UNCOMPARED
MBZZLI	750	100	1/2	753,750.00	04/23/86	04/24/86	0024	T/T	05/20/86	ADVISORY

TOTAL BUYS 0 TOTAL SELLS 1,500 TOTAL SIDES 2

UNCOMPARED CREATED 1 ADVISORIES CREATED 1 UNCOMP/ADV DROPPED 0 VALID ADV/UNCOMP 0

FIGURE 8–4 (cont'd).

Uncompared/Advisory List

The Uncompared and Advisory List reflects transactions for five (5) business days pending resolution. The entry date is considered the first day of the five day suspense cycle. If a transaction is left unresolved, it drops off the report on the sixth business day. The following information is reflected on the Uncompared and Advisory List:

1   Participant NAME, ADDRESS and SYMBOL
2   SECURITY DESCRIPTION
3   CLASS – Code denoting settlement month, coupon rate, security type and trade type.
4   CONTRA-SIDE SYMBOL – MBSCC Participant Symbol.
5   BUYS
6   SELLS
7   PRICE – Contract price in whole dollar and fraction.
8   CONTRACT VALUE – Contract price multiplied by face value.
9   TRADE DATE
10   ENTRY DATE
11   ADVISORY NUMBER – Each advisory is assigned a four digit number. This field is blank for uncompared transactions.
12   TRADE TYPE – Settlement Option

> Blank   =   SBO Destined
> T/T   =   Trade-for-Trade

13   SETTLEMENT DATE – First date on which assigned pools will be able to be cleared.
14   TRADE NUMBER – Assigned by MBSCC upon comparison.

FIGURE 8-5. MBS Clearing Corporation Advisory Notice Reentry Blotter

ENTRY DATE **04/29/86** ①

CONTACT **John Smith** ②

TELEPHONE # **(212)555-2300** ③

SUBMITTING FIRM SYMBOL **MBXX** ④

⑤ ADVISORY #	⑥ CONTRA SIDE	⑦ CLASS	⑧ ORIGINAL ENTRY DATE
0024	MBZZ	B172FA1	04/24/86
	MB		
	MB		
	MB		
	MB		
	MB		
	MB		
	MB		
	MB		
	MB		
	MB		

ADVISORY #	CONTRA SIDE	CLASS	ORIGINAL ENTRY DATE
	MB		
	MB		
	MB		
	MB		
	MB		
	MB		
	MB		
	MB		
	MB		
	MB		

DATA INPUT

5MO REV 12/84

for a net loss on a participant's position resulting from a change in the current market price versus the original contract price. The MMD calculation is figured daily and is equivalent to 130% of the potential losses for the total obligations of a participant in each of the following categories:

❑ All forward and immediate TBA positions.
❑ Option positions.
❑ Unpaid SBO market differential payments.
❑ SBO fails.
❑ Unpaid cash amounts (fines, cash adjustments, etc.).

Note: Credits are not given on either immediate or fail positions.

The MBSCC Board of Directors has begun discussions on rule changes which would require each participant to maintain a minimum MMD contribution at all times. This minimum amount could be as high as 2.5 million dollars per participant. An exemption from this minimum requirement is being considered for broker's brokers. Subject to SEC approval, it is anticipated this change could become effective during the second quarter of '89.

SETTLEMENT NETTING SERVICES

At this stage of processing, thousands of trades have been compared and are awaiting settlement. Because dealers constantly buy and sell the same TBA type or class throughout the trading cycle, many of the compared trades can be paired off. This pairing-off process is called *netting*. Netting takes all buys and sells into consideration regardless of whether they were done with the same or different contra-parties; the resulting pair-offs could conceivably result in a single instruction to receive or deliver.

If you have never worked with a netted comparison system, trying to follow the MBSCC netting flow can be difficult. It will be useful to review the concept and procedures by applying the principles of netting, on a broad generic basis, to a single day's trading activity in a specific issue. Let's assume that on October 10, 1988, five dealers traded GNMA I SF 30-yr, 10% coupon. Each of the dealers reports its trades to a fictitious Central Comparison Corporation, which takes all the information and produces for itself an executed trade report (see Table 8–1). Each trade has an

TABLE 8–1.

EXECUTED TRADE REPORT				TRADE DATE ACTIVITY 10-10-88		
DEALER	BOUGHT	SOLD	PRICE	VALUE and CONTRA-SIDE DEALER		
A	1MM		102	$1,020,000.00	vs.	DEALER B
A		1MM	103	$1,030,000.00	vs.	DEALER D
B		1MM	102	$1,020,000.00	vs.	DEALER A
B		1MM	101	$1,010,000.00	vs.	DEALER E
C	1MM		102	$1,020,000.00	vs.	DEALER E
D	1MM		103	$1,030,000.00	vs.	DEALER A
E	1MM		101	$1,010,000.00	vs.	DEALER B
E		1MM	102	$1,020,000.00	vs.	DEALER C
TOTALS	4MM	4MM		$8,160,000.00		

originating dealer and a contra-side. Buyers must receive the issue purchased; sellers must deliver it. The goal of a netting system is to reduce all activity to the least number of receivables and deliverables. The Central Comparison Corporation (CCP) takes the following steps to achieve that goal.

Step 1

Calculate an average price for all trading activity by dividing the total contract value by the total quantity value:

$$\$8,160,000.00/8MM \ = \ 102 \text{ (the average price)}$$

Why is this necessary? If an average price were not assigned to every transaction, only purchases and sales executed at the same price could be paired off (netted); the advantage of netting is maximized only when the same average price is associated with every contract.

Step 2

For each firm or dealer, the CCP must pair off (net) the buys and sells for each security traded (in this case GNMA I SF 30-yr, 10% coupon) (see Table 8–2). Dealer A bought and sold 1MM; CCP pairs these trades off leaving Dealer A with a net R&D requirement of zero. If it did not, Dealer A will receive 1MM from Dealer B (the contra-dealer) and then redeliver the same 1MM to

Dealer D (the contra-dealer). What would the net effect of the R&D process be to Dealer A? A zero position! So, by netting, you relieve Dealer A of the need to take in (receive) securities and then redeliver them without changing Dealer A's final net position, zero. The same net zero position is achieved by pairing off the trades and their associated R&D requirements. Continue the pairing-off process for the day's trades. Because Dealer B was only a seller on the day and Dealers C & D were only buyers, nothing can be paired. Dealer E bought and sold 1 MM and, as with Dealer A, can be netted to zero.

TABLE 8–2.

EXECUTED TRADE REPORT				TRADE DATE ACTIVITY 10-10-88	
DEALER	BOUGHT	SOLD	PRICE	VALUE and CONTRA-SIDE DEALER	
A	~~1MM~~		~~102~~	~~$1,020,000.00 vs. DEALER B~~	} Pair
A		~~1MM~~	~~103~~	~~$1,030,000.00 vs. DEALER D~~	Off
B		1MM	102	$1,020,000.00 vs. DEALER A	
B		1MM	101	$1,010,000.00 vs. DEALER E	
C	1MM		102	$1,020,000.00 vs. DEALER E	
D	1MM		103	$1,030,000.00 vs. DEALER A	
E	~~1MM~~		~~101~~	~~$1,010,000.00 vs. DEALER B~~	} Pair
E		~~1MM~~	~~102~~	~~$1,020,000.00 vs. DEALER C~~	Off

Step 3

The dealers whose positions do not net to zero must either receive or deliver the unnetted portion of their day's trades. The clearing corporation now advises each dealer of its netted quantities and advises each one of the quantity to be received or delivered *as well as the identity of the contra-dealer* from whom the dealer will be receiving the issue or to whom they must deliver. Carefully examine Dealer B's trades. The contra-parties to the original sales executed by Dealer B were Dealers A and E, both of whom were netted to a zero position. So, although it is true that Dealer B would ordinarily deliver 1MM GNMA I SF 30-yr, 10% coupon to each of them, Dealers A and E both have a flat (zero) net trading position for the day. The clearing corporation will instruct Dealer B to deliver to Dealers C and D 1MM each. Dealers C and D are the only dealers left with a net long (buy-side) position after the netting process. This explains why you can "lose" the identity of the original contra-party in a netting system.

The format of the R&D instructions issued by the clearing corporation to the dealers with open positions is called a *settlement balance order* (SBO). Each SBO identifies the contra-party to the R&D instruction. The contract value on the SBO is calculated using the *average price* calculated in Step 1. In this example, four instructions are issued as follows:

1. Dealer B must deliver 1MM to Dealer C versus payment of $1,020,000.
2. Dealer B must deliver 1MM to Dealer D versus payment of $1,020,000.
3. Dealer C must receive 1MM from Dealer B versus payment of $1,020,000.
4. Dealer D must receive 1MM from Dealer B versus payment of $1,020,000.

Step 4

When the SBOs are issued, the contract value is the amount of money that will change hands when the securities are delivered. The contract value, known as the *settlement amount*, is calculated by multiplying the average price times the quantity ($102 \times 1MM$). But the original trades were executed at prices ranging from 101 to 103; the P&L realized on the original trades is lost if everything is settled at 102. Step 4 is the calculation of the clearing corporation adjustment known in the MBSCC Clearing Corporation as the *SBO Market Differential* (SBOMD). In effect, the clearing corporation compares the prices for each day's compared trades (including trades that were netted) to the average settlement price. The contract value of each execution is compared to its settlement value at the average price, and the differences are credited or debited to each dealer involved in the netting process (see Table 8–3).

TABLE 8–3.

				CONTRACT		AVG SETL	
DLR	BOT	SOLD	PRICE	VALUE		VALUE	DIFFERENTIAL
A	1MM		102	$1,020,000.00	vs.	$1,020,000.00	0.00
A		1MM	103	$1,030,000.00	vs.	$1,020,000.00	$10,000.00 CR
B		1MM	102	$1,020,000.00	vs.	$1,020,000.00	0.00
B		1MM	101	$1,010,000.00	vs.	$1,020,000.00	$10,000.00 DR
C	1MM		102	$1,020,000.00	vs.	$1,020,000.00	0.00
D	1MM		103	$1,030,000.00	vs.	$1,020,000.00	$10,000.00 DR
E	1MM		101	$1,010,000.00	vs.	$1,020,000.00	$10,000.00 CR
E		1MM	102	$1,020,000.00	vs.	$1,020,000.00	0.00
TOT	4MM	4MM		$8,160,000.00		$8,160,000.00	0.00

EXECUTED TRADE REPORT   *TRADE DATE ACTIVITY 10-10-88*

Step 5

On the settlement date for this day's trades, the Central Comparison Corporation will collect the debit differential amounts from Dealers B and D and pay the credit differential amounts to Dealers A and E. These sums must change hands on the settlement date; they are not contingent upon the actual receipt or delivery of the settled trades.

Do you understand what the differential (SBOMD) represents? It is each dealer's P&L for that day. Dealer A's trades paired off, but when Dealer A sold 1MM at 103, Dealer A realized a 1-point profit on the 1MM face quantity of the trade, or $10,000.00. Broker B sold a lot at 101 but will receive the equivalent of 102 when he delivers to Dealer D. That is $10,000.00 more than the amount to which Broker B is entitled, and it must be returned so that it can be paid to the dealer to whom it is due. There is no differential for Dealer C because his execution value equals the averaged settlement contract value. You can apply similar logic in calculating the differentials for Dealers D and E. Finally notice, once again, that debits equal credits. The $20,000.00 payment to be made to the clearing corporation by the debited dealers will be paid out to the dealers with the credited differentials.

In the preceding examples, 50% of the executed trades were paired off. The MBSCC has stated that during a typical TBA settlement period, participants can expect to net or pair off about 90% of the TBA dollar volume for SBO destined trades. The elimination of all those deliveries represents an enormous savings of time and money. There are two reasons for such a large percentage of netted trades. First, TBAs are actively traded in and out of position before settlement is reached. Second, when the TBA netting cycle begins, you are not working with a single day's trading activity but with the cumulative reported executions during weeks of trading. You are able to net on the basis of an overall firm position that is based on a dealer's long-term trading strategy as opposed to netting a single day's work.

Now we are going to return to the real world of the MBS Clearing Corporation and examine the way that they perform this netting process. Figure 8–6 is from the MBSCC–GNMA settlement procedures manual and provides a graphic explanation of the netting process. You will notice that the MBSCC uses two terms relative to the calculation of the market differential. The Class Average Price (CAP) is the average price of all trades, for all dealers, for the entire TBA trading cycle and is equivalent to Step 1 in the preceding example. The Firm Class Average Price (FCAP) is similar except that it is based on the trades of the individual dealers and a separate FCAP is calculated for each dealer for its trades with like contra-sides.

The question remains, "How is the netting process controlled internally?" When an MBSCC–SBO eligible issue is bought for a firm's trading account, an offsetting entry is automatically generated to an MBSCC omnibus account. An omnibus account is one that reflects all transactions on a continuous balance forward basis. Therefore internally at your firm, the net position in this omnibus account should always equal the net positions being reported to your firm on its open commitment reports after adjustments have been made for the uncompared trades. It is imperative that the balances in the omnibus account be proven daily to the MBSCC's figures.

SBO PROCESSING AND THE DAILY CASH ADJUSTMENT

For the purpose of protecting its participants from the failure of another participant, MBSCC marks to the market all open forward and SBO positions on a daily basis. Marking to the market consists of applying the current market value of a participant's transactions against the participant's original contract value. If

HBSCC utilizes The Open Commitment Reports
at the close of business On Trade Input
Cutoff to perform netting

MBS CLEARING CORPORATION
OPEN COMMITMENT REPORTS
02/01/82

BEGINNING POSITIONS PRIOR TO NETTING

MBXX

SECURITY DESCRIPTION	TRADE DATE	BUYS	SELLS	PRICE	CONTRACT VALUE	BUYER/SELLER	ENTRY DATE	TRADE NO.
0021500J3 FEB 13 G/R	12/28/81	3,000		95-45/64	2,871,093.70	MBYY	12/29	023789
	12/28/81	1,000		95-28/32	958,750.00	MBZZ	12/29	023790
	01/04/82	1,000		95-20/32	956,250.00	MBYY	01/04	028639
	01/04/82		2,000	95- 4/32	1,902,500.00	MBZZ	01/05	028732
	01/05/82		2,000	95- 9/32	1,905,625.00	MBYY	01/06	029847
	01/06/82		1,000	97-16/32	975,000.00	MBZZ	01/07	030021
	01/08/82		1,000	98	980,000.00	MBYY	01/09	039726

MBYY

SECURITY DESCRIPTION	TRADE DATE	BUYS	SELLS	PRICE	CONTRACT VALUE	BUYER/SELLER	ENTRY DATE	TRADE NO.
0021500J3 FEB 13 G/R	01/05/82	2,000		95-9/32	1,905,625.00	MBXX	01/06	029847
	01/08/82	1,000		98	980,000.00	MBXX	01/09	039726
	12/28/81		3,000	95-45/64	2,871,093.70	MBXX	12/29	023789
	01/04/82		1,000	95-20/32	956,250.00	MBXX	01/04	028639

MBZZ

SECURITY DESCRIPTION	TRADE DATE	BUYS	SELLS	PRICE	CONTRACT VALUE	BUYER/SELLER	ENTRY DATE	TRADE NO.
0021500J3 FEB 13 G/R	01/04/82	2,000		95-4/32	1,902,500.00	MBXX	01/05	028732
	01/06/82	1,000		97-16/32	975,000.00	MBXX	01/07	030021
	12/28/81		1,000	95-28/32	958,750.00	MBXX	12/29	023790

FIGURE 8–6 (cont'd).

SBO NETTING PROCESS

The SBO netting process is herein detailed to provide you with an in-depth understanding, which is crucial to reconciliation.

STEP # 1 – CLASS AVERAGE PRICE DETERMINATION

The Class Average Price (CAP) is an average price of all Participants SBO destined trades in a given class. It is calculated by determining the average aggregate price of SBO destined trades recorded in a given class prior to the performance of SBO netting.

Listed below is an example of all the prices of Participants SBO destined trades in the F130NC1 class.

Price	Decimal Equivalent	Trade Quantity	Total Price
95– 45/64	95.703125	6,000	5,742,187.50
95– 28/32	95.875000	2,000	1,917,500.00
95– 20/32	95.625000	2,000	1,912,500.00
95– 4/32	95.125000	4,000	3,805,000.00
95– 9/32	95.281250	4,000	3,811,250.00
97– 16/32	97.500000	2,000	1,950,000.00
98	98.000000	2,000	1,960,000.00
		22,000	21,098,437.50

FORMULA:

Total Contract Price	divided by	Total Trade Quantity	=	Class Average Price
21,098,437.50	divided by	22,000	=	95.901989

FIGURE 8–6 (cont'd).

STEP # 2 – TRADE SEGREGATION PROCESS

In the trade segregation process the system separates each SBO destined trade into one million dollar increments. For example, a trade with a quantity of $5,000,000 becomes 5 × $1,000,000. The original contra-sides are retained throughout this process.

Next, BUY trades with like contra-sides are independently grouped as well as SELL trades with like contra-sides. Below is an example of the trade segregation process using MBXX's SBO destined trades.

Contra-Side Seller	Trade Quantity	Original Price	Contract Value
MBYY	1,000	95–9/32	952,812.50
MBYY	1,000	95–9/32	952,812.50
MBYY	1,000	98	980,000.00
TOTAL PER CONTRA-SIDE	3,000		2,885,625.00

Contra-Side Seller	Trade Quantity	Original Price	Contract Value
MBZZ	1,000	95– 4/32	951,250.00
MBZZ	1,000	95– 4/32	951,250.00
MBZZ	1,000	97–16/32	975,000.00
TOTAL PER CONTRA-SIDE	3,000		2,877,500.00

Contra-Side Buyer	Trade Quantity	Original Price	Contract Value
MBYY	1,000	95–45/64	957,031.25
MBYY	1,000	95–45/64	957,031.25
MBYY	1,000	95–45/64	957,031.25
MBYY	1,000	95–20/32	956,250.00
TOTAL PER CONTRA-SIDE	4,000		3,827,343.75

Contra-Side Buyer	Trade Quantity	Original Price	Contract Value
MBZZ	1,000	95–28/32	958,750.00
TOTAL PER CONTRA-SIDE	1,000		958,750.00

FIGURE 8–6 (cont'd).

STEP # 3 – FIRM CLASS AVERAGE PRICE (FCAP) DETERMINATION

Firm class average prices are the average contract price of **each** Participant:

– BUY trades with like contra-sides

– SELL trades with like contra-sides

Contra-Side Seller	Total Contract Value	Total Buys		FCAP/ Million
MBYY	2,885,625.00	3,000	=	96.187500
MBZZ	2,877,500.00	3,000	=	95.916667

Contra-Side Buyer	Total Contract Value	Total Buys		FCAP/ Million
MBYY	3,827,343.75	4,000	=	95.683593
MBZZ	958,750.00	1,000	=	95.875000

FIGURE 8–6 (cont'd).

STEP # 4 – NETTING PROCESS

The MBSCC netting process attempts to simulate an ex-clearing environment as closely as possible. To accomplish this MBSCC performs two (2) types of pair-off functions.

NETTED

BUY and SELL trades are paired off with the **like** contra-sides. Positions which cannot be eliminated in this process are carried over to next pair-off function.

NET OUT

BUY and SELL trades are paired off with **unlike** contra-sides. Positions which cannot be eliminated in this process are considered the remaining NET OPEN positions.

NET OPEN

NET OPEN positions are the remaining BUYS **or** SELLS which could not be eliminated through the netting process. Because MBSCC's netting process eliminates the original SBO destined trades, the newly created SBO trades replace all original transactions. This results in the creation of new delivery/receive obligations at the CAP.

NETTED
(PAIR-OFFS WITH LIKE CONTRA-SIDES)

CONTRA-SIDE	—	MBYY		CONTRA-SIDE	—	MBZZ
SELLS		*BUYS*		*SELLS*		*BUYS*
1,000	(NETTED)	1,000		1,000	(NETTED)	1,000
1,000	(NETTED)	1,000		1,000	(CARRYOVER)	
1,000	(NETTED)	1,000		1,000	(CARRYOVER)	
	(CARRYOVER)	1,000				

NET OUT
(PAIR-OFFS WITH UNLIKE CONTRA-SIDES)
(CARRYOVER FROM NETTED CYCLE)

CONTRA-SIDES

MBYY		MBZZ
BUYS		*SELLS*
1,000	(NET OUT)	1,000
	(CARRYOVER)	1,000

NET OPEN
(REMAINING OPEN BUY <u>OR</u> SELL POSITIONS)
(CARRYOVER FROM NET OUT CYCLE)

CONTRA-SIDE	—	MBZZ
SELLS		
1,000		

FIGURE 8–6 (cont'd).

STEP #5 – SBOMD CALCULATION

The SBOMD calculation is an integral part of the SBO netting process. This is illustrated below using the netting information detailed on the preceding pages.

NETTED

(SBOMD for a NETTED position is the cash differential in FCAPs between **like** contra-sides.)

Contra-Side — MBYY

Sells	FCAP	Buys	FCAP		SBOMD
1,000	96.187500	1,000	95.683593	=	$5,039.07 CR
1,000	96.187500	1,000	95.683593	=	$5,039.07 CR
1,000	96.187500	1,000	95.683593	=	$5,039.07 CR
		1,000	95.683593		(CARRYOVER)

Contra-Side — MBZZ

Sells	FCAP	Buys	FCAP		SBOMD
1,000	95.916667	1,000	95.875000	=	$416.67 CR
1,000	95.916667	(CARRYOVER)			
1,000	95.916667	(CARRYOVER)			

NET OUT

(SBOMD for a net out position is the cash differential in FCAPs between **unlike** contra-sides.)

Contra-Side — MBYY / Contra-Side — MBZZ

Buys	FCAP	Sells	FCAP		SBOMD
1,000	95.683593	1,000	95.916667	=	$2,330.74 CR
		1,000	95.916667		

NET OPEN

(SBOMD for a remaining open buy or sell position is the difference in FCAP and CAP.)

Contra-Side — MBZZ

Sells	FCAP	CAP		SBOMD
1,000	95.916667	95.901989	=	$146.78 CR

this calculation results in a deficit, the participant is required to make an additional collateral deposit equal to 130% of the deficit. If the result is a credit, the participant will be overcollateralized but may not withdraw this amount without the permission of the MBSCC.

The SBOs that have been distributed to the members are still in a generic format. Each participant who has received them is now actively engaged in the allocation, or pool assignment, process.

Once one or more pools have been assigned to each TBA SBO, delivery or settlement of the assigned pools will begin to occur on settlement date. As each pool is delivered both the buyer and seller are obligated to notify the MBSCC that delivery has taken place. This notification must contain the details of the delivery and the identification number of the original SBO. Since each pool assigned to an SBO is considered a separate deliverable contract, delivery of one pool frequently is only a partial settlement of the original SBO. Notification of settlement by the members accomplishes two things.

First, it advises the MBSCC that the buyer and seller have completed their contractual obligations. MBSCC at this point will remove the SBO from its open commitments (partial removal is accomplished if the pool information does not completely satisfy the SBO quantity). Once the SBO, in whole or in part, is removed, all margin requirements cease for that particular trade. Second, notification triggers the calculation of the final *cash adjustment* which the MBSCC will debit and credit to all participants who were involved in the *net out cycle* for the particular SBO being reported. Do you recall that each firm either pays or collects an SBOMD based upon the class average price? Because SBOs are created prior to actual pool allocation the SBOMD has to be based upon an assumed delivery quantity of $1,000,000.00 per contract. A cash adjustment must be made whenever the amortized quantity delivered in settlement of the SBO is greater or less than the SBO par amount. The *cash adjustment on amortized value is calculated by multiplying the SBOMD by the percentage of the amortized value amount above or below par.* Table 8–4 discloses the conditions under which you can expect to receive either a debit or credit cash adjustment and provides specific examples.

TABLE 8–4.

Amortized Value	SBOMD	Amortized Adjustment
Over par	Debit	Debit
Over par	Credit	Credit
Under par	Debit	Credit
Under par	Credit	Debit

Examples:

Amortized Value	Percent ± Par	SBOMD	Cash Adjustment
999,887.91	0.00011209	(4,062.50)	0.46
1,020,575.94	0.02057594	(1,250.00)	(25.42)

Several points should be made concerning this adjustment. *All* firms whose trades were involved in the net out cycle are subject to cash adjustments, not just the firms who received SBOs. Since this adjustment cannot be calculated until the final delivery associated with a particular SBO is made (MBSCC must know the total quantity delivered against the SBO), the cash adjustment can occur months after the original settlement date. Keep a file of all SBOMDs associated with each class and settlement date if you intend to verify adjustment figures when they are received from MBSCC. These cash adjustments are calculated weekly and are payable on the Friday following notification; the average cash adjustment during volatile markets ranges in the area of $200.00–$300.00. Except during periods of volatile prices, a firm should experience a minimal net effect from this adjustment. However, there are circumstances under which it can be a significant amount and a firm policy must be established as to whether these funds are to be applied against the trading P&L or the allocations P&L.

Transactions compared through the T/T program are excluded from the cash adjustment process. However, as with SBO trades, the MBSCC must be notified when delivery is made so that they can be deleted from the participant's margined positions.

9

Allocation Processing

As has previously been explained, TBAs are forward contracts for MBS pools that are due for settlement during a specific contract month. Allocation is the process of assigning specific mortgage-backed issues to the original TBA contract, thus fulfilling the terms of the contract and making it deliverable. The allocations group has the responsibility for keeping all TBA positions in balance, netting out settling TBA positions, and assigning pools to open positions.

When the allocations group assigns a specified issue to a TBA contract, the assigned security *must* have the same characteristics as contracted for in the TBA. The group cannot match (assign) a GNMA I pool to a GNMA II TBA or to an FNMA TBA, nor can they assign a fixed-rate, single-family GNMA I pool with an original maturity of 30 years to a GNMA I 15-year TBA. Each individual characteristic of a TBA plays a role in the yield and pricing of the trade. Dealers hedge TBA positions against existing and future inventory. In addition to being unacceptable to the purchaser, incorrect assignment would play havoc with both the P&L and the firm's balancing of positions. Therefore, the features of the issues assigned during the allocation process *must meet and completely satisfy* the description of the type of MBS contracted for in each TBA trade. The matching criteria are as follows:

❑ Guarantor of the issue (GNMA, FHLMC, FNMA, etc.).

❑ Type of underlying collateral (single or multifamily, etc.).

❑ Interest payment type (fixed level pay, GPM, adjustable, etc.).

❑ Coupon rate (10%, 10.50%, etc.).

❑ Maturity range of the underlying loans (15, 20, 30 years, etc.).

THE PUBLIC SECURITIES ASSOCIATION (PSA)

The confirmation, allocation, and clearance processing of mortgage-backed securities is governed by rules established by the Public Securities Association (PSA). The PSA is a national trade association with three divisions: the government securities division, the municipal securities division, and the mortgage-backed securities division. Each division addresses trading and operating practices associated with its product group. Membership in the MBS division includes most of the hundreds of banks, brokers, and dealers who trade MBS. Among its many contributions, it has developed through its membership the rules governing MBS operations. These rules are published in its recently revised book, *Uniform Practices for the Clearance and Settlement of Mortgage-Backed Securities and Other Related Securities*. The PSA is not a federal agency and does not have enforcement powers; its rules are guidelines. However, because the rules were formulated through its committees, which were comprised principally by members of the association, the rules are voluntarily accepted as standard industry practice.

THE PSA ALLOCATION RULES

The following lists give TBA assignment rules in effect as of January 2, 1989. These rules relate strictly to the assignment of specific securities to a TBA transaction and do not apply to secondary market trading of specified issues.

Generic Assignment Rules

❏ The original terms of the TBA and the assigned MBS must be the same.

❏ It is the obligation of the seller to advise the buyer of the specific issue(s) that will be delivered in settlement of the TBA. This notification must be made no later than 3:00 P.M. EST two business days before the settlement of the TBA.

❏ No one certificate or combination of smaller certificates may exceed $1,024,999.99 in *amortized* value as applied *to each 1MM* portion of a TBA contract.

❏ Actual deliveries (amortized quantity value) may not vary more than plus or minus 2.499999% of the *dollar amount* (quantity value) of the original TBA trade.

❏ Deliveries for a 1MM TBA shall consist of a maximum of four issues if the coupon rate is 12% or above. If the coupon rate is below 12%, the maximum number of issues is three. If the TBA is a multimillion dollar trade, these parameters apply to each 1MM lot.

❏ Deliveries for TBA trades having a value *greater than 500M but less than 1MM* shall consist of a maximum of three issues if the coupon rate is 12% or above, or two issues if the coupon is below 12%.

❏ Deliveries for TBA trades having a value *equal to or less than 500M* shall consist of a maximum of two issues if the coupon rate is 12% or above, or a single issue if the coupon rate is below 12%.

❏ When more than one issue has been assigned to a TBA contract, delivery of the individual issues may be made independently of each other and on different dates if necessary.

Allocation Rules for Issuer-Specific MBS

❏ The minimum original face value of a physical certificate (GNMA program) that may be delivered is $25,000.00.

❑ Custom pools and Jumbo pools (GNMA II program) may
not be combined for assignment to a single 1MM allocation. However, if the trade is a multimillion dollar
GNMA II TBA, custom and Jumbo pools may be assigned as long as the allocation integrity is maintained
within each 1MM segment of the trade and no restricting
specification was made on the TBA.

Other Restrictions on Issuer-Specific Allocation

❑ FHLMC PCs having a prefix number 43 through 48 may
not be assigned to any generic FHLMC TBA unless
specifically identified at the time of trade.

❑ FHLMC PCs having prefix numbers 21 and 50 (15-year
non-GNOMES) may not be assigned to a FHLMC
GNOME TBA (prefixes 20 and 38).

The two foregoing rules apply to TBA settlements for all GNMA,
FNMA, and FHLMC securities. Exceptions must be agreed to by
both parties at the time the TBA is executed and should be so noted
in the trade confirmation and comparison. Such transactions are
referred to as *specified TBAs* and must be given priority attention
during the allocation process.

GOALS OF THE ALLOCATION PROCESS

The TBA settlement date is the date on which the actual
delivery and payment of specific issues (that is, fulfilling the terms
of the TBA forward contract) are expected. TBAs are traded for
settlement during a specified month. The PSA has attempted to
spread out the settlement process by classifying TBAs into five
distinct groups, and it assigns to each classification a particular
day each month as its group settlement date. The settlement days
associated with this five-tiered structure are fully described in
Table 7–2 on page 121.

The four goals of an allocations group are the following:

1. Assign specific issues to every settling TBA contract.
2. Make all assignments in conformity with PSA regulations.

3. Generate profits and/or avoid losses through the prudent allocation of inventory.

4. Ensure timely delivery and therefore optimize cash flow.

Before you are able to begin assigning specific issues to TBA contracts, you must have all the information that affects the process. To determine what is necessary, ask yourself two questions.

1. What are the forward contracts that must be allocated?

2. What inventory is available to allocate to these sales?

The answer to the first question is: "Every open TBA sale contract that is approaching its assigned settlement day." It is the seller of a TBA contract who is obligated to advise the purchaser which specific issues will be allocated to the TBA and ultimately delivered in settlement of the contract. The purchaser must accept whatever issues are assigned as long as the assignment is made in accordance with the terms of the TBA contract and the rules governing it. The allocation must be made no later than 3:00 P.M. EST or EDT two days before the established settlement date; this is the "48-hour rule."

There are two answers to the second question. Both the current inventory of previously issued, secondary market, mortgage-backed securities and the new issues that will be received in settlement of open TBA purchases can be used. Each of these two categories of inventory evokes some thoughts about the complexity of the allocation process. If you use existing secondary inventory, the issues may have been substantially paid down. True! That is why the rules allow multiple issues to be assigned to a single TBA. The total amortized value of the three issues that may be used to fulfill a 1MM TBA contract with a 10% coupon must be within the variance of plus or minus 2.499999% permitted by the PSA.

Let us reiterate the trade computation process. In the settlement of a trade, the three principal components of the calculation are the amortized amount, the price, and the accrued interest. A buyer must pay the seller accrued interest from the first of the month up to, but not including, the settlement date of the trade.

This is the interest that the seller has earned on the investment. The buyer will recoup that amount at the end of the month. At that time the purchaser will be the holder on the P&I record date and will receive a full month's interest check from the issuer within two to three weeks. Computations for the sale (as principal) of MBS Pool No. 123456 10% due 08-15-2011, original face value 1MM, price 99 1/8, TD 11-11-88, SD 11-18-88, current factor of 0.87654321, are as follows:

Face amount × factor = amortized amount (or quantity)
$1,000,000.00 × 0.87654321 = $876,543.21

Face × factor × price = principal + accrued interest = net
1MM × 0.87654321 × 0.99125 = $868,873.46 + $4,139.23 = $873,012.69

Accrued interest for this trade will be calculated as follows:

$1,000,000 × 0.87654321 × 0.10 × (17/360) = $4,139.23

Note: Accrued interest is never considered in determining the permissible 2.499999% PSA variance.

Therefore, if this pool is used to fulfill a 1MM TBA contract, the allocators must locate one or two other pools having an aggregate value ranging from $98,456.80 to $148,456.78. These figures are arrived at as follows:

PSA variance × TBA face amount = acceptable difference
0.02499999 × $1,000,000.00 = $24,999.99

TBA face amount − acceptable difference = lowest permissible allocation
$1,000,000.00 − $24,999.99 = $975,000.01

TBA face amount + acceptable difference = highest permissible allocation
$1,000,000.00 + $24,999.99 = $1,024,999.99

Lowest figure − assigned value = minimum required remainder
$975,000.01 − $876,543.21 = $98,456.80

Highest − assigned value = maximum permissible remainder
$1,024,999.99 − $876,543.21 = $148,456.80

Now, turn your thoughts to the second source of the allocator's inventory, the securities that will be received in settlement of TBA purchases. If you thought that the identity of the issues being delivered may not be known at the time you need it, you are correct. The seller needs only to comply with the 48-hour rule, and herein lies another complication for the allocators. The identity of inventory available to the allocators is constantly changing with each notification by a seller. A quick, accurate method must be available to keep track of this incoming information. It must be merged with existing inventory records so that an allocator may have optimum use of all known issues.

THE ALLOCATION PROCESS

Step 1

The first step in the allocation process is to sort your TBA trade files according to the following parameters:

- ❑ Common settlement date.
- ❑ Buys and sells.
- ❑ Specified transactions by program (GNMA, FHLMC, etc.).
- ❑ Generic transactions by program (GNMA, FHLMC, etc.).
- ❑ Retail customer trades.
- ❑ Institutional customer trades.
- ❑ Broker trades.
- ❑ Dealer trades.
- ❑ Face value (highest to lowest).*
- ❑ Price (highest to lowest).

Step 2

The next step is to identify all possible pair-offs of matching buys and sells in each category. If you identify the pair-off as being for an institutional customer, you must contact that customer to secure an agreement to the pair-off. Simultaneously con-

---

*Files of actual inventory are sorted by amortized value (highest to lowest).

firm the net amount of funds to be paid or received as a result of the pair-off. Most of the pair-offs for streetside transactions will have been accomplished through the netting process at the MBSCC. However, there may be settlement balance orders and trades executed after the MBSCC cutoff date of SD – 7 that can be paired; authorization from the contra-party is required to do so. Journals should be pre-prepared for *all* authorized pair-offs so that they can be processed on the settlement date, and these trades should be removed from your work files, leaving updated files consisting of only the open contracts to be received or delivered.

Step 3

The next step is to provide a ready access to all issues that you will be able to assign to your TBA trades. You will need a TBA listing reflecting your firm's buy-side. These are the TBAs for which you will be receiving pool assignments from the street and customers. These issues, together with the issues in your firm's secondary trading inventory accounts, are the source (available inventory) of the pools you must assign to your firm's sales.

Step 4

The last preparatory step involves what I refer to as "reserving inventory." The practice of trading TBAs on a specified basis has become increasingly prevalent. A specified TBA is one with restrictions, agreed to by the trader(s), over and above those required by the PSA regulations. These restrictions usually apply to a special definitive feature of the issue assigned to the contract. A TBA contract may require delivery of a single issue, it may require delivery of a new issue, it may require delivery of an issue collateralized with loans originated in a specific geographic region of the country, it may require delivery of a specific maturity date. There is some stipulation on the TBA that restricts the allocation beyond the normal regulatory scope. The criteria established by the specified trade must be met for the contract to be deliverable. It is important that these situations be identified at the onset of the allocation process so that either buy-side/sell-side TBAs having the same criteria can be matched or inventory that can fulfill the special requirements of the trade can be reserved and not assigned to a TBA for which any generic issue may be used. Here again is yet another coding requirement—specified TBAs.

PRIMARY ALLOCATION CONSIDERATIONS

The PSA rules governing allocations have been outlined, and the computation process has been explained (an allocator must know the amortized value of available pools). Throughout the allocation process, an allocator must be constantly alert to the following:

❑ PSA rules.

❑ Current TBA and secondary market inventory.

❑ Assignment information received from sellers.

❑ Direct and indirect impact on the P&L of each allocation.

❑ Denominational breakdown ("pieces") if physical.

❑ Clearance turnaround capability.

❑ Open items (fails).

❑ Account type (dealer, broker, customer).

Earlier in this chapter we identified the four goals of the allocations department. The first two goals have been discussed. Now let's concentrate on what has to be considered the bottom line of the allocations process: generating profits and ensuring maximum cash flow for the firm.

OPTIMIZING PROFITS

Through careful use of the 2.499999% variance, additional profits can be made on a trade. A 1MM TBA can be satisfied with an issue or issues having an amortized value of anywhere between $975,000.01 and $1,024,999.99, a variance of nearly $50,000.00 per million. The goal of the allocator is to control the available inventory in a manner that results in the *assignment of the largest amortized trades to the firm's sales with the highest dollar price.*

Assume that your firm purchases two lots of 1MM 10% GNMA I 30-year TBAs, one lot at 98 and the second at 99. You then sell 1MM at 99 and 1MM at par. When you receive your assignment information from the sellers, you are told that the amortized value of the pool being assigned to the TBA purchased at 98 will be $1,020,000.00 and that $980,000.00 in amortized amount will be delivered against the TBA contract done at 99. It's your lucky day. You now have to assign these pools to the accounts to whom you have sold the TBAs. Remember that it is your option, your right, as the seller, to determine what inventory will be assigned to each open TBA. The more inventory you deliver at the highest contract values, the more profits your firm will realize.

In this example, the firm's profit on the original TBA transactions is $20,000. The allocator has properly assigned the pools to the purchasers. That is, the $980,000 pool is assigned to the sale done at 99 (gross proceeds $970,200), and the $1,020,000 pool is assigned to the sale done at par (gross proceeds $1,020,000). The profit on this transaction is now $20,400—an additional $400.00 over and above the original trading profit is brought to the bottom line of the firm (see Table 9–1).

TABLE 9–1. Calculation Recap

TBAs		Assigned Pools		
B 1MM @ 98	$ 980,000.00	B 1,020,000 @ 98	$	999,600.00
B 1MM @ 99	990,000.00	B 980,000 @ 99		970,200.00
Cost	1,970,000.00	Cost		1,969,800.00
S 1MM @ 99	990,000.00	S 980,000 @ 99		970,200.00
S 1MM @ 100	1,000,000.00	S 1,020,000 @ 100		1,020,000.00
Proceeds	1,990,000.00	Proceeds		1,990,200.00
Total Proceeds	1,990,000.00	Total Proceeds		1,990,200.00
Total Costs	1,970,000.00	Total Costs		1,969,800.00
Net Profit	$ 20,000.00		$	20,400.00

Notice in Table 9–1 that accrued interest on the pools assigned to the TBAs was not considered during the allocation assignment process. However, it must be figured into the transaction for confirmation and settlement purposes. Notice also the principal contract value of the assigned pool executed at 99, $970,200.00. Never compare the principal contract value of an assigned trade to the original face value of a TBA contract for purposes of determining compliance to the 2.499999% variance rule. Instead, compare original face to the assigned amortized value, which is sometimes referred to as the current face amount.

The example discussed and given in Table 9–1 was made deliberately simple to clearly demonstrate the impact of the allocation process on the P&L. Realistically, an allocator deals with thousands of transactions. Mismatching buys and sells can, under certain circumstances, actually reduce the original TBA trading profits. The need for sorting the trade records in the sequence described at the beginning of this chapter is now obvious; the size and price parameters are very important in P&L optimization. Sorting secondary market inventory is easy; keeping amortized and price information that is being received during the day from other firms is not so easy. Some form of real-time, on-line computerized support is a necessity.

Let us skip to customer considerations for a moment. If you are an investor, you may have a concern at this point. It may seem that your final settlement costs may be higher than expected at the time you purchased a TBA and that the higher cost is exclusively beneficial to your broker or dealer. Yes, it is true that you may be required to accept a higher amortized value (and therefore higher cost) than was stated in the TBA confirmation. You do receive the benefits from this higher cost, however. Your investment and interest income will be proportionately higher. Your overall yield is not affected; you are simply receiving additional interest income for an increased dollar investment.

CASH FLOW CONSIDERATIONS

Obviously, the primary goal of an allocations department is to increase trading profits. If the department personnel had all the necessary information needed to complete this process on a timely basis, the job would be simple. However, they do not. They do have pool numbers and factors on positioned inventory, but this is a small percentage of what they must allocate. Every dealer on the street is performing the same function at the same time, and all assignments must be made by 3:00 P.M. EST on SD – 2. Most of the information for thousands of trades is being transmitted verbally throughout a two-to-three day period. You do not obtain all incoming assignment information on a basis that is timely enough to optimize the firm's profits on 100% of its TBA trades. When it is approaching cutoff time on the 48-hour day, allocators must keep in mind the cost of financing. If the current cost of money is 8%, it will cost a firm almost $225.00 a day to finance 1MM. If an allocator fails to meet the 3:00 P.M. pool assignment deadline, the trade cannot be settled on its assigned settlement date. The contra-party is entitled to a 48-hour notice before delivery can be made. So a judgment is frequently required as to whether to wait for more pool information on the chance that you might better optimize the assignment or whether to assign on a first-in, first-out basis, thus avoiding the risk of a potential fail with its attendant financing costs.

Another consideration to keep in mind is the constraints under which the clearance department must operate. The delivery of mortgage-backed securities must be accomplished daily no later than the PSA-established cutoff times. Presently (and probably until mid-1989 when the PTC is scheduled to be fully functional) this can create a problem for dealers relative to the physical deliveries of GNMAs not eligible for the depositories (see Table 9–2).

TABLE 9–2. Delivery Cutoff Schedules (EST/EDT) for Physical Deliveries

Classification	Cutoff Time (P.M.)
Nondealer to dealer	2:15
Dealer to broker	2:30
Broker to dealer	2:45
Dealer to dealer	3:00
Nondealer to nondealer	3:15
Dealer to nondealer	3:15

Given the constraints shown in Table 9–2, dealers must be careful to avoid assigning a pool coming from a dealer to a trade with a broker. If the contra-dealer were to deliver that pool after 2:30 P.M., the purchasing dealer could not redeliver to the broker and a costly fail would result. When there are serious concerns about a potential financing situation, the safest route is to assign the pool to a retail custody account. The next safest route is to assign it to a nondealer account (a customer COD account), which will give you until 3:15 P.M. to redeliver the securities.

TRADING CONSIDERATIONS

Reduction of the firm's small odd lot inventory should be considered during the allocation process. Odd lot trades are normally transactions having an original face value of less than 1MM. Dealers do not want to build up their inventory in odd lots of the 100M, 200M, 300M size, etc. because these positions are not readily marketable. Numerous odd lots can add up to a substantial amount of inventory that cannot be sold quickly if necessary; it's an unwanted risk. So, even if there seems to be no P&L advantage to allocating "high," there may be a market advantage. Whenever possible, small odd lots should be added to larger pieces. For example:

50M + 924M = 1,024M (maximum allowed per 1MM)
100M + 100M + 800M = 1,000M

Another issue related to trading is the assignment of seasoned versus unseasoned issues. An *unseasoned issue* is generally an MBS that has been outstanding for less than two to three years. The issue has not been outstanding for a sufficient time to predict accurately the paydown rate of the issue through the use of one of several models available in the industry. Because of this, there is more potential for fluctuation in the outstanding amortized value of the issue, and it is generally considered less desirable as trading inventory than is a seasoned issue. Unseasoned issues should be used to the fullest extent possible during the allocation process.

CONSIDERATIONS FOR FHLMC AND FNMA ISSUES

FHLMC PCs and FNMA MBS must be delivered through the book-entry facilities of the Federal Reserve. The first consideration is regulatory: The Fed will not accept delivery instructions for a single transaction the face value of which exceeds 50MM. The second consideration is one of professional courtesy which, by the way, is usually repaid in like manner. For example, only whole-dollar quantities can be processed through the Fed system. Under PSA regulations, the minimum acceptable delivery on a 1MM TBA is $975,000.01; the constraints of the Fed system mandate a minimum delivery of $975,001.00. If you made an amortized delivery for this amount and if the purchaser had in turn sold that $1 million in two lots of 500M, the recipient would be unable to make a good delivery on one of its trades. The minimum acceptable delivery against the 500M TBA is $487,501; $975,002 is needed to ensure the ability to turn around both the odd lots. Adding the extra dollar to an allocation will not, in 99.9% of all cases, hurt your firm's position. The courtesy makes a friend and keeps the overall industry clearance process running smoothly.

The fact that most FHLMCs and FNMAs are wireable facilitates the allocation function and affords you good opportunities to increase your profits. Assume that you have purchased 100MM FHLMC TBAs 30-year 10% PCs from a dealer at par and sold 10MM at par, 45MM at 99, and the final 45MM at 101; the dealer who sold to you allocates 100 PCs each having an amortized value of 1MM. You can bring an additional $22,498.20 profit to your bottom line through the allocation shown in Table 9-3.

TABLE 9–3. The Allocation of Wireable Securities

	Buy-Side				Sell-Side		
#PCs	Amort Val	Price	Cost	#PCs	Amort Val	Price	Proceeds
100	1,000,000	100	100,000,000	10	1,000,000	100	10,000,000.00
				45	975,002	99	43,436,339.10
				45	1,024,998	101	46,586,159.10
	100,000,000		$100,000,000		100,000,000		$100,022,498.20

This is a situation which you can avail yourself of with issues that are either book-entry or Fedwire eligible. If you did this with securities which required physical delivery you would have to re-register the certificates into appropriate denominations. The transfer process would most likely take two days which could force you to fail on your deliveries. A single day's financing cost on the 100MM would exceed the allocations profit. Unless you are able to guarantee that your transfer turnaround time will meet your settlement schedule, do not attempt this type of an allocation when a physical delivery is necessary.

THE NOTIFICATION AND CONFIRMATION PROCESS

Once the decision has been made as to which issue(s) are to be allocated to a TBA sale, the next step is to notify the purchaser as to which issues will be delivered in settlement of the TBA contract. Notification must be made no later than 3:00 P.M. EST two days before settlement date. If the notification is made after the cutoff time, the purchaser does not have to pay for the delivery on settlement date. Delivery is extended one day for each day that the allocation notification is late so that purchasers always have 48 hours after notification before they must pay for a delivery. This extension applies only to the delivery and payment for the transaction; no change of the settlement date used to calculate accrued interest is permitted. Therefore, late notifications result in an economic loss to the seller in an amount equivalent to one day's interest on the net proceeds of the sale for each day late.

Information must be transmitted either verbally or electronically (mutual agreement is required for electronic transmissions). The information must include the following:

❑ Specific identification of each assigned issue (e.g., pool number).

❑ Face value of each assigned issue.

❑ Coupon rate, price, trade date, and settlement date.

❑ Issuer's name, issue date, and maturity date. (The maturity date is required only if the assigned security is a newly issued GNMA.)

❑ Issue date and maturity date for FHLMC and FNMA issues.

The obvious problem is meeting the 48-hour rule. Everyone is attempting similar transmissions at the same time. When you approach the 3:00 P.M. deadline, it is very important that you consolidate the information being transmitted to a contra-party. If you have assignments relative to four different TBAs, advise the purchaser of that *before* you begin to transmit the specifics of the issues to be delivered. If you do that and the 3:00 P.M. bell rings, the purchaser must continue to take the information on the trade being discussed and must accept delivery on settlement date.

Subsequent information is subject to delayed payment as discussed in the previous paragraph. The identification of all TBAs to be assigned in order to protect the 3:00 P.M. deadline can be a two-way street. If you happen to be a purchaser receiving such a call and you know that you have information to transmit to the party presently on the phone, you can and must state that fact immediately to preserve your rights under the 48-hour rule. Once both you and the other party have stated your intentions, the conversation can continue to 3:15 (or later if necessary), and both parties will be obligated to accept deliveries on the settlement date.

There will be times when it will be beneficial or necessary to change an allocation on which you have already transmitted the information to the buyer. This is permitted. However, if it is done after 12:15 P.M. EST or EDT on a 48-hour day, then the purchaser has an extra day before payment is required. If the change is made after a 48-hour day (changes will sometimes be necessary weeks after the original allocation and settlement), the purchaser will always have two business days after notification before payment is required; three days if the notification occurs after 12:15 P.M. EST.

All verbal notifications must be confirmed in writing by both parties. If within 10 days of the trade or notification date you do not receive a confirmation on a trade you have confirmed, you must contact the contra-party to receive both a verbal and written confirmation of the transaction. In these situations, make sure that you keep a careful record of the dates, times, phone number, and full name of the person(s) with whom you have spoken as well as a brief indication of the text of your conversation(s).

MISCELLANEOUS CONSIDERATIONS

Allocation processing is exciting, interesting, and challenging, and it has a significant impact on the P&L of the dealer firm. It is also a tedious process for which there is relatively little system support in the industry. In years past, automation was resisted, but the elimination of "firm yield maintenance contracts" several years ago also eliminated much of the valid opposition to the development of automated allocation systems. The time to step up this effort is now. Aside from supporting the processing steps that have just been described, current systems efforts should take the following issues into consideration.

1) Why would anyone buy MBS? What would attract some one to buy MBS than any other debt

→ Risk is less as it is guaranteed by fannie (Gov't)

PACKING SLIP:
Amazon Marketplace Item: Processing Mortgage-Backed Securities by Karcher, Louis J.
Listing ID: 0910W099451
SKU: 5304993
Quantity: 1

Purchased on: 28-Oct-2005
Shipped by: excelsiorbayco@aol.com
Shipping address:

Ship to: Nisha Kripalani
Address Line 1: 60 Jared Dr
Address Line 2:
City: North Brunswick
State/Province/Region: NJ
Zip/Postal Code: 08902-5518
Country: United States

Buyer Name: Nisha Kripalani

- - - - - - - - - - - - - - - - - - -

Monday, October 31, 2005 America Online: ExcelsiorBayCo

Under certain circumstances as many as four issues may be assigned to a single 1MM TBA trade; each of those four issues is deliverable independently of the others. TBA trades for 5MM, 10MM, 20MM are not uncommon. As many as 80 issues could conceivably be delivered on a $20 million TBA. Customers and traders frequently inquire about the status of a TBA. What issues were assigned to it? When were the assigned issues delivered, and what portion of the original TBA, if any, remains unsettled? The answers to these questions are ascertainable, but quite a bit of effort and time are required. Automation efforts in developing allocation systems should address the need for establishing a unique TBA group number to be assigned to the original TBA and to identify each individual trade that is processed in connection with the allocation of that TBA. This kind of ID number would save many days of work each month. If the reference number were incorporated into the confirmation process, it could also serve as an audit trail for a firm's customers and provide the firm with a competitive marketing tool.

The goal of an allocations division is to increase the trading P&L. There must be some measure of the success or failure of an allocations group. Even if all P&L is booked into a single account, some thought should be given to creating an interim accounting system that could track the efficiency of each member of the allocations team. Ideally, such a system could capture the inventory available at the time the actual allocation was made and then perform a Saturday night quarterbacking routine that could be studied to determine where improvements need to be made.

Persons working in systems development should keep in mind that the PSA rules are flexible and under constant review. It is conceivable that the five-tiered settlement cycle could change depending on volume changes and the addition of new products. As time progresses, the amortized value of the older issues steadily decreases. It may be necessary to increase the number of allowable issues per $1 million from the current three or four. And if you understand the concepts behind some of the automated clearance systems available today, you will see some interesting challenges and opportunities for systems enhancements that could tie directly into the allocation function.

10

The Clearance Process: Overview

The securities clearance area, commonly referred to as the receive and deliver (R&D) department, is the group responsible for receiving and delivering securities. It is part of an operation's cashier's division. The name of the department seems self-explanatory, but the name fails to capture the principal objective of the area, which is to maximize the cash flow of a firm. *Cash flow* is a general term used to describe the amount of money (cash) received or anticipated each day, the sum of which is used to support the normal functions of a business. In the investment industry, that business is buying and selling securities. Every instruction that an R&D clerk handles has an effect on the cash flow of the firm. To achieve the objective of the clearance department, every security that is scheduled and available for delivery on a particular settlement date must be delivered or cleared by the close of business on that date. If it is not, the cash expected to have been available had the delivery been completed will not be there. That means that those missing funds must be borrowed because they have probably already been invested in anticipation of receipt. The cost of borrowing these uncollected funds to cover the investment has a negative impact on a firm's P&L.

A second objective is closely related to the first: to preserve the capital of the firm. In the R&D department's function, capital preservation is (1) making sure that cash in an amount equal to the original contract value of the trade is received for every delivery and (2) receiving negotiable securities for every cash payment made by the firm.

Now that you know the principal objectives of an R&D department, can you identify what the principal concern should be? The answer can be expressed in a single word: Control! *Control requires initiative.* An R&D department that merely reacts to the instructions and events of the day will not succeed. You must initiate actions that will ensure that all deliveries will be made and that the attendant cash flow will be achieved.

Several chapters will be required to complete the discussion of the R&D process. This chapter, however, focuses on the following aspects of that process:

❑ The origin of clearance instructions.

❑ Presettlement controls.

❑ The identification of the four methods used to clear MBS.

Subsequent chapters will explain the characteristics and processing requirements of each of the four MBS clearance methods. Capital preservation will be discussed in Chapter 15, which discusses the control of fails. However, two basic and simple rules cover the essentials. *First,* in terms of cash flow, every delivery instruction should be considered as an instruction to deposit cash in the bank at the end of the night. Unless that deposit is made, the person responsible has not done the job. *Second,* in terms of capital preservation, never give up a "freebie." No free deliveries! When you deliver securities, make certain payment is ensured. When you pay out cash, you must receive securities having an equivalent value.

From the standpoint of a clearance operation, there are two types of accounts: retail and nonretail. From firm to firm, retail accounts are identified by different terms. "Consumer market accounts," "custody accounts," "hold accounts," "safekeeping accounts"—all are terms that refer to retail accounts. These accounts may be carried on a cash or margined basis. This is important to the credit department, but it is not a significant factor in terms of clearance. The first step in clearance is the accumulation of receive and deliver instructions. When an account is opened, the instructions for it are entered into the name and address file. For retail accounts, the payment for transactions and the delivery of the securities are independently controlled by the credit department and the cashier's department, respectively. Because of this, plus the fact that retail processing can continue internally after all other delivery processes have been stopped because of daily cutoff schedules, we will discuss only nonretail accounts, which are the trades for institutional customers (the capital markets trades), brokers, and dealers. These accounts are delivered on a collect-on-delivery (COD) basis. The implication of COD is a simultaneous exchange of securities for cash, although the amount of time that elapses between delivery and payment can vary greatly. Terms used in lieu of COD are RVP/DVP (receive versus payment/deliver versus payment) and DAC/RAP (deliver against collection/receive against payment).

ORIGIN OF CLEARANCE INSTRUCTIONS

Clearance instructions are generated from the NAMSTR file in the form of a multipart instruction ticket referred to by most firms as a *delivery manifold*. Some firms generate delivery manifolds for every COD transaction regardless of whether it is a customer or streetside trade; the manifolds are usually made available on the morning of SD – 1. A manifold recaps the details of each trade plus its R&D instructions. A manifold serves a dual purpose. First, it is used as a delivery bill and is attached to certificates being physically delivered. A delivery bill identifies the details of the delivery for the recipient. Second, a manifold serves as a source document from which to input the information concerning the delivery into a firm's computer system. The days of manifold-based delivery systems are numbered. Once the physical delivery process is eliminated, and assuming other computerized support processes are in place, the delivery manifold will no longer be required.

All the information required to identify and clear this trade is available on the manifold. Much of the information is identical to that contained in the trade confirmation and comparison; the numbered fields are specifically clearance information.

FIGURE 10-1.

PaineWebber GOVERNMENT SECURITIES COMMERCIAL PAPER CONFIRMATION

GOVERNMENT SECURITIES DEPARTMENT
120 BROADWAY, NEW YORK, N.Y. 10271
TELEPHONE: (212) 437-2121

TO BE DELIVERED

AGAINST PAYMENT OF FEDERAL
FUNDS UNLESS OTHERWISE NOTED.

AS PRINCIPAL WE HEREBY CONFIRM   OUR SALE TO   YOU TODAY OF THE FOLLOWING SECURITIES

CLIENT NUMBER	TRADE I.D. #	REF. #	TRADE DATE	AS OF DATE	SETTLEMENT DATE		
	F 005	602270	11/11/88		11/18/88	FACTOR .87654321	

PAR VALUE	SECURITY					DISCOUNT/BASIS	PRICE
1,000,000.00	GNMA POOL 123456 SF LEVEL PAY FIXED RATE 10% DUE 08-15-2011						99 1/8

PRINCIPAL	INTEREST/DISCOUNT PERIOD	INTEREST/DISCOUNT	CHARGES	TOTAL
$ 868,873.46		$ 4,139.23		$ 873,012.69

SECURITY NO.	HOUSE ACCOUNT NO.	CUSIP NO.	DELIVERY INSTRUCTIONS
			① DVP-BANK OF NY 110 WASHINGTON CLEAR DIV 19th FLOOR AC XY ZEE MBS FUND INC
			② WIRE FUNDS TO: CHEM NY ABA021000128 AC PWJC AC 0660077

☐ WE BOUGHT   SIGNED _____
☐ WE SOLD   DATE _____
    BY _____

IT IS EXPRESSLY UNDERSTOOD AND AGREED THAT TITLE OF THESE SECURITIES SHALL REMAIN VESTED IN PaineWebber Incorporated UNTIL FULL PAYMENT IN CASH OR ITS EQUIVALENT SHALL HAVE BEEN MADE THEREFOR.

GNS-1298 REV. 8/87 PTG 4/88

RECEIVING INSTRUCTIONS/MESSENGER'S RECEIPT

175

Delivery Instructions ①

Delivery instructions are used by the R&D clerk to determine where to send purchased securities for payment. They must include the following:

- ❑ The name and address of the firm to whom the delivery will be made.
- ❑ The identity of the department, floor, and/or room number to which the delivery is to be directed.
- ❑ The required identification number of the firm (such as an ABA number or a clearinghouse number) if the transaction is eligible for book entry.
- ❑ The title and account number of the account for which the securities are being delivered as they appear on the books of the receiving firm.
- ❑ If possible, the name and phone number of the person who compared the trade.

Payment Instructions ②

Payment instructions are intended for the receiving firm. They identify the information needed to ensure prompt payment for the delivery and include the following:

- ❑ The name and ABA number of the bank to whom payment is to be made.
- ❑ The firm name and number to which payment is being made as they appear on the bank's records.
- ❑ The name and phone number of the individual at the delivering firm who should be called if there is a problem.
- ❑ If possible, a trade ID or reference number to be included on the payment wire to facilitate identification.

PRESETTLEMENT CONTROLS

To ensure that the goal of optimizing cash flow is met, a presettlement analysis of the upcoming day's work is extremely important. Having such an analysis available 24 to 48 hours before settlement gives you the opportunity to answer the following questions:

- ❑ Do you have all your instructions? Do they appear to be correct and complete?

- ❑ Are the securities that need to be delivered available? Have proper instructions been given to remove them from a custody location? If physical, are proper pieces available? Do the economics of the settlement call for a rush transfer?

- ❑ Is a large block of securities coming in from a customer or another broker? Do the circumstances require a call to ensure against a major fail?

- ❑ Would a substitution of a similar pool enable you to clear an item?

- ❑ Have all possible pair-offs been made?

- ❑ If a conflict exists between availability and requirement, have efforts been made to determine if the securities will become available on a timely basis? If not, have instructions been given to deliver the item that will have a more favorable impact on cash flow.

Each of these questions is directed at a common goal, ensuring that as many deliveries as possible are made on the original settlement date of a trade. It should be obvious that the answers to each question are not available from a single source. You must examine multiple records in the pending trade file and the stock record file to obtain them.

The fuel required to feed the initiative that has to be taken to answer these questions is in the form of a special report that summarizes the necessary information. That report is the *delivery requirement analysis*, which is produced daily for each issue in which a sale is due to settle within two days or less and/or for each issue in which a sale has previously settled but remains undelivered (a fail). Issues for which only purchases or activity and positions not related to trades are recorded are not included in the delivery requirement analysis report.

The delivery requirement report provides clearance personnel with all the information they need to ensure that deliveries are made on a timely basis. Does that mean that the report will enable an R&D clerk to make all deliveries on settlement date? If not, what is a timely basis? Frequently, there are legitimate reasons for being unable to make a delivery on settlement date. The most common one is that the securities purchased and resold to a customer have not been received; it is therefore impossible to deliver them. In such a situation, there is no negative impact on cash flow. Because the purchased issue has not been received, the firm has not had to pay for it. Street fails such as this are paid for only when received (RVP); remember, no freebies. Because cash has not been paid out, the fact that you haven't taken in cash from a DVP account has zero impact on cash flow. Knowing this, we can define *delivery on a timely basis* as a delivery made no later than the date on which the securities bought on behalf of the customer have been paid for.

A delivery requirements analysis report can be divided into four parts. Under each security description or header record, delivery requirements, receive requirements, a receive and deliver recap, and a location recap should be provided. Study the example in Figure 10–2. What relationships do you see between the delivery requirements (sales) and the remaining information on the report?

A quick review of the contents of the report will be helpful.

Item 1 is the header line, which contains a complete description of the issue for which details are being reported. Additional information that might appear here includes the current market price, an internal security number, method of delivery (Fedwire, physical, etc.), and the current P&I rate. A new header is printed for every issue for which there is a delivery requirement.

Item 2 is the original settlement date of the trade.

Item 3, the account number, is the internal number assigned to the customer by the broker or dealer making the delivery.

Item 4 shows the original face value ("F") of the trade, the amortized value ("A") of the trade on the date of sale, and the net contract value ("$") of the trade.

Item 5 shows the name of the clearing agent to whom the delivery is to be made. The lines following the name contain a street address, the floor or room number plus the identification of the area being delivered to (CUS = custody; TR = trust), and the

FIGURE 10–2. A Delivery Requirements Analysis

```
Mtg Backed Securites Clearance Department              COB 10-28-88
                              ①
GNMA Pool 185850  9% 10-15-16    CUSIP 362167L71    Factor .52324929
```

DELIVER				**RECEIVE**			
SD	ACCT	QTY/VALUE	INSTRUX	SD	ACCT	QTY/VALUE	INSTRUX
③		④	⑤				
0916	4444	1000,000.00F	US TRUST	0830	5432	1000,000.00F	CHASEBK
Principal		523,249.29A	130 John	Principal		533,290.19A	1 CMPlz
#6543		$499,010.42	5flr CUS	#5213		$480,123.01	BLvl TR
PD 10-15		7950.00	ac 77777	PD 09-15	15,850.00		ac68686
				PD 10-15	7,950.00		
1101	1225	250,000.00F	BKRS TR	1031	0614	150,000.00F	BKRS TR
Principal		130,812.32A	1BT PLZ	Principal		78,487.39A	1BT PLZ
#8892		$129,504.19	Retail	#8857		$77,715.22	Retail

Margin call-outs on left: ② ⑥ ⑦ ⑧

OPEN ITEM RCAP (CONTRACT VAL)			LOCATION RECAP COB 10-28-88		
	Deliver	Receive	Account	Face Amt	Mkt Value
COD BLOT			SUSPN P&S		
RTL BLOT			SUSPN CAGE		
BKR BLOT			SUSPN SR	100M	53M
COD FAIL	499M	480M	DK		
RTL FAIL			RECLAIM		
BKR FAIL			TRACCT SHORT		
SubTotal	499M	480M	BANK LN		
			REPO		
NEXT DAY			EXCESS SEG		
			BOX	250M	130M
COD			FIRM TFR		
RETAIL		78M	CUST TFR		
BROKER			TRANSIT	150M	78M
FUTURE					
COD					
RETAIL	130M				
BROKER					
TOTALS	629M	558M			

internal account number of the customer as shown on the records of the clearing agent.   Other useful information would be the clearinghouse ID number or the ABA number of the agent.

Item 6 indicates the role of the firm in the transaction. A principal trade is one in which securities are bought or sold directly through a firm's trading accounts. On days when only principal trades are executed, there will be no broker's blotter.   Agency transactions are those in which the contra-side of a customer's trade is another firm.

Item 7 is a transaction identification number (reference number) assigned to each trade confirmation. It can be used in research or to process a trade.

Item 8, PD, refers to the payable date for a P&I distribution due on the indicated trade. The actual date of the distribution as well as the full P&I amount are indicated. This alerts clearance personnel that due bills and/or P&I checks are required on receipt or delivery.

By analyzing this report, an R&D clerk knows that two deliveries have to be made for GNMA Pool 185850. The first is for account number 4444, which settled over a month ago. Why wasn't the delivery made? Because, as the report shows, the issue was originally purchased from customer 5432 back on 08-30. Because the pool has not been received (or paid for), it cannot be delivered. Normally RVP and DVP trades would not be open this long, but they can be. Someone should certainly be following up with the customer who sold this issue to find out when the securities will be received.

The second delivery requirement is for a trade that will not settle for two more business days. This is a principal trade, so there will be no fail to receive; the trading account is the offset to this transaction. If you look at the box position, you will see the $250,000.00 face amount in position. The securities will be removed from the box the night before settlement to ensure timely delivery. This report will be discussed further in Chapter 15.

METHODS FOR CLEARING MORTGAGE-BACKED SECURITIES

At the close of 1984, there was only one way to deliver a mortgage-backed issue: physically. Since then, an enormous amount of effort has been expended to improve the clearance process. There are presently four methods for clearing mortgage-backed issues. There is more than $1 trillion worth of MBS out-standing; on a normal TBA settlement day, more than $40 billion worth of securities clear. Efforts have been and continue to be focused on developing systems designed to eliminate the massive physical flow of certificates by creating book-entry clearance facilities. Current clearance methods are shown in Table 10–1; these are broad categories and there are exceptions.

TABLE 10–1. Clearance Methods

Type of Issue	Method of Clearance
GNMAs ("noneligible" coupons only)	Physical
GNMAs (depository eligible only)	Book entry via MBSCC depository
FNMA and FHLMC issues	Book entry via the Fedwire system
CMOs and REMICs	Book entry via SDFS or NDFS system of DTC
Others	Physical or SDFS/NDFS system of DTC

The remaining paragraphs in this chapter are meant for those who require a broad explanation of physical clearance versus book-entry clearance. Physical clearance is accomplished by the delivery of an actual physical certificate. Each trade that is cleared physically requires a separate delivery of certificates to the clearing agent of the purchasing account. This means that messengers are continually transporting certificates back and forth between firms. Payment is received subsequent to delivery. This method is extremely time-consuming, costly, and prone to error.

Book-entry clearance has none of the disadvantages of physical clearance. If this is the first time that you have come across the concept of book-entry clearance, consider it as being analogous to your personal checking account. When you open a demand deposit (checking) account, you take your cash and deposit it under the control of a custodian, a bank. That cash is credited to your account at the bank. When you want to use all or some of your cash, you write a check. That check becomes your bank's authorized instruction to withdraw (debit) your account for the amount indicated on the check and to pay (credit) that amount to the payee's agent bank. The actual cash does not necessarily move. The entire process can be accomplished by debit and credit entries that do nothing more than identify the true owner of the immobilized cash. All book-entry clearance systems are designed along the same concept. Every member firm of a book-entry depository takes the security inventory belonging both to its customers and to the firm and deposits these securities at some central location. When the securities are sold, the firm instructs the depository to remove the appropriate quantity from its own account and deliver them to another firm as designated on the instructions. This delivery may be "free"—that is, no cash exchanges hands in the transaction. Or most likely, delivery is made versus payment. In that case, the receiving party's account is debited the contract value of the delivery as designated by the firm that initiated the delivery instructions; the deliverer's account is credited cash. Information on processing through the book-entry systems operated by the Fed, the DTC, and the MBSCC follows in the next chapters.

To assist you in understanding the basic concepts underlying physical and book-entry clearance, Figures 11-2 and 12-2 graphically depict the clearance processing cycle for both methods. In the book-entry scenario, the manner in which end-of-day cash payments are made will be explored in greater depth in later chapters.

11

Fedwire Clearance

Because there are multiple ways to clear MBS, each will be discussed in a separate chapter. This chapter addresses the Fedwire system. It is this system, the same one that is used for the clearance of U.S. agency and Treasury issues, that *must* be used to clear most FNMA and FHLMC mortgage-backed issues.

The Fedwire is too frequently regarded as being mysterious and fearsome. These reactions have to be attributed to a lack of understanding of the system. Have no fear! The principle behind the system is rather simple. It involves transmitting clearance instructions and balancing the entries made in connection with the execution of the instructions. The Fedwire is a combination of a communications system and an accounting system for securities and cash (Fed funds). When you want to deliver a security through the Fedwire, you transmit a delivery instruction (a message) to the communication system. The system accepts this message and then transmits it to an internal accounting module in the Federal Reserve system. There it is translated into a series of debit and credit entries executed in the accounts of the receiving and delivering participants for both securities and cash. The basic concept is that simple. It is the administration of Fedwire clearance that becomes burdensome but only because of the extremely heavy volume and the same-day settlement feature of many of the trades cleared through the Fed.

STRUCTURING A CLEARANCE ACCOUNT

Any person who is familiar with the clearance operations of a broker or dealer knows that such a firm must always employ the services of a clearing bank to clear its government and government agency trades. Only depository institutions that are members of the Federal Reserve system have direct access to the Fedwire, so all broker-dealers use the services of an intermediary. They enter into a clearing agreement with a bank which then sets up a series of clearing accounts within the bank, not with the Fed, for the broker-dealer. It is the bank—the depository institution— that has the Fed accounts. Movements within the Fed system are debits and credits made to the accounts of the depository institutions that are direct members acting on behalf of their customers. The instructions originating from the broker-dealers are directly related to the trading activities of the broker-dealer's customers, who become another accounting layer in this interwoven scenario. Figure 11–1 depicts the various interrelationships.

THE ISSUANCE AND CLEARANCE CYCLE

Let's play the "what if?" game. What if the FHLMC issues a new pool, $250,000.00 #18–0003298, which it sells at 99 to the broker-dealer, Basic, Inc., which clears through Bank B. Basic, Inc., in turn sells the issue at par to a COD account, MBS Fund, Inc., which clears through Bank A. Who does what, and to whom? Following the execution and booking of the trades, the following steps take place (see Figure 11–2).

Step 1

The FHLMC's escrow agent notifies the Fed that all documents in connection with the creation of issue #18–0003298 have been properly filed and escrowed. The Fed places an entry in the FHLMC's original issuance account reflecting the creation of the $250,000.00 pool. The offsetting entry is made to the position (box) account of the FHLMC agency. The credit position booked as an original face amount in the position account remains the same for

FIGURE 11–1. The Fedwire System

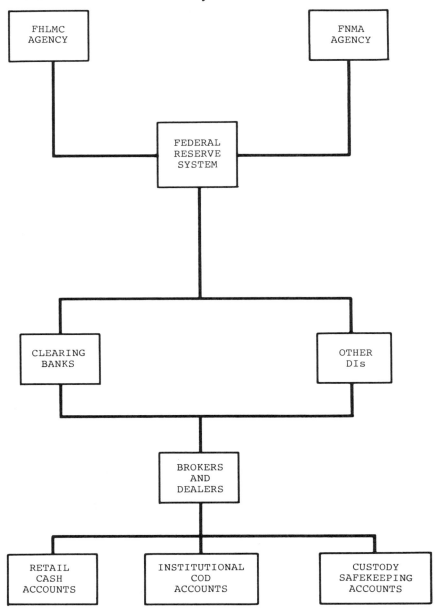

FIGURE 11-2. Federal Reserve Book-Entry System: Dealer-to-Dealer Transfer Using Different Clearing Banks

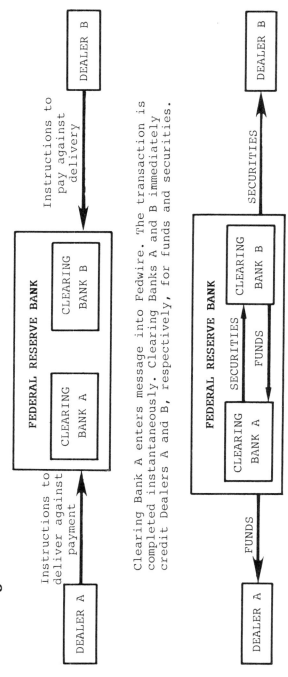

the outstanding life of this issue. It is important to recognize that this is a book-entry issuance; physical certificates are not required, not created, do not exist, and therefore cannot be deposited. A carefully controlled accounting process replaces the physical issuance of a certificate.

Step 2

The FHLMC transmits a message to the Fed authorizing the delivery of the $250,000 pool #18–0003298 to Bank B for the account of Basic, Inc. versus payment of $247,500.00. Basic, Inc. transmits two instructions *to Bank B*, not to the Fed. The first advises Bank B to receive (through the Fed a/c FHLMC) 250M FHLMC #18–0003298 versus payment of $247,500.00. The second advises Bank B to deliver 250M #18–0003298 to Bank A for the account of MBS Fund, Inc. versus payment of $250,000.00. The MBS Fund, Inc. transmits instructions to Bank A to receive 250M FHLMC #18–0003298 from Bank B versus payment of $250,000.00.

Step 3

Bank B transmits a message to the Fed (see Figure 11–3, p. 192) authorizing the delivery of 250M FHLMC #18–0003298 to Bank A for the account of MBS Fund, Inc. versus payment of $250,000.00.

Step 4

The Fed executes the instructions from the FHLMC and from Bank B. The Fed system validates the existence of a sufficient position in the FHLMC's position account, delivers the issue off the account to Bank B. It simultaneously credits the FHLMC's account and debits Bank B's cash reserve account with $247,500.00. Once the securities are received into Bank B's account, the Fed executes the bank's instruction to deliver the position to Bank A and makes the appropriate security and cash entries to the accounts of both Banks A and B.

Step 5

Banks A and B receive, through the Fed system, notification of the actions taken by the Fed in Step 4.

Step 6

Bank A processes internal accounting records for the account of MBS Fund, Inc. that reflect receipt of the securities and a debit of $250,000.00 for same. Bank B processes internal accounting records for the account of Basic, Inc. The securities are received in, the account is debited $247,500.00, the securities are delivered out, and the account is credited $250,000.00

Step 7

Banks A and B advise their customers (MBS Fund, Inc. and Basic, Inc., respectively) of the activity that has taken place on their behalf, and they both make the appropriate entries on their internal ledgers. We need to discuss only the entries made at Basic, Inc.

Basic, Inc. records the receipt of securities from the FHLMC in the FHLMC account that had to be set up to record the FHLMC's sale (Basic's purchase); the cash payment is recorded in the same account. The offset to these entries is the clearance account that is set up internally to reflect the activities and positions as reported to Basic by its clearing bank, Bank B. Basic must also record the activity relative to the delivery to its customer, MBS Fund, Inc.

Step 8

For this step you need to take a broader approach. In the preceding steps, accounting entries were made at clearing Bank B to Basic's account; the broker-dealer made corresponding entries internally. Now, envision not only the transactions that we have been focusing on, but realize that hundreds of other instructions are being processed on any particular day. Every time one of these instructions is executed, accounting entries are generated on the records at the Fed, on the records at the clearing banks, and on the records of the broker-dealers and their customers. Focus on Bank

B and Basic. The bank has processed hundreds of entries for the account of Basic and has advised Basic who responds by processing corresponding entries internally. At the end of the day, there will be a net debit or a net credit in Basic's clearance account at the bank. This is the amount the bank will be expecting to collect from Basic (if a debit) or pay to the broker-dealer (if a credit). Basic must now finish processing all its internal entries so that it too is able to arrive at a net debit or credit figure in its internal clearance account. If that figure agrees with the figure reported by the bank, Basic assumes that it is in balance with the bank and either pays the bank or collects from the bank the amount of the balance. If the balances do not agree, the individual advices received from the bank during the day must be compared to the individual entries made at Basic to determine where the discrepancy originated. Depending on the degree of sophistication of your automated support, this can be either a totally manual process or an automated one in which the individual systems of both organizations "talk" to each other, compare entries, and identify the differences.

Step 9

This step is a repetition of Step 8, the difference being that it takes place between the clearing banks and the Fed. The "real" movements of money and securities occur in the Fed system. The Fed members are the depository institutions, and they are the ones who have to settle at the end of the day with the Fed, not the brokers, the dealers, or the customers. So the clearing bank performs the same validation process with the Fed and settles the balance in its reserve account, normally by 6:30 P.M. each business day.

Step 10

In addition to reconciling its clearance cash balance each day, Basic will also reconcile every one of its positions, long and short, with its clearing bank. Again, the degree of automation that is available to a firm determines how tedious this job is.

THE INSTRUCTION PROCESS

If your clearing bank does not have instructions from your firm, no securities will be received or delivered on behalf of the firm. Chapter 6 explains the importance and role of the internal name and address master file relative to the origin of clearance instructions for customers. The discussion here, therefore, focuses on the implications of Fedwire clearance rather than on the origin of the instructions.

Having followed the previously outlined 10-step clearance process, you recognize the necessity for an interface between the broker-dealer and its clearing bank. In terms of instructions, this interface must address five main issues, as follows:

❑ Identity of the clearing agent.
❑ Eligibility of the traded security.
❑ Accuracy of the clearing instructions.
❑ Format of the clearing instructions.
❑ Speed of transmission to the clearing agent.

Identity of the Clearing Agent

Identifying the clearing agent may seem like a nonissue. Not so, if you consider the automation needs of a major dealer who maintains an active market in a broad range of products. This type of firm probably has clearing agreements, assigned by product, with several or more agents. So the first consideration is routing instructions for MBS trades to the correct clearing bank.

Eligibility of the Traded Security

The second issue, eligibility, is tied very closely to the first. Only those instructions for the trades eligible for Fedwire delivery should be transmitted to the appropriate clearing agent. As of the first quarter of 1989, Fedwire-eligible mortgage-backed issues consisted of all FHLMC PCs under their swap and guarantor programs, FHLMC mortgage cash flow obligations, FHLMC stripped mortgage-backeds, FHLMC CMOs, and FHLMC REMICs (the CMO and REMIC residual classes are not eligible). The FNMA has similar eligible programs. Negatively amortized issues are not eligible in the Fed.

Accuracy of the Clearing Instructions

The need for accuracy of instructions is self-explanatory. The main obstacle jeopardizing accurate instruction processing is the fact that three distinct entities—the broker-dealer, its clearing bank, and the Fed—must always be in synch for the settlement process to be accomplished. The ideal situation is to have a direct computer-to-computer (CPU-to-CPU) link between the dealer and the clearing bank. When the dealer enters a trade into its system, all trade details and clearance information are generated programmatically and "sent" directly to the bank with no manual intervention. The bank's system then automatically reformats the trade message for the Fed. All records have to be the same because they were all created from the original trade. Few firms have reached this degree of sophistication. Many dealers take extracts of their trade records and reenter the trades and instructions into a subsystem or simply wire the details to the bank. This is a second manual processing of an original trade—an opportunity for an error to be made. Whenever additional manual steps must be taken to complete the instructional process, verification procedures should be implemented to ensure the accuracy of the information. Such verifications can range from a manual trade-by-trade comparison to the accumulation of "hash" totals for all key fields and the comparison of the primary and secondary file totals.

Another important consideration relative to the accuracy of clearing instructions is the processing of corrections involving changes in the original trade instructions. It is imperative that instructions previously issued be easily identifiable by means of a unique trade or systems transmission number. In the absence of a unique identifier, all details of the original trade should be transmitted with a clearly discernible "Cancellation" announcement. Regardless of the method used, as soon as you become aware of a change in instructions, notify the agent to cancel the original instructions and simultaneously provide the corrected instructions. If the cancellation and/or change is processed on or after the settlement date, this information should be immediately transmitted to the clearing agent by phone; the conversation should be immediately followed up with a system-generated or wired verification of the change. Also, under these circumstances it should be ascertained whether the erroneous delivery instructions have already been executed. If so, the receiving party should be immediately contacted to arrange for a prompt reversal of the delivery so that the securities will be available for proper routing on the same day.

Format of the Clearing Instructions

Delivery instructions that are input into the Fedwire must be formatted in accordance with the Fed's specifications. Although this is the responsibility of the clearing agent, it is beneficial for the dealer community to be aware of the format. The less restructuring that the clearing agent has to do, the quicker and more accurate will be the overall delivery process. The Fed-formatted message that would be produced in Step 3 is as shown in Figure 11–3.

FIGURE 11–3. A Message in the Fed Format [a]

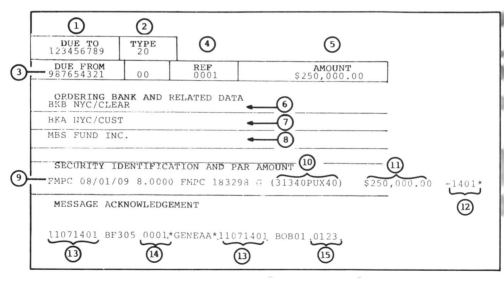

[a] Numerals in circles are keyed to the explanation of the Fedwire format on the next page.

Explanation of Fedwire Format:

1. The unique nine-digit American Bankers Association (ABA) number assigned to depository institutions; required on clearance communications. This is the number of the recipient of the wire.

2. The Fed message type code: 20 = a secondary market security transfer (reversal code 2002); 25 = original issuance security transfer from the account of the issuer (reversal code 2502).

3. The ABA number of the originator of the wire instruction.

4. A system-assigned reference number.

5. The net contract or delivery value of the trade.

6. Standardized mnemonic abbreviation of the bank plus the identity of the division within the bank responsible for the origination of the instruction.

7. Identification of the recipient of the securities that uses a standardized mnemonic abbreviation of the bank plus the identity of the division within the bank.

8. The party on whose behalf the trade was executed.

9. Security descriptions use standardized mnemonics, some examples of which are FMPC = FHLMC Participation Certificate, FMMO = FHLMC Collateralized Mortgage Obligation, FNST = FNMA Stripped Mortgage-Backed Security.

10. The universal CUSIP number.

11. Original face amount of transaction.

12. Time of day of the origination of the message.

13. Date and time of message origination.

14. See #4 above.

15. A system acknowledgment number for process verification.

Note: In this example both the original face value of the certificate as indicated under "SECURITY IDENTIFICATION AND PAR AMOUNT" and the contract/settlement value as indicated under

"AMOUNT" were the same $250,000.00. These figures represent different values. One is a quantity amount; the other is a monetary amount.

Speed of Transmission to the Clearing Agent

The last of the five considerations relative to instructions is speed. Here again, systems support is a key factor and the CPU-to-CPU environment enables a firm to transmit its instructions on a real-time basis. Lacking this advantage, the key to success lies in sorting trading activity from highest priority to lowest as follows:

❑ Postsettlement corrections and cancellations.
❑ "Cash" trades.
❑ Next-day trades.
❑ All others.

Instructions for trades covered in the first two categories must be transmitted as soon as received. For these trades, many firms forward a copy of the trader's ticket directly to an operations support group, usually trade processing. The trade is calculated, and instructions are wired or phoned to the clearing agent before the trade has been formally processed and confirmed. Both speed and accuracy are important; all clearance agreements contain a stipulation stating the time needed by the agent to guarantee execution of an instruction on a same-day basis. The majority of cash trades in MBS are either repos or reverse repos. Trade clearance receives a copy of the trade and matches it to the confirmation and delivery instruction, which is produced later that same day. Instructions for the remaining two categories can be forwarded in a batch mode to the clearing agent at the end of the day.

GENERAL CONSIDERATIONS

It was only a few years ago that all MBS were issued in definitive form (physical certificates), and all clearing involved the physical delivery of certificates to the purchaser. When the Fed accepted Fannies and Freddies into their security transfer system, the rules of clearance became simpler but different. So let's go through the rules of the road.

- ❑ Securities must be eligible, and instructions must be formatted.
- ❑ Securities must be transferred within designated periods.
- ❑ Under certain circumstances, the Fed will approve one or more extensions of the normal daily cutoff times.
- ❑ No single instruction for a secondary market transfer can exceed 50MM in original face value.
- ❑ On trades exceeding 50MM, partials in amounts divisible by 50MM must be accepted. If there is a remainder not equally divisible by 50MM, that entire remainder may be partially delivered at any time regardless of the settlement status of the remainder of the trade.
- ❑ Redelivery of securities is to be made in a timely manner to reduce the size of intra-day overdrafts.
- ❑ Deliveries using a reversal code must be valid reclamations or a mutually agreed-on late delivery. All others are illegal and incur penalty and interest charges.
- ❑ All reversals (reclamations) must be processed within 120 calendar days from the date of original receipt.
- ❑ Physical due bills evidencing P&I payments need not be delivered. A copy of the Fedwire transfer is considered adequate evidence of P&I payments due.
- ❑ Physical securities may not be withdrawn from the system.
- ❑ If physical securities are received from a customer in settlement of a sale, they must be deregistered and deposited with the Fed. Clearance cannot be accomplished until the conversion is completed and delivery is effected through the Fedwire system.

Cutoff Schedules for Fedwire Processing

There are three cutoff schedules for processing through the Fedwire system: (1) the normal schedule (for securities transfers),

(2) the dealers' schedule (for securities transfers), and (3) the schedule for the funds-only wire.

Normal Schedule—Securities Transfers

Opening for transfers	9:00 A.M. EST
Closing for transfers	2:30 P.M. EST
Closing for reversals	3:00 P.M. EST

Dealers' Schedule—Securities Transfers

Opening for transfers	9:00 A.M. EST
Final nondealer-to-dealer transfer	2:15 P.M. EST
Final dealer-to-dealer transfer	2:30 P.M. EST
Final dealer-to-broker transfer	2:30 P.M. EST
Final broker-to-dealer transfer	2:30 P.M. EST
Final dealer-to-customer transfer	2:45 P.M. EST
Final reversal	3:00 P.M. EST

Funds Transfers

Opening transaction	9:00 A.M. EST
Final interdistrict for customers	5:00 P.M. EST
Final intradistrict for customers	6:00 P.M. EST
Final reserve account settlements	6:30 P.M. EST

Member banks may request an extension of time from the Fed. Extensions are requested when there is a substantial backlog of instructions created by computer problems occurring at the member banks, the offices of the banks' customers (the broker-dealer community), or at the Fed itself. The Fed will grant a 15-minute extension or a series of extensions if it deems that a serious financial hardship will be incurred by its members if the extension was not granted. While the rule today, they will soon become the rare exception.

Intra-day Overdraft Exposure

During the step-by-step review of the Fedwire processing procedures, it was mentioned that debits and credits are entered into the cash reserve accounts of its members by the Fed and that each member in turn enters similar debits and credits into the accounts of its customers. The debits represent the contract value of securities received, whereas the credits represent the contract value of securities delivered. Brokers and dealers buy securities that they must first receive (a debit to their cash position) before they can redeliver against their sales. So the very nature of the business results in intra-day debit or overdrafts pending a subsequent credit resulting from a turned around delivery. It has also been customary to "hold" deliveries aside until additional securities become available, thus permitting larger deliveries and a better cash flow.

It is this holding pattern that plays a large role in the extent to which intra-day overdrafts exist. The overdrafts represent uncollected funds. As such, they are considered by the Fed to be a risk to the entire system that must be carefully monitored to prevent serious losses from occurring. There is the risk of a domino effect from the failure of a major participant. When everyone waits until the last minute to optimize deliveries, the potential for incurring an unmanageable debit increases. There is no time to correct errors, no time to recover from system failures, and possibly not enough time to execute all delivery instructions. The Dealer Surveillance Department of the Fed monitors the clearing practices of the dealers. It is the responsibility of the clearance personnel in the dealer community to understand the underlying concerns and the actions that they must take to keep the system safe and to avoid burdensome and costly regulations that will be implemented if voluntary cooperation is not achieved. The following Fed communique of April 1988 addresses the issue and the ground rules of conduct that the Fed hopes will be voluntarily observed. **(See Appendix, page 306, for PSA Guidelines effective 2/1/89 relative to the reduction of overdraft exposure.)**

Dealer Clearance Behavior and the Reduction of Payments System Risk

This statement describes how the Federal Reserve Bank of New York (FRBNY) monitors the dealer clearance practices of primary dealers in U.S. Government securities and the criteria used in evaluating those practices.

Background

A continuing issue for the Federal Reserve in the management of payments system risk has been the need to control daylight overdrafts. Book-entry daylight overdrafts occur on Fedwire as the result of timing gaps between the receipts and subsequent deliveries against payment of securities by depository institutions. Dealers incur daylight overdrafts at their clearing banks until securities held in the dealers' positions are delivered against payment later in the day. The practice of accumulating intra-day positions of securities gives rise to increased levels of daylight overdrafts on the Federal Reserve's wire transfer system (Fedwire), which represent a direct financial risk to a Reserve Bank. Moreover, the subsequent bunching of deliveries of securities later in the day poses risks to the effective functioning of the clearance system by increasing late afternoon congestion on Fedwire and increasing the risk of "fails" to all market participants.

In January 1988, the Federal Reserve placed a $50 million par-value limit on secondary market securities transfers over Fedwire. That transfer cap is designed to reduce incentives for intra-day position building in government securities and to encourage market participants to deliver securities earlier in the day, thereby allowing them to operate with lower levels of book-entry daylight overdrafts and less risks of late-day fails. The efforts by this Bank to encourage sound clearing practices among primary dealers are intended to complement the transfer cap and to further the effective functioning of the payments system, consistent with the July 1987 policy statement of the Board of Governors of the Federal Reserve System.

Dealer Clearance Practices

Primary dealers are expected to establish policies and procedures aimed at controlling risks associated with clearing book-entry U.S. Government securities and avoiding practices that adversely affect the payments systems. Firms should have the operational capabilities and systems required to process transactions efficiently and accurately. Dealers should be willing to commit the resources needed to upgrade those capabilities in order to increase the efficiency of the clearing process and to achieve proper integration between the dealers' trading, financing, back-office, and clearance systems.

Dealers are expected to make timely redeliveries of securities in order to minimize the size and duration of their overdrafts at the clearing banks and to help maintain liquidity in the clearing system. While there are no hard and fast rules on what constitutes timely redelivery, experience at firms with sound clearing practices suggests that dealers should be able to release a meaningful percentage of the day's deliveries by noon and more than half by 2 p.m. Moreover, dealer management should discourage clearing practices that tend to increase the overall level of financial and operational risk within the system, even if such practices seem to work to the benefit of their individual firm. For example, dealers should avoid deliberately delaying deliveries in order to insure "positive fails".

If a seller of securities fails to make delivery, the seller must finance the securities overnight while passing to the purchaser the accrued interest on those securities. Hence, sellers have an incentive to build intra-day securities positions so that they will be able to complete delivery of their largest orders first and thus minimize overnight financing costs.

The activation of account "holds" on pending deliveries is a normal business practice designed to provide dealers with time to arrange collateral positions for their daily financing activity and to schedule delivery of their largest order first. At some point in the day, however, the continued adherence to such practices poses risks to the effective functioning of the overall government securities clearance system and interferes with efforts by the Federal Reserve and other market participants to manage risks effectively. As a general matter, dealers are encouraged to release account holds at the earliest practical time in the clearing day. While operational and financing desk arrangements can vary somewhat from one firm to another, experience suggests that the continued utilization of "holds" beyond 1:00 p.m. is neither necessary to ensure adequate coordination in a well-run dealer financing operation nor consistent with each participant's responsibility to clear securities in a way that works to reduce the general levels of risk to all participants in the system. Accordingly, the FRBNY believes that considerable additional attention to clearing operations is warranted by those firms and their clearing banks that appear to place delivery holds on a significant portion of the day's deliveries after 1 p.m. each day.

Primary dealers are expected to follow both the letter and spirit of the PSA's Good Delivery Guidelines regarding the $50 million limit on secondary market transfers over Fedwire, effective January 14, 1988. Cooperation with the transfer limit implies the acceptance of partial deliveries from counterparties, as well as the avoidance of practices that delay a series of large deliveries until late in the day. For example, a participant's continued use of "holds" against $50 million deliveries is not consistent with Federal Reserve policy because it limits the effectiveness of the transfer cap in reducing market illiquidity, overdrafts, and congestion on the wire system.

Controlling the risks associated with large-dollar payments systems depends on the cooperation of all market participants, including dealers, brokers, clearing banks, and customers. The Federal Reserve encourages individual firm and industry efforts to control those risks and maintain the integrity of the book-entry clearing system.

Monitoring Dealer Clearance Behavior

The FRBNY evaluates the practices of primary dealers in government securities during on-site reviews of dealers' clearance operations. FRBNY also contacts primary dealers for information on clearing activities as the result of periodic reviews of clearing patterns over Fedwire or in response to unusual developments in the market. Particular attention is focused on aspects of a firm's performance which are inconsistent with good clearing practices or appear deficient in relation to the levels of performance achieved by similar firms.

Those factors evaluated during visits to the dealers include the efficiency of ticket processing, pair-off and trade confirmation procedures, as well as the general level of sophistication of computer systems and controls. During the visits, delivery patterns are observed first-hand in order to assess dealers' commitment to clearance timeliness. Finally, discussions with management provide insight into the extent of coordination between the financing desk and the clearance area, the autonomy of clearance personnel over the delivery process, and the overall "industry-orientation" of individual dealers with regard to clearance practices.

Federal Reserve Bank of New York
Dealer Surveillance Department
April 1988

Reclamations and the Fedwire Reversal Code

A delivery reclamation is made when the receiving party does not know the transaction that is being delivered or does not agree with the one or more details of the delivery. The contract value could be incorrect, the quantity being delivered could be incorrect, the settlement date could be incorrect, and so on. The receiving party is charged with the delivery. However, the receiving party then instructs its clearing agent to reverse the delivery back to the originator. Special Fed codes identify these kinds of transactions; 2002 identifies the reversal of a regular security transfer, and 2502 identifies the reversal of a new issue to the issuer.

Barring extensions, reversals must be completed by 3:00 P.M. EST. Now, the zinger: illegal reversals! Technically, an *illegal reversal* is a delivery that is being made for the first time using a 2002 code and/or a redelivery of a reversal using a 2002 code. In practice, the reversal code is frequently used to make a late delivery of regular trades and late repos *but* only on receipt of an agreement from the contra-party to accept the late delivery. Erroneous reversals are also reversed back in the final minutes and seconds of the same day (reversals end at 15:00:59 EST). Technically, these transactions are illegal reversals and could be subject to costly penalty assessments. Whenever a mutually agreed-on delivery is made by a reversal code, you must carefully record and maintain all the information concerning the time and source of authorization for the reversal. Penalty charges can be and have been charged to firms months after the fact. All charges associated with illegal reversals should be booked to an account established for that purpose. Charges in this account should be reviewed to determine whether authorization for the reversal had in fact been received, and if so, efforts must be made to reverse the penalty.

Penalties are costly and consist of the following:

- ❑ An FRBNY assessment of 5% of par, plus
- ❑ interest compensation at the Fed funds rate, plus
- ❑ a processing fee imposed by the clearing agent.

The message is clear: Control reclamations!

BALANCING DAILY CLEARANCE ACTIVITY

A statement was made at the beginning of this chapter to the effect that Fed clearance simply involved an instruction process and a balancing process. Balancing is more than merely making sure that debits equal credits. It is making sure that you are paying only for securities that have been received and that you are being paid for everything that you have delivered. And it is making sure that you have all the securities that you are supposed to have in your account. To arrive at this point, it is necessary to account for the following:

- ❑ Deliveries and receipts versus original contract value.
- ❑ Internal pair-offs.
- ❑ Money differences between contract value and actual receipts.
- ❑ Cancellations and corrections.
- ❑ Receipt and payment of funds unrelated to the clearing process.

Deliveries and Receipts Versus Original Contract Value

Keep in mind the eighth and ninth steps of the 10-step clearing process reviewed earlier in the chapter. The sources of the hundreds (for some firms, thousands) of instructions that a clearing bank begins to execute each day at 9:00 A.M. are threefold: (1) the uncleared settled trades in the open fail file as of the close of business the previous evening, (2) previously executed trades settling on the current day, and (3) the trades that will be executed on the current day on a cash or same-day settlement basis. Collectively, these three sources constitute the entire instruction base for the current day's clearance processing. Every instruction executed by your clearing bank represents a trade cleared through the Fedwire; cash and securities changed hands not physically but beneficially on the books and records of the Fed and its participating members. Every time one of these instructions is executed, an accounting entry is generated on the records at the Fed and on the records at the clearing banks. The clearing bank advises each of its clients, the brokers and dealers, of the activity then. The broker-dealers respond by processing corresponding internal entries reflecting delivery or receipt of the trade. Let's ignore the entries being processed at the Fed and the clearing bank and examine the internal entries of the broker-dealer by using the example in Figure 11–3.

The BD Basic, Inc. buys a new pool, $250,000.00 #18–0003298 at 99 from the issuer FHLMC. Basic, Inc. clears through Bank B. Basic, Inc., in turn sells the pool at par to a COD account, MBS Fund, Inc., which clears through Bank A. All trades clear on settlement date. The cash entries reflected in Figure 11–4 were made on the cash ledgers of Basic, Inc. on the settlement date. Interpret the entries for yourself before reviewing the explanations that follow.

FIGURE 11–4. Accounting Entries Recording Purchase and Clearance of Pool #18–0003298 on the Records of Basic, Inc.

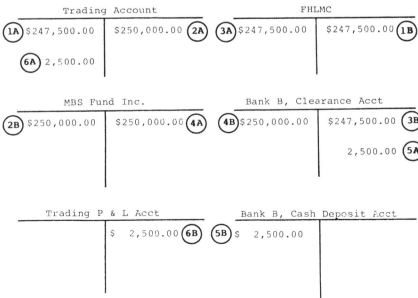

Explanation of Figure 11–4:

1a. This debit reflects Basic's original trade with the FHLMC; it is the cost of the purchase from the FHLMC.

1b. This is the offsetting entry to the firm's purchase. It is posted to the internal account set up for the FHLMC, and it reflects the net proceeds of the FHLMC's sale.

2a. This credit reflects Basic's sale from its inventory account. It is the net proceeds of the sale.

2b. This is the offsetting entry to the firm's sale. It represents the purchase made by MBS Fund, Inc. and represents the net amount owed to Basic—the amount that will be paid on delivery.

3a. This entry was posted onto Basic's records when it was advised by Bank B that the FHLMC had delivered (through its clearing agent) the securities it purchased (entry 1a). The debit indicates that payment was made to the FHLMC for the proceeds of the sale (entry 1b). This entry is known as a "cleanup" (of an outstanding transaction).

3b. When cleanups are processed, they must be offset (usually done automatically) by an entry to the clearance account. Debits are receivables; credits are liabilities. This offsetting credit represents Basic's liability to pay to Bank B the amount that Bank B must pay to the Fed at the end of the day. It is the proceeds of the FHLMC's sale that were simultaneously exchanged when FHLMC delivered the securities. Remember that at this stage all movements of securities and cash are nothing more than accounting entries that will be netted at the end of the day. Once the entries are netted, an actual movement of cash will take place at the end of the cycle in an amount equal to the balance in the clearance account at the end of the day. This entry also exemplifies how intra-day overdrafts originate.

4a. This entry was posted onto Basic's records when it was advised by Bank B that it had delivered to MBS Fund's agent the securities that the fund had purchased (entry

2b). The credit represents payment to Basic for the delivered securities; it too is a cleanup.

4b. This is the system-generated offset to entry 4a. This offsetting debit is a receivable that represents funds due to Basic from Bank B as a result of clearance activity. At this point, all instructions have been executed; there is a $2,500 net debit balance in the clearance account reflecting the clearance activity of the day. Basic will now wait for the bank to report its clearance balance. If the figures agree, the two firms are in balance with each other. In this case, the bank owes Basic $2,500. You may have already noticed that this amount coincides with the profit reflected in the trading account. The profit has been there from the trade date; now it has been collected because the trades have cleared. If the bank's and the broker-dealer's balances do not agree, all activity of the day will be reviewed to determine which transaction(s) created the discrepancy. Appropriate adjustments will then be processed.

5a. This is the final entry of the day to the clearance account. Once the account has been balanced, the net amount in the account must be paid to the bank (if there was a net credit) or received from the bank (if there was a net debit). Because there is a net debit balance of $2,500 in the account, a credit entry in the equivalent amount is processed. This entry represents payment by the bank to Basic of the net clearance activities of the day. Because of the simplistic nature of the example, the amount does correspond with the P&L, a coincidence that rarely occurs. The clearance account must be flattened to a zero balance each evening. Each day's activities must stand alone to facilitate the end-of-day balancing process.

5b. This is the offsetting entry to 5a. Cash was not actually received from the bank in payment of the clearance balance but, rather, moved to Basic's regular demand deposit account.

The entries reflected in 6a and 6b are shown for reference only. They reflect the movement of the trading P&L from the inventory trading account to an income account, an accounting process that is not normally handled by the clearance personnel of a firm.

Internal Pair-Offs

Broker-dealers and some institutional accounts actively trade their positions, and there are times when a firm finds that it has open buy and sell transactions in the same issue with the same contra-party. Pairing off a trade involves crossing the buy against the sell by means of journal entries that effectively deliver off the open positions. If the quantities of the buy-side and the sell-side are equal, the only thing that remains open on your records is a cash amount equal to the difference between the contract values of the pair-off transactions. Arrangements are made for the collection of this amount by a wire transfer of funds to be completed on the day the pair-off is executed.

Pair-offs are accomplished by processing cleanups, which in most firms create offsetting entries to the clearance account. In the case of pair-offs, the bank is unaware of the activity so it will not be incorporated into the end-of-day bank figure to which you have to balance. Therefore, it is necessary to segregate pair-offs through the use of a special blotter code or journal so that the figures involved in these transactions and the separate wire payments associated with them can be accounted for in the balancing process. Remember to cancel your bank instructions after a pair-off has been accomplished.

Always, always, *always* try to get consent from the contra-party to pair off matching open items. You reduce your open fails, you reduce your clearing costs (agents charge a fee for every delivery they make), and you reduce the possibility of jeopardizing the timeliness of other deliveries.

Money Differences: Contract Value Versus Actual Receipts

A frequent contributor to out-of-balance cash positions is money differences. If a delivery is made to you for an amount that does not correspond with your internal records, you have the option to have your bank reverse the delivery. Many times, however, the amount of the difference is insignificant when compared to the value of the transaction. Many firms have authorized their agents to accept any item having a difference less than a predetermined maximum amount. In such cases, cleanups are processed with internal figures, which do not correspond to the figures that are processed by the bank. Procedures should be established to provide for the identification of all such differences as soon as possible after the Fedwire has closed. All such differences must be journaled into an account designated for the purpose—both for balancing and for facilitating the collection (or payment) of the differences.

Cancellations and Corrections

The specific concern with cancellations and corrections is the processing of changes on trades that have already settled. The details of these trades will already have been included in the clearing agent's system. Should the original trade have been cleared before the changes were effected, it will be necessary to process adjusting entries internally to correspond to the action taken by the bank. As with pair-offs, this type of processing should be isolated on a specific blotter so that each entry can be easily isolated and examined should you be out of balance at the end of the day. Postsettlement changes frequently contribute to out-of-balance records.

Receipts and Payments Unrelated to Clearance

Most firms maintain several different accounts at a single bank. There are times that funds are received into and/or paid out of the clearance account when they should have been directed through some other account. Whenever you are out of balance with the clearance account, examine all money-only transfers in the account to determine whether they actually belong in the clearance account or should be swung into a different account.

POSITION BALANCING

The discussion of balancing has thus far deliberately focused on cash to avoid muddying the waters by jumping back and forth between cash accounting and securities accounting. Although very little space is given here to the topic, balancing your positions on a daily basis is equally as important, perhaps even more important, than balancing your cash daily. If you understand the principles covered in connection with cash balancing, however, you can simply apply them to position balancing.

Several quick observations: First, when you process a cleanup, use a single entry for both the securities side and cash side of the trade. It is important to realize that this does not mean that if you have balanced your cash position, your inventory position must necessarily be in balance. Two different systems and two sets of master files are processed—the broker's and the agent's files. Either could have an erroneous security description. Early FHLMC PCs in the 16 and 17 group range had pool numbers that were issued in duplicate to issues with different maturity dates. These issues are still traded and are sometimes involved in position discrepancies. This is just one of the problems that can result in position differences.

The second point to consider is that your inventory positions are usually in several accounts. The clearance account normally contains your uncommitted trading inventory, which is available for any purpose need. The seg account contains inventory that belongs to fully paid custody accounts; these positions cannot be delivered unless sold or otherwise authorized by the beneficial owner. The collateral loan account contains positions used to secure your bank loans. The triparty repo account contains positions used to collateralize open repo contracts (see Chapter 15). It is important to confirm daily that the internal records of the broker-dealer and the internal records of the agent bank reflect not only the same overall quantity per each positioned issue but also that the securities are booked into the proper accounts. If you find that a position has been erroneously posted into the wrong account, you must immediately process an adjustment to prevent improper and possible illegal use of the securities.

Physical Clearance

Within a year after the publication of this book, the physical clearance of MBS should be a historical chapter in the evolution of MBS processing. For now, it needs to be addressed because the clearance of current coupon GNMA securities through the MBSCC depository (PTC) has not yet been mandated. Furthermore, one of the topics to be discussed—certificate negotiability—must be understood and dealt with until all the currently outstanding physical certificates have matured or been paid down.

PHYSICAL SETTLEMENT OPTIONS

No matter what method of clearance is used, the most important step is always the analysis of the presettlement delivery requirements. This chapter concentrates solely on the procedures and the concerns associated with *physical* clearance. Before we get into specifics, you should realize that there are different options, or methods, that each firm individually chooses as the method it wants to use to clear its physical mortgage-backeds. A firm can perform all clearance functions itself (that is, be a self-clearing organization), or it can employ the services of a clearing agent and/or bank to clear on its behalf.

A self-clearing firm uses its own employees to receive and deliver all certificates on its own premises. Payments for deliveries are made after the fact by a Fed funds wire that originates from the firm's bank contingent on the bank's receipt of an authorized instruction. Think about the risk that is involved here! If you were the delivering firm, you would have taken your assets (the securities), given them to another firm, and received a receipt. And then you sit and wait for that firm to instruct its bank to initiate a wire payment. You have no securities, you have no cash, you have no recourse to the bank if payment is not received. There is no simultaneous exchange of securities and money as there is in the Fedwire system. There is no secured fund backing the intra-day debits and credits being posted to members' accounts as there is in the MBSCC depository. There is exposure! Herein is the main reason for the move to book-entry-only clearance and also for the need for internal credit committees to monitor the financial health of the firms and customers with whom we do business. (See Figure 12–1.)

The second option involves entering into an agreement with a clearing agent or bank. When this option is chosen, physical deliveries are accomplished at the clearing bank. Because the bank is directly accepting securities on behalf of its clearing clients, there is an additional layer of credit protection inasmuch as the bank is now directly responsible for either payment or the return of the securities it has accepted. However, history has shown us more than once that clearing banks also fail and are unable to meet their obligations. (See Figure 12–2.)

Regardless of whether your firm self-clears or uses an agent, the following is a listing of the major concerns and problems associated with the physical clearance of mortgage-backeds:

- ❑ Instruction processing.
- ❑ Availability of proper denominations.
- ❑ Good delivery guidelines.
- ❑ Maintaining records of certificate numbers.
- ❑ Delivery processing and reclamation processing.
- ❑ Controlling delivery routes.
- ❑ Payment processing.
- ❑ Vault security.

FIGURE 12-1. Physical Settlement: Dealer-to-Dealer Transfer Direct Delivery

In a wire payment transaction, Dealer B gives Dealer A a window receipt specifying the amount of payment that will be sent by wire later on.

Dealer B instructs its bank to wire funds to Dealer A's bank; transaction becomes final.

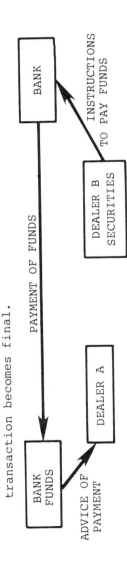

FIGURE 12-2. Physical Settlement: Dealer-to-Dealer Transfer Using Different Clearing Banks

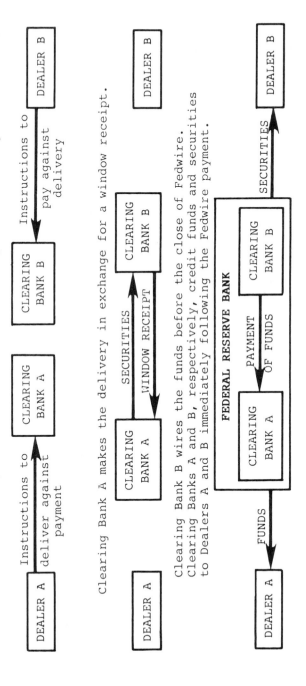

Dealers A and B give instructions to their respective clearing banks.

Clearing Bank A makes the delivery in exchange for a window receipt.

Clearing Bank B wires the funds before the close of Fedwire. Clearing Banks A and B, respectively, credit funds and securities to Dealers A and B immediately following the Fedwire payment.

INSTRUCTION PROCESSING

The issues concerning content, accuracy, timeliness, and corrections that have been previously discussed are the same for physical clearance. The format and method of transmitting instructions *do* differ. Instructions for securities that have to be cleared physically must serve two purposes: (1) to provide the necessary clearance information and (2) to serve as the delivery bill that must be attached to the securities when they are delivered.

Instructions for a physical delivery must be explicit. Because you are not using the Fedwire or a depository to execute your delivery, you must clearly identify the entity to which the delivery is to be made, its street address, the floor and room numbers or the identity of the area to which the securities are to be delivered. Avoid using specific names in your general instruction file; people change departments and change firms. Identifying departments can avoid costly delays. Because there is no simultaneous exchange of securities and cash as in the Fedwire or the debit/credit posting of the MBSCC depository, you must give clear instructions as to how payment is to be accomplished. The normal payment method is by a Fed funds wire. If this is the method to be used, your instructions must provide the receiving party with adequate information to complete the funds transfer. The information should contain the identity of the bank, including its ABA number, to which the transfer is to be directed as well as the mnemonic identity and the internal bank account number of the beneficiary of the transfer (the delivering party).

Instructions should be printed on a multipart form, the delivery bill, or the delivery manifold. The information on the delivery bill mirrors that confirmation information and includes the settlement instructions (see Figure 12–3). Some firms produce their confirms and delivery bills simultaneously by simply adding a top confirm copy to their delivery bills. A delivery bill form should have a minimum of five parts. Two parts (preferably three if it is a six-part form) are attached to the securities when they are delivered, one part is kept by the messenger dispatcher, one part is kept by the clearance unit for balancing and reference, and one part is sent for centralized processing and/or permanent storage in the firm's record files.

FIGURE 12-3. A Delivery Bill for Physical Clearance

PaineWebber

GOVERNMENT SECURITIES / COMMERCIAL PAPER CONFIRMATION

GOVERNMENT SECURITIES DEPARTMENT
120 BROADWAY, NEW YORK, N.Y. 10271
TELEPHONE (212) 437-2121

TO BE DELIVERED

AS PRINCIPAL WE HEREBY CONFIRM

OUR SALE TO

AGAINST PAYMENT OF FEDERAL FUNDS UNLESS OTHERWISE NOTED.

YOU TODAY OF THE FOLLOWING SECURITIES

CLIENT NUMBER	TRADE I.D. #	REF. #	TRADE DATE	AS OF DATE	SETTLEMENT DATE		
	F005	602270	11/11/88		11/18/88		

PAR VALUE	SECURITY					DISCOUNT/BASIS	PRICE
$ 1,000,000.00	GNMA POOL 123456 SF LEVEL PAY FIXED RATE 10% DUE 08-15-2011				FACTOR .87654321		99 1/8

PRINCIPAL	INTEREST/DISCOUNT PERIOD	INTEREST/DISCOUNT	CHARGES	TOTAL
$ 868,873.46		$ 4,139.23		$ 873,012.69

SECURITY NO.	HOUSE ACCOUNT NO.	CUSIP NO.

DELIVERY INSTRUCTIONS

① DVP-BANK OF NY 110 WASHINGTON
CLEAR DIV 19th FLOOR
AC XY ZEE MBS FUND INC
② WIRE FUNDS TO: CHEM NY
ABA021000128 AC PWJC AC 0660077

SIGNED _____
DATE _____
BY _____

☐ WE BOUGHT
☐ WE SOLD

IT IS EXPRESSLY UNDERSTOOD AND AGREED THAT TITLE OF THESE SECURITIES SHALL REMAIN VESTED IN PaineWebber Incorporated UNTIL FULL PAYMENT IN CASH OR ITS EQUIVALENT SHALL HAVE BEEN MADE THEREFOR.

GNS-1298 REV. 8/87 PTG 4/88

RECEIVING INSTRUCTIONS/MESSENGER'S RECEIPT

AVAILABILITY OF PROPER DENOMINATIONS

When MBS securities are originated, the face value reflects the principal value of the mortgages securitizing the issue on the date of issuance. There can be dollar and penny amounts involved that are not evenly divisible by the incremental unit of trading, $5,000.00. These odd amounts are known as *tails*. The entire amount of a tail must always remain with a single certificate, which can never be less than $25,000.00 face value (the minimum trading denomination). As a result of this odd issuance amount, it is frequently difficult to match sales to the exact denominations of the physical certificates that are deposited in a firm's inventory vault. All other kinds of securities are issued in evenly divisible amounts and are traded in round lot denominations that are predictable and controllable. Physical MBS are neither.

Part of the process of preparing for physical clearance, therefore, must be to determine if the denominations of the securities in the vault, referred to as *pieces*, match your delivery requirements. If not, you must send the securities to the transfer agent (Chemical Bank for all GNMA issues) for a denominational breakdown by means of the transfer (reregistration) process.

If the delivery to be made is for a sizable contract value, you should request a special rush transfer for which you must pay a fee. You must base this decision on a comparison of the financing cost that you will incur if you fail versus the cost of the fees charged for the rush transfer. This is another example of why presettlement planning is required. This problem will be eliminated, however, except perhaps for a few of the new asset-backed securities, when the MBSCC programs are fully implemented and all MBS are cleared through some form of book entry.

GOOD DELIVERY GUIDELINES

The obvious requirements for a good delivery are that the securities being delivered to the purchaser's agent fulfill the terms of the trade contract. Securities, quantity, contract value, customer identity must be correct; the delivery can be made on or after the settlement of the trade. No single certificate may have an original face value of less than $25,000.00. Due-bill requirements will be discussed separately. All deliveries against payment must be in good deliverable format; they must be properly endorsed and may not be registered in a name that is considered to be a legal transfer. Briefly, legal transfers include securities registered in the name of a deceased person, a corporate entity, or the like. Any certificate that requires the filing of legal papers over and above a standard form of endorsement can be considered a legal transfer. Such certificates, even if delivered with the required legal papers, should not be accepted as a good delivery. They are what is known as a good transfer but not a good delivery. Such certificates need to be reregistered into the street name (i.e., the name of the delivering broker or dealer) after which the reregistered certificates may be delivered.

Since we are talking about the physical delivery of mortgage-backed securities, let's examine a GNMA Single-Family Pool certificate and a GNMA II Jumbo certificate. (See Figures 12–4 and 12–5.)

Explanation of Figures 12–4 and 12–5:

1. Issue date. The date that the pool was officially created; the first day that benefits began to accrue on the issue.

2. Pool number and type of mortgage. The unique number assigned to and identifying the individual pool of mortgages collateralizing all the certificates issued under this number.

3. Interest rate. The coupon rate that is passed through to the registered owners of the pool. It is lower than the actual rates being paid on the underlying mortgages.

4. Initial/original principal amount. The original face amount of the certificate representing a proportionate share in the overall pool. After the first P&I record date, the actual outstanding amortized amounts for these types of pools will always be less than the amount shown on the certificate.

5. Initial/original aggregate amount. The total principal value of the entire pool on the date of issuance.

6. Maturity date. The date on which the final payments of P&I are officially scheduled to be paid. Actually, the total

FIGURE 12–4. GNMA Single-Family Pool Certificate

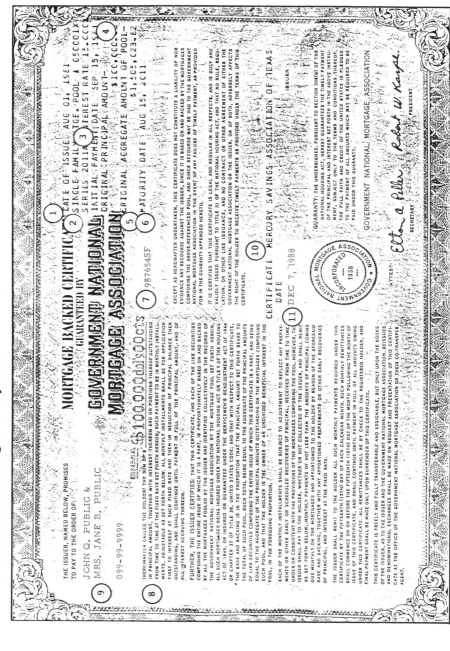

FIGURE 12-5. GNMA Jumbo Certificate

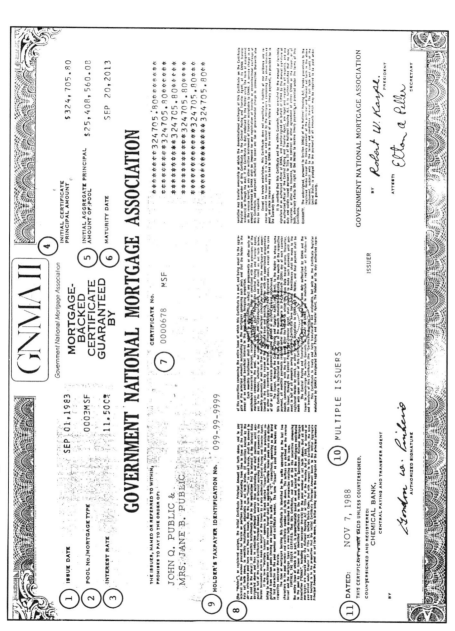

217

repayment of principal will almost certainly occur before the maturity date.

7. Certificate number. The unique number assigned to each certificate issued by the transfer agent; it has no relationship to the pool number.

8. Registration information. The name(s) of the owners of the certificate as recorded on the books of the transfer agent. The registered owner is the party to whom all P&I payments will be made.

9. Taxpayer identification number. The Social Security number of the individual whose name appears first in the registration (John Q. Public) or the assigned tax ID number if a corporation is the owner.

10. Issuer name. The identity of the mortgage banker or other entity that requested the issuance of the pool; the organization that is servicing the pool (i.e., collecting and distributing P&I). The GNMA II pool has multiple issuers; Chemical Bank distributes the P&I for this kind of a Jumbo pool.

11. Dated date. The date on which this particular certificate was issued by the transfer agent. This is the day on which the registered owner is recorded on the books of the transfer agent as being the owner of the certificate.

Registered certificates are not negotiable unless they are signed. To be deliverable on settlement of a sale, registered physical certificates must be properly endorsed by the registered owner(s) and have the appropriate guarantees affixed by a commercial bank or trust company having a New York City office or by a member of a national securities exchange. Figures 12–6 and 12–7 show the backs of GNMA certificates; there are two illustrations because certificates currently exist in two different formats. Frequently, certificates are signed through the use of a detached assignment, which also comes in two formats (see Figures 12–8 and 12–10). The P.D. 1832 format corresponds to the old certificate format, and the HUD format corresponds to the new certificate format. Explanation of the way assignments of P.D. 1832 and HUD forms are executed follows (see Figures 12–9 and 12–11). Notice, however, that the HUD format of detached assignment

FIGURE 12–6. Back of Certificate—New Format

POOL NUMBER SUFFIXES

X — GNMA I (as third from last character)   SF — Single family, level payment mortgages (as last two characters)

REGISTERED HOLDER ABBREVIATIONS

The following abbreviations, when used in the inscription on the face of this instrument, shall be construed as though they were written out in full according to applicable laws or regulations.

TEN COM — as tenants in common

TEN ENT — as tenants by the entireties

JT TEN — as joint tenants with right of survivorship and not as tenants in common

UNIF GIFT MIN ACT ....
(Cust.)

Custodian ....
(Minor)

Under Uniform Gifts to Minors
Act ....
(State)

Additional abbreviations may also be used though not in the above list.

ASSIGNMENT

FOR VALUE RECEIVED, the undersigned hereby sell(s), assign(s) and transfer(s) unto

PLEASE INSERT SOCIAL SECURITY OR OTHER
IDENTIFYING NUMBER OF ASSIGNEE

(12) (Please print or typewrite name and address including postal zip code of assignee)

the within Certificate and all rights thereunder, hereby irrevocably constituting and appointing

(13) _____ attorney
to transfer said Certificate on the books of the issuer with full power of substitution in the premises.

Dated_____

(14)

NOTICE: The signature of the individual Holder or the name of the corporate Holder must correspond with the name as written upon the face of the within Certificate in every particular without alteration or enlargement or any change whatever

(signature if Holder is an individual, name if Holder is a corporation)

By _____
(signature and title if Holder is a corporation)

Signature, and ownership or authority to act on behalf of owner(s), must be guaranteed below by a member firm of any national stock exchange or commercial bank having a correspondent in New York City

GUARANTEE

I CERTIFY that the above named person(s) as described, whose identity (or the identity of each of whom) and whose ownership or whose authority to act on behalf of the holder(s) of the within Certificate is well known or proved to me, personally appeared before me this

_____ day of _____ 19____

at _____
(City and State)

and signed the above assignment.

GUARANTEED
By _____

(15) (Signature and title of certifying officer)

_____
(Address)

IMPORTANT: The present principal balance of this Certificate is not necessarily the Initial Certificate Principal Amount shown on its face. The present principal balance of this Certificate may be ascertained from the Transfer Agent or a dealer in such securities.

FIGURE 12–7. Back of Certificate—Old Format

ASSIGNMENT

I AM THE OWNER, OR THE DULY AUTHORIZED REPRESENTATIVE OF THE OWNER, OF THE WITHIN
MORTGAGE BACKED CERTIFICATE AND FOR VALUE RECEIVED HEREBY ASSIGN THE SAME TO

_____
(ASSIGNEE)

AND AUTHORIZE THE TRANSFER THEREOF ON THE BOOKS OF THE ISSUER.

_____
(SIGNATURE OF ASSIGNOR)

PERSONALLY APPEARED BEFORE ME THE ABOVE NAMED PERSON, WHOSE IDENTITY IS WELL KNOWN
OR PROVED TO ME, AND SIGNED THE ABOVE ASSIGNMENT, ACKNOWLEDGING IT TO BE HIS FREE ACT AND
DEED. WITNESS MY HAND, OFFICIAL DESIGNATION, AND SEAL.

_____   _____
(SIGNATURE OF WITNESSING OFFICER)   (OFFICIAL DESIGNATION)

SEAL   DATED AT_____   _____, 19_____.

ASSIGNMENT

I AM THE OWNER, OR THE DULY AUTHORIZED REPRESENTATIVE OF THE OWNER, OF THE WITHIN
MORTGAGE BACKED CERTIFICATE AND FOR VALUE RECEIVED HEREBY ASSIGN THE SAME TO

(12) _____
(ASSIGNEE)

AND AUTHORIZE THE TRANSFER THEREOF ON THE BOOKS OF THE ISSUER.

(14) _____
(SIGNATURE OF ASSIGNOR)

PERSONALLY APPEARED BEFORE ME THE ABOVE NAMED PERSON, WHOSE IDENTITY IS WELL KNOWN
OR PROVED TO ME, AND SIGNED THE ABOVE ASSIGNMENT, ACKNOWLEDGING IT TO BE HIS FREE ACT AND
DEED. WITNESS MY HAND, OFFICIAL DESIGNATION, AND SEAL.

(15) _____   _____
(SIGNATURE OF WITNESSING OFFICER)   (OFFICIAL DESIGNATION)

SEAL   DATED AT_____   _____, 19_____.

INSTRUCTIONS

TO ASSIGN THIS MORTGAGE BACKED CERTIFICATE, THE OWNER, OR HIS DULY AUTHORIZED REPRESENTATIVE, SHALL APPEAR
BEFORE AN OFFICER AUTHORIZED TO WITNESS ASSIGNMENTS, ESTABLISH HIS IDENTITY TO THE SATISFACTION OF SUCH
OFFICER, AND IN HIS PRESENCE EXECUTE THE ASSIGNMENT, USING ONE OF THE ABOVE FORMS. THE WITNESSING OFFICER
MUST THEN AFFIX HIS SIGNATURE, OFFICIAL DESIGNATION, AND SEAL, IF ANY, AND ADD THE PLACE AND DATE OF EXECUTION.
OFFICERS AUTHORIZED TO WITNESS ASSIGNMENTS INCLUDE EXECUTIVE OFFICERS OF BANKS AND TRUST COMPANIES IN-
CORPORATED IN THE UNITED STATES OR ITS ORGANIZED TERRITORIES, AND THEIR BRANCHES, DOMESTIC AND FOREIGN.
IF ADDITIONAL ASSIGNMENTS ARE REQUIRED, A FORM SIMILAR TO THE ABOVE MAY BE WRITTEN OR TYPED HEREON. FULL
INFORMATION REGARDING ASSIGNMENTS MAY BE OBTAINED FROM GOVERNMENT NATIONAL MORTGAGE ASSOCIATION.

IMPORTANT

THE PRESENT PRINCIPAL BALANCE OF THIS MORTGAGE BACKED CERTIFICATE IS NOT NECES-
SARILY THE ORIGINAL PRINCIPAL AMOUNT SHOWN ON ITS FACE. THE PRESENT PRINCIPAL
BALANCE OF THE CERTIFICATE MAY BE ASCERTAINED FROM THE ISSUER NAMED THEREON OR A
DEALER IN SUCH SECURITIES.

FIGURE 12–8. Detached Assignment, P.D. 1832 Format

FORM PD 1832
Dept. of the Treasury
Bur. of the Public Debt
(Rev. Mar. 1977)

**SPECIAL FORM OF DETACHED ASSIGNMENT FOR
UNITED STATES REGISTERED SECURITIES**

1

FOR VALUE RECEIVED I assign to _____
(Name)

(Taxpayer identifying number and address of assignee)

the following-described registered securities of which I am (we are) the owner(s) or the duly authorized representative of the owner:

TITLE OF LOAN and/or ISSUE _____   2
(Include interest rate, series, issue date and call and maturity dates)

DENOMINATION	SERIAL NUMBERS	REGISTRATION (Exact inscription on each security)
		3
		4
		5

and hereby authorize discharge of registration thereof on the books of the Department of the Treasury.

6

(Signature by or on behalf of owner)

(Additional signature, if required)

I CERTIFY that the above-named person(s) as described, whose identity (or the identity of each of whom) is well known
or proved to me, personally appeared before me this _____ day of _____, 19___,   7

at _____, and signed the above assignment.
(City and State)

8

(SEAL)
_____
(Signature and title of certifying officer)   9

(Address)
(See other side for list of officers authorized to certify assignments)

FIGURE 12–9. Explanation of P.D. 1832 Format

Detached Assignment (P.D. 1832)

1 ASSIGNEE – See Line # 1 on certificate rear (Exhibit A 1).

2 TITLE OF LOAN AND/OR ISSUE – Full description of security –
     pool number, maturity date, rate, and issuer.

3 DENOMINATION – Face amount of the certificate.

4 SERIAL NUMBERS – Certificate numbers.

5 REGISTRATION – Exact inscription on each security.

6 ASSIGNOR – Manual signature of the registered holder of the
     certificate or his duly appointed representative.

7 LOCATION – Date and site of assignment.

8 SIGNATURE OF WITNESSING OFFICER – See reverse side of P.D. 1832.

9 SEAL – The seal of the witnessing bank must be affixed here
     in lieu of the bank seal, either the banks savings
     bond validating stamp or a signature guarantee stamp
     can be used.

FIGURE 12–10. Detached Assignment, HUD Format

U. S. DEPARTMENT OF HOUSING AND URBAN DEVELOPMENT
GOVERNMENT NATIONAL MORTGAGE ASSOCIATION
MORTGAGE-BACKED SECURITIES PROGRAM

FORM OF DETACHED ASSIGNMENT

FOR VALUE RECEIVED the undersigned hereby sell(s) and transfer(s) unto

Please Print or Type Name and Address Including Zip Code of Assignee | Please Insert Social Security, Tax Identification or Other Identifying Number of Assignee

The following described GNMA Mortgage-Backed Certificate(s) and all rights thereunder of which I am (we are) the owner(s) or the duly authorized representative of the owner(s).

| Pool Number | Issue Date | Maturity Date | (Pass-Through Rate) |

| Certificate Principal Balance (As shown on face of certificate) | Certificate Number(s) | Registration (Exact inscription on each certificate) |

(Signature if holder is an individual, name if holder is a corporation)

By _____

(Signature and title if holder is a corporation)

Notice: See reverse side for signature guidelines

Guaranty

I CERTIFY that the above-named person(s) as described, whose identity (or the identity of each of whom) and whose ownership or whose authority to act on behalf of the owner(s) of the above described Certificate(s) is well known or proved to me, personally appeared before me this _____ day of _____, 19___, at _____ . and signed the above assignment.

(City and State)

(SEAL)

GUARANTEED:

By _____

(Signature and title of certifying officer)

(Address)

_____ IMPORTANT _____

The present principal balance of the Certificate(s) is not necessarily the original principal amount shown on its face. The present principal balance of the Certificate(s) may be ascertained from GNMA or a dealer in Certificates.

FIGURE 12–11.   HUD Format Instructions

INSTRUCTIONS

> NOTE: USE OF THIS FORM MUST BE SPECIFICALLY AUTHORIZED BY A FEDERAL RESERVE BANK OR BRANCH, OR THE BUREAU OF THE PUBLIC DEBT.

Registered transferable securities may be assigned in blank, to bearer, to a specified transferee, to the Secretary of the Treasury for exchange for coupon securities, or to the Secretary of the Treasury for redemption or for exchange for other securities offered at maturity, upon call or pursuant to an advance refunding offer. Nontransferable securities may be assigned only in the manner and to the extent provided in the offering circulars or special applicable regulations. The owner or his authorized representative must appear before and establish his identity to the satisfaction of an officer authorized to certify assignments, and execute the assignment in the presence of that officer. The officer must then fully complete the certification form. If the securities are assigned to a specified transferee, the name, taxpayer identifying number (social security account number or employer identification number), and the address of the assignee should be shown on the form in the space provided.

OFFICERS AUTHORIZED TO CERTIFY ASSIGNMENTS

(1)   IN THE UNITED STATES:

    (a)   Any and All Assignments:

        Officers and employees of banks and trust companies incorporated in the United States, its territories or possessions, or the Commonwealth of Puerto Rico, and Federal Savings and Loan Associations, or other organizations which are members of the Federal Home Loan Bank System, who have been authorized to (i) generally bind their respective institutions by their acts, (ii) unqualifiedly guarantee signatures to assignments of securities, or (iii) expressly certify assignments of securities. A complete list of classes of authorized officers may be obtained from any Federal Reserve Bank or the Bureau of the Public Debt.

        CAUTION: NOTARIES PUBLIC HAVE ONLY LIMITED AUTHORITY. SEE (b) BELOW.

    (b)   Limited Authority:

        Assignments for redemption for the account of the assignor, or for redemption-exchange, or pursuant to an advance refunding offer for other securities to be registered in his name, or in his name with a joint owner, may be certified by;

        (i)   Justices of the peace and notaries public in the United States, in territories and possessions, the Commonwealth of Puerto Rico and the Canal Zone.

        (ii)   Postmasters, acting postmasters, assistant postmasters, inspectors-in-charge, chief and assistant chief accountants, and superintendents of stations of any post office in the United States, its territories and possessions, the Commonwealth of Puerto Rico and the Canal Zone.

(2)   IN FOREIGN COUNTRIES, Any and All Assignments:

    (a)   United States diplomatic or consular representatives.

    (b)   Managers, assistant managers and other officers of foreign branches of banks or trust companies incorporated in the United States, its territories or possessions, or the Commonwealth of Puerto Rico.

    (c)   Officers authorized to administer oaths, including notaries public, but their official position and authority must be certified by a United States diplomatic or consular representative under the seal of his office.

INSTRUCTIONS TO CERTIFYING OFFICER

The owner or his authorized representative must appear before you and establish his identity to your satisfaction. The signature to the assignment or certification must be executed in your presence. Then you should fully complete and sign the certification form provided for your use.

If you are an employee (rather than an officer) authorized to certify assignments and certifications, insert the words "Authorized Signature " in the space provided for the title. Insert the place and date, as required, on the form. Impress the seal of your organization, or imprint in the space provided a "signature guaranteed" stamp, if your organization is a bank, or the issuing agent's dating stamp, if your organization is an authorized issuing agent for United States Savings Bonds of Series E. If assignment or certification is one a notary public is authorized to certify and you are a notary, impress your seal and insert the expiration date of your commission.

> NOTE: THE FURNISHING OF SOCIAL SECURITY NUMBERS IS REQUIRED BY THE GENERAL REGULATIONS GOVERNING UNITED STATES SECURITIES, I.E., DEPT. CIR. NO. 300, CUR. REV. THE NUMBERS ARE USED TO MAINTAIN OWNERSHIP RECORDS OF THE BONDS. OTHER INFORMATION REQUESTED BY THIS FORM IS ALSO REQUIRED UNDER THE ABOVE REGULATIONS TO ESTABLISH THE RIGHTS, AUTHORITY AND/OR ENTITLEMENT OF THE SIGNERS. FAILURE TO FURNISH ANY OF THE REQUESTED INFORMATION MAY PREVENT COMPLETION OF THE TRANSACTION.

can be used on all certificates whether they are in the old or new format. If you need to obtain a detached assignment form, always opt for the HUD form if your firm is a member of a national securities exchange. In this case, your own firm will be able to directly guarantee certificate endorsements. The P.D. 1832 is much more cumbersome to use.

Explanation of Assignment Procedures:

12. Assignment lines and tax ID number. The Social Security number or the tax ID number and the full name and address of the party in whose name this certificate is to be reregistered is recorded here. This area is not filled in when the certificate is going to be delivered in settlement of a sale, as in this example. It is used only when a certificate is going to be reregistered into a new name. A detached assignment form known as a transfer manifold is frequently used for this purpose.

13. Power of attorney line. Once a registered certificate is endorsed, it is negotiable. To prevent illegal negotiation of the certificate, the identity of the receiving broker or dealer is inserted on this line. Until the entity that has been granted power of attorney in this fashion signs a power of attorney release, the certificate cannot be transferred or otherwise negotiated even if the registered owner(s) have signed the certificate. Securities firms delivering certificates by messengers and customers mailing certificates to their brokers should both avail themselves of this protection.

14. Signature line. This is where the registered owner(s) of the certificate must sign the certificate when it is sold or otherwise being transferred. If a customer erroneously signs the certificate in any other area, an additional guarantee, known as a valid endorsement guarantee, must be added below other required guarantee endorsements. All signatures must correspond exactly to the form of the name as it appears on the face of the certificate.

15. Signature guarantee. All certificate endorsements must have a signature guarantee placed below the signed en-

dorsement. This guarantee must be signed by an authorized officer of a banking institution or brokerage firm that is a member of a national securities exchange. If the signature(s) that are guaranteed differ in any manner from the way that the certificate is registered, *OR* if the signature(s) are illegible, additional signed guarantees will be required.

MAINTAINING RECORDS OF CERTIFICATE NUMBERS

One of the advantages of a book-entry-only clearance mandate is that you no longer have to be concerned about losing a physical certificate. Envision a totally physical environment for a moment. All deliveries involve the physical delivery of one or more certificates. Hundreds, probably thousands, of certificates pass through the hands of a single employee in the course of a week; there may be dozens of employees involved in a large MBS processing area. Another firm calls the manager of the clearance area in your firm stating that they have never received the certificates you claimed you delivered the previous afternoon. Or your internal audit department advises you that a spot-check of your inventory in the vault indicates that $1 million par value MBS are missing. What would you do? Place a stop transfer on the missing securities! Right! But what are the specific certificates that are missing? The security that appears to be short has been actively traded back and forth dozens of times since the last audit. To place a stop you need to advise the transfer agent of the specific certificate number you want stopped. Obviously, you need to maintain a complete historical record of the certificate numbers received into and delivered out of your firm. You need to be able to relate those numbers to specific transactions so that you can isolate the particular certificates that are missing.

Every time a physical certificate is received into or delivered out of the firm, a record of the certificate number must be retained. Once the certificate is inside the firm, every time it moves from one area of responsibility to another, the number of the certificate must be recorded. All certificate numbers of securities moving into or out of the vault must be recorded. You must maintain these tight internal controls for two reasons. First, if a mechanical or human failure results in the unavailability of a number at a particular point in the processing cycle, you can reconstruct the flow if you have picked up the number at some other point. The chances of everyone making the same error with the same certificate are very slim. Second, there is always the possibility of internal loss and even theft. If a particular certificate number can be traced through its internal processing cycle, losses will be negligible and probably nonexistent.

Some firms accomplish the recording of certificate numbers by having their clerical staff record the numbers manually on the copies of their delivery manifolds and on their vault movement journals. It is far preferrable to microfilm each certificate. You retain not only certificate number information but also registration and date information, which is very important not only in loss situations but also for P&I claim purposes.

Microfilming is important, and there are several considerations about it to keep in mind. Always develop film promptly and examine it immediately to ensure that film has been properly exposed. Corrective measures must be taken if the film is blank. Several copies of each roll of film should be available with one copy being stored off the premises for emergency purposes. The final point on microfilming concerns firms that do not have their own microfilm equipment. Even if it is necessary to rent cameras for a day or two, all physical inventory should be microfilmed at least once a year.

DELIVERY AND RECLAMATION PROCESSING

When the actual receive or deliver process is being performed, your main concern should be "Is this a good delivery?" Does the certificate in your hands match the requirements of your instructions as to description and quantity? The quantity value instructions and the quantity value recorded on a certificate are both "face" so they must match. There is no need to be concerned about the current amortized amount. It is usually sufficient to match pool numbers to determine if you have the correct issue. The early FHLMC series 16 and 17 need to be closely examined, however, because identical numbers were assigned to issues with differing coupons and maturities. CMOs and REMICs usually have multiple classes per issue, so these classifications must be carefully matched. Remember to check the CUSIP number on the certificate with the number on the delivery bill. If they do not match, there is a good chance that you have a problem. Due-bill requirements also come under the heading of good delivery. Due bills are promissory notes that must accompany deliveries that settled on or before the P&I record date but are being delivered after the record date. The rationale is that the purchaser bought the issue with distribution but that delivery was not made in time to reregister the certificate by the record date. Therefore, the seller must provide payment.

All deliveries must be made on a timely basis in accordance with the schedule of delivery cutoff times shown in Table 12–1.

TABLE 12–1. Delivery Cutoff Schedules for Physical MBS Deliveries

Participant Classification	EST (EDST)
Customer to dealer	2:15
Dealer to broker	2:30
Broker to dealer	2:45
Dealer to dealer	3:00
Nondealer to nondealer	3:15
Dealer to customer	3:15
Reclamations	3:30

Establish delivery priorities according to this schedule. A dealer should complete its broker deliveries, dealer deliveries, and customer deliveries in that order. That is a general rule of thumb. Circumstances may necessitate failing on a less important broker delivery to ensure that a larger dealer delivery is made. Another problem frequently encountered is that certain customers may have been given dealer status (for delivery purposes) by senior management. Keep this list current to avoid serious fail problems resulting from "too late" delivery reclaims. The personnel in a firm's clearance department frequently become the first and only ones in the firm to learn about changes in its customers' settlement instructions. They become aware of these changes when a delivery that they made is returned to them DKed. A procedure should be in place to ensure that such information is properly communicated so that the name and address master files can be updated to reflect the required changes—thus avoiding additional and unnecessary financing costs.

While on the topic of DKs, let's discuss reclamations. A reclamation is the return of a delivery previously made because of an error or because you "don't know" (DK) the trade. The PSA has specific guidelines relative to the processing of reclamations that should be reviewed and understood. All reclamations must be made on a timely basis, must be acompanied by a copy of the contra-party's original delivery bill, and must contain the reason (and proof if applicable) of the validity of the reclamation. Many "recs" are done on a same-day basis. In such a situation, the receiving party does not return the certificates against payment. It simply does not make the wire payment the deliverer was expecting and advises the deliverer to pick up its securities, or it might redeliver them "free." Whichever method is used, the party initiating the reclamation should notify the contra-party as soon as it realizes it does not intend to pay for the delivery. Courtesy (or lack of it) is usually repaid. An acknowledgment of the reclamation in the form of a receipt for the returned securities should be obtained so that the reclaiming party can prove that the certificates were returned.

CONTROLLING DELIVERY ROUTES

Only if you have experienced the frenetic pace of a clearance department on a major settlement day can you appreciate the importance of managing the resources of your messenger staff. When you are dealing with physical deliveries, coordination between the clearance staff and the messenger staff is very important. On peak days, arrangements must be made beforehand to bring in temporary workers to handle the extra work load. During such periods, there must be close communication between the R&D and messenger departments to ensure that all major deliveries are made. It can take 30 minutes or more to make a physical delivery, so routing has to be carefully planned to enable a single messenger to make as many 'drops' in as narrow a geographic area as possible. The R&D people must advise the dispatcher of what their requirements are going to be, especially in the closing hour, to ensure the delivery of all transactions. As more GNMA issues are mandated for clearance through MBSCC, however, this becomes less of a problem.

PAYMENT PROCESS

When securities are physically delivered over the window, they are taken to the central receive window of the purchasing firm. Almost all such deliveries are accepted subject to examination and count, and only a receipt is given in exchange. Payment does not coincide with delivery. This practice is necessary for several reasons. Nonauthorized personnel do not have access to the people who will actually process and pay for securities; they work in a secured area that is protected by alarms and guards. Therefore, there is a need for an accessible central drop point for all securities and clearance-related materials. Because the receive window must function as an internal distribution center for a variety of materials, the person at the window has neither the time, the skills, nor the authority to execute the payment for a receive-versus-payment (RVP) transaction.

Once the delivered securities have been counted, the endorsements examined, and every other aspect of the delivery has been found to conform to the rules and terms of the trade, payment is authorized by using the firm's internal trade manifold as the authorization form. This is an important point. Cash payments must be controlled. All security movements and cash movements must have proper authorization, and trade tickets are a sufficient form of authorization. Very briefly, the reason they can be used to authorize cash payments is that all trading activity goes through several balancing steps in independent areas of the firm. Any fictitious or invalid trade would cause a break that would prevent further processing. In the absence of a trade instruction, manual cash payment requests are prepared. However, all such manual instructions must be properly authorized according to the procedures established by each individual organization.

Payment authorization takes the final form of a message to your bank to wire funds in accordance with the instructions that have been received from the delivering party. These instructions can be entered into your master files, and on entry of the proper authorization code, payment instructions can be preformatted and sent electronically to the bank without any manual intervention. Most payments will be made by a Fedwire. A Fed funds check is also an acceptable method of payment, but the process is cumbersome, time-consuming, and not the normal method of payment.

VAULT SECURITY

Whenever physical certificates are involved, vault facilities must be available. The vault (box) is always in a separate secured area of the cashier's department. Cashiering as a whole is a secured area, and only authorized personnel may enter it. Even authorized personnel may not enter the vault area unless they are part of the vault staff or have special authorization. A signature log should be provided to record the entry of such authorized persons.

Movement of securities out of the vault may be accomplished only under authorized instructions. Such instructions should be computerized so that the physical movement of certificates coincides with cage delivery requirements associated with trading activity. Miscellaneous movements of all customers' securities may be accomplished only on receipt (*not* the promise of receipt) of an authorization from the credit department. All movement in and out of the vault must be recorded and the certificates filmed or photostated. There are normally three separate areas in a vault, each represented by its own account (i.e., the box account, the seg account, and the safekeeping account). Certificates that are in the box can be in firm name, street name, or customer name, and they normally represent "working inventory." Working inventory could be used from sales, repos, deposits to a book-entry facility, and so on. Certificates in a seg location are registered in the name of the firm and represent certificates being held by a firm on behalf of its customers. Certificates in safekeeping are registered in the names of a firm's individual customers for whom the firm is providing custodial services.

When recording movements, accounting entries must be made to the proper box, seg, or safekeeping account. Debit, or "long," entries reflect a withdrawal of certificates, whereas credit, or "short," entries reflect a deposit. If the box account reflected a short position of 5MM GNMA Pool 58473, you would expect to find 5MM physical certificate(s) stored in the box area of the vault. Firms that carry retail customer accounts always have an inflow of securities from its customers, and these certificates are always stored in the vault. All inventory must be checked daily to determine if any of the securities deposited the previous day were eligible for a book-entry depository. If they are, they should be immediately removed from the firm's vault and deposited where appropriate. Never maintain possession of physical certificates unless there is no other alternative.

Because the inventory in any vault is a constantly moving flow of certificates, it is necessary to ensure that the physical inventory in the vault corresponds to your accounting records. Toward this end, periodic counts of all certificates must be made and the count totals matched to the totals for each issue as reflected on the records of the firm. These counts should not be executed by vault personnel; an internal audit staff is excellent for this purpose. Such counts, however, should be supervised by the supervisory staff of the vault for control purposes. In addition to these periodic counts, a full count must be made annually to coincide with the firm's year-end audit. This count is controlled by the firm's outside independent auditors. Any differences that are discovered as a result of a security count must be immediately reported to senior management and steps taken to locate the missing certificates. Because the certificate numbers of all physical securities are recorded, it is possible to reconstruct all activity and identify any particular certificate that may be missing. Once that has been determined, an immediate stop transfer must be filed with the transfer agent to prevent the reregistration of the certificate by an unauthorized party. Replacement proceedings should not be initiated until all efforts to find the missing certificate have been exhausted.

A final point to be made in connection with missing certificates is that SEC Regulation 240.17f–1 requires that all "reporting institutions" (which includes securities dealers) report the discovery of missing certificate(s) within one business day of the discovery. Such reports must be made to the Securities Information Center, Inc. (SIC) in Wellesley Hills, Massachusetts. People who are responsible for this function must thoroughly acquaint themselves with Regulation 17f–1 and the reporting procedures. Computerized linkage to the SIC data bases is available.

13

Book-Entry Depository Clearance

THE MBSCC DEPOSITORY DIVISION

Book-entry depositories were created to deal with the paper crunch that resulted from the ballooning volume of the 1960s. The purpose of a depository is to immobilize certificates and to create an environment in which deliveries can be made without physically handling a certificate. The best analogy available to explain a securities depository is your personal checking account. You and all other bank customers deposit your negotiable cash in a demand deposit account at a bank. The bank becomes a custodian for your funds. When you need your money, you draw a check to the payee. The check is your instruction to the bank to remove your funds from your account and give them to someone else. Provided funds are available in your account, your instructions will be honored; you never have to handle the actual cash. Even your deposits are probably rarely in the form of cash.

A securities depository works the same way. All members deposit their physical certificates which become part of a fungible mass available to each member to the extent of its own position. Instructions to deliver positions, either free or against payment, are executed. The contract values of the transactions received and delivered during the day against payment are netted at the end of the day, and a single dollar amount is paid or collected daily through the depository by each of its members.

The depository becomes the custodian for the securities that each member firm deposits into its proprietary, seg, agency, or pledgee account. The MBSCC has a custodial relationship with Chemical Bank, which is also the transfer agent for all GNMA issues. The physical certificates that are deposited are stored at Chemical as agent for the depository; all physical processing (i.e., depositing, withdrawing, transferring) is done at Chemical. However, all certificates are held in the depository's nominee name "MBSCC & Co." Positions are held in Jumbo certificate form. There is no readily available inventory to draw on, and physical withdrawals are almost totally prohibited.

MBSCC Depository Eligibility List

This listing indicates the specific GNMA products that are eligible and those in which trading is sufficient to produce daily closing prices. Specific coupons within each GNMA product have been previously designated by PSA. Those products in which trading is inadequate to produce daily closing prices are marked by an asterisk.

BD/GNMA I*	BD	=	Buydowns
CL/GNMA I*	CL	=	Construction Loans
GA/GNMA I* GA/GNMA II* }	GA	=	GEMs (Growing Equity Mortgages) which have payment increments of 4% per annum per life.
GD/GNMA I* GD/GNMA II* }	GD	=	GEMs (all others)
GP/GNMA I GP/GNMA II }	GP	=	GPMs (Graduated Payment Mortgages) which experience monthly payment increments for no more than the first five years after origination.
GT/GNMA I* GT/GNMA II* }	GT	=	GPMs which experience payment increases for no more than the first ten years after origination.
MH/GNMA I* MH/GNMA II* }	MH	=	Manufactured (Mobile) Homes
PL/GNMA I*	PL	=	Level payment Project Loans
PN/GNMA I*	PN	=	Non-level payment Project Loans
SF/GNMA I SF/GNMA II }	SF	=	Single Family
ARM/GNMA I* ARM/GNMA II*}	ARM	=	Adjustable Rate Mortgages

Clearance is accomplished through instructions that can be prefiled or issued the same day by paper, tape, on-line terminal, or automatic file transmissions. Participants can prioritize their instructions, which gives them the opportunity to maximize their turnarounds (fail control). The MBSCC will settle regular trades, repos and reverses, option transactions, and trades resulting from exercised options. The PSA has issued a ruling that if an issue is eligible for a book-entry depository, delivery must be effected in book-entry form. Most inventory positions are marked to the market daily, which enables the MBSCC to perform an exposure analysis by comparing intra-day cash debits to the marked value of the positions of each participant. Each participant is required to maintain sufficient collateral to offset the net amount of its market exposure. Deficits in required margin that are revealed during this analysis must be satisfied by the member with an immediate collateral deposit.

All deliveries and receipts that have been made during the day are netted into a single pay or collect figure that is settled with the MBSCC at the end of each day. This eliminates the present need for multiple wire payments and attendant fees.

The MBSCC also provides P&I services. Holders of record are guaranteed timely payment, regardless of receipt from the issuer. In the event the depository has not received payment from the paying agent, the MBSCC borrows the funds on behalf of its members and prorates the cost to the recipients of the payments. An interim accounting system will keep track of all receipts and deliveries requiring due bills, thus eliminating due-bill and claim processing. There is a repo accounting system that maintains the separate identities for both the contra-side and the beneficial owner, thereby eliminating P&I distribution problems associated with repo trading. Finally, the system provides for the use of a unique transaction identification number (TID). This number is assigned by the MBSCC system when you issue an instruction, and it is made known to both the initiator and contra-side of the instruction. It is useful in resolving problems between members because it is a common reference. It can also be used to call up a previous day's instruction that has not been processed. If you are referencing a TID number on a date other than the origination date, the original date must be included with the number.

In an effort to ensure an orderly conversion, book-entry processing is being phased in over an extended period; full implementation is expected by mid-1989. During the start-up phase, members can make bulk deposits of 200 or more pools. Bulk deposits are economical; the MBSCC has temporarily waived the

$10.00 reregistration fee and the $7.75 deposit fee that are ordinarily charged. The depository must be advised in writing of your intent to make a bulk deposit. It then notifies Chemical Bank, which prepares a sequential listing of certificates in each pool in your name that are outstanding. No sooner than two weeks later the certificates can be deposited (it must be on a Friday) using the computer listing as the deposit ticket. Nondeposits must be crossed off the listing. Bulk deposits may also be initiated via your MBSCC terminal, eliminating the need to update the hardcopy listing. The deposit must be completed by 11:00 A.M., and credit will be available on Monday morning. Deposits other than bulk deposits must be made no later than 11:00 A.M. daily; credit is given on the same day. Up to 10 certificate numbers for a single pool may be entered on a single deposit ticket. When depositing a GNMA II with multiple tails, you must deposit each tail on a separate ticket. Only the GNMA II Jumbos have multiple tails because the underlying loans (or pools) have multiple issuers. All nonbulk deposits are examined at the window. If there is a problem with any certificate, the entire deposit can be rejected.

Withdrawals can be made only by transfer reregistration to your customer's name. Withdrawal instructions must be accompanied by a letter from the initiating firm, explaining the reason for the withdrawal request. Unless there is a legal requirement for the issuance of physical certificates, the withdrawal request will be rejected. If accepted, a firm's transfer instructions can be for either same-day or future-day processing; a unique code is used for each. When a transfer instruction is entered, the system produces an audit print, which serves as a window ticket that the messenger presents to Chemical along with firm ID. Physical certificates will not be available for seven days.

The system provides the capability of building an instruction file that permits you to do an automatch on your receives and that gives you the opportunity to examine each incoming item and make individual decisions on each. The auto/pend instruction is set up by account. So it may be wise to pend all transactions for your proprietary account, and use the auto feature only for your seg items.

Pending receive and deliver instructions can be input as much as one year in advance of settlement. The system can bind (i.e., associate a particular TID with another) so that only completion of a particular transaction will trigger the execution of the

Book-Entry Depository Clearance

contra-instruction. You can bind as many as ten different transactions to each other; care must be taken to ensure that the aggregate face amounts of your deliveries do not exceed the aggregate face amount of the receive instructions. Instructions may be canceled at any time provided they have not yet been processed. When an item is DKed through the system, multiple codes are available to identify the reason for the DK. There is also room for additional free-form trailer information that can be used to provide the contra-party with additional information or to record information that may be useful in your own internal processing. All securities that are fully paid for customer positions *must be segregated* from the remainder of your inventory positions. Any position that is in your seg account may not be used by the MBSCC for *any* reason. There is no provision in the system for the execution of a buy-in. The term buy-in as used by the MBSCC refers to *the receive process*.

TABLE 13–1. MBSCC Depository Cutoff Schedule for Designated Coupons[a]

Opening of Business	6:45 A.M.
(Inquiries & pended transactions)	
Book-Entry Movements	7:00 A.M.
Deposits	11:00 A.M.
(Same-day credit for a maximum of 200 pools per day per participant)	
Withdrawals	3:00 P.M.
(Availability in 2 calendar days)	
Book Entry	3:00 P.M.
Reclamations	3:30 P.M.
Pay & Collect (Final)	3:45 P.M.
Wires to MBSCC (Debits)	4:15 P.M.
Wires from MBSCC (Credits)	5:00 P.M.
Seg Movements (Same Day)	6:00 P.M.
Pended Transactions (Next Day)	6:00 P.M.
Hard Copy & Tape Output	8:00 P.M. to 10:00 P.M.
Tape Input	12:00 A.M. (midnight)

[a]All times are EST and are subject to change depending upon the needs of the depository and its participants.

FINANCING SUPPORT THROUGH
THE COLLATERAL LOAN FACILITY

One area that is particularly cumbersome for participants is the collateralizing of loans in today's physical environment. Borrowers, lenders, and the depository are all concerned with credit and risk issues as well as the need to efficiently complete a substantial number of activities in a very short time.

The Collateral Loan Facility (CLF) was designed to make the loan process efficient and straightforward while maintaining the individual controls required by each entity. Further, credit/risk concerns were paramount in the design of this function.

The depository's system for collateral loans provides for credit verification, transfer of control of the collateral securities from the pledgor to the pledgee, principal and interest processing, and appropriate pledgor and pledgee control. The system also provides for audit trails and ensures the maintenance of adequate collateralization and margin.

CLF provides participants with an automated means of identifying securities a borrower pledges, via book entry, to a participating lender. It can also be used to maintain records of the collateral a borrower has pledged to a nonparticipant (Held-in-Custody Repos and Tri-Party). In addition, CLF provides for documentation, selection, and the application of customized lender margin requirements. CLF transactions may be versus payment or free.

For any CLF executed the borrower must satisfy the minimum margin requirements of the depository. This minimum margin of 5% must be satisfied even if the lender's requirements are more liberal.

CLF loans are secured through the following steps.

Loans with a Depository Participant as Lender

1. Borrower identifies the terms of the loan, the collateral, and the lending participant's pledge account through the

CLF command. Collateral may be selected automatically by the system according to specifications given by the borrower, or pools may be individually allocated.

2. The lender participant reviews and accepts or rejects the collateral listed. Rejected collateral may be substituted by the borrower.

3. The lender accepts the CLF, creating a credit for the loan amount to the account of the borrower and a corresponding debit to the account of the lender. CLFs may be executed free with payment arranged outside the depository.

4. At the termination of the loan the lender returns the CLF, relinquishing control of the securities and reversing the account debits and credits.

Loans with a Nondepository Participant as Lender

1. The borrower identifies the terms of the loan, the collateral, and the borrower's hold in custody account through the CLF command.

2. Upon or prior to the execution of the CLF the borrower may produce a report for the nonparticipant lender which identifies the terms of the loan and the exact collateral pledged.

   Multiple CLF transactions may be executed to one or more HIC accounts while still maintaining complete records of the segregation of collateral. Each loan can be identified and the collateral which corresponds to the loan is listed, in a report, for each lender.

3. When the loan is repaid the borrower executes the instruction to return the collateral from the HIC account.

FIGURE 13-1. Loans with a Depository Participant as Lender

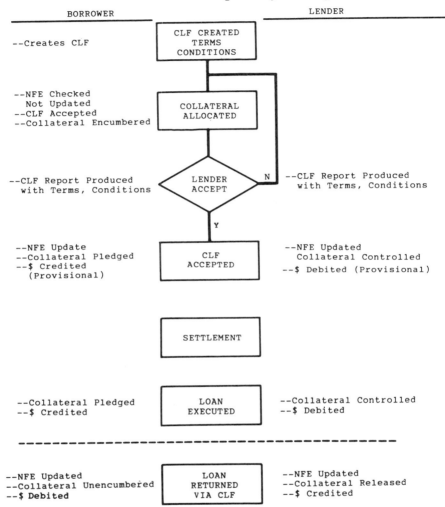

FIGURE 13–2. Loans with a Nondepository Participant as Lender

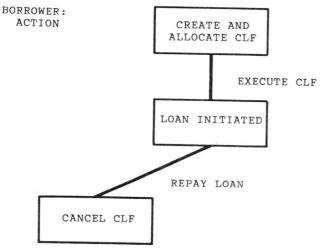

BORROWER:
    ACTION

CREATE AND
ALLOCATE CLF

EXECUTE CLF

LOAN INITIATED

REPAY LOAN

CANCEL CLF

PENDING CORPORATE STRUCTURAL CHANGES FOR MBSCC DEPOSITORY

Negotiations are continuing aimed at changing the structure of the MBSCC Depository. It is anticipated that it will become a participant-owned organization in the second quarter of 1989. At the time that this is accomplished the name of the depository will be changed to Participants Trust Company or PTC. Upon completion of the transfer of ownership to the membership, PTC will become both a limited purpose trust company and a member of the Federal Reserve Bank of NY.

14

Clearance—Special Product Considerations

There are two final clearance topics which need to be addressed. The first is the latest product addition to the securitized debt marketplace, namely, asset-backed securities. The second is the latest addition to the list of clearing entities who are involved in the mortgage-backed and asset-backed marketplaces—The Depository Trust Company (DTC).

ASSET-BACKED SECURITIES

The principal behind an asset-backed security (ABS) is similar to the principal behind the formation of a collateralized mortgage obligation. An ABS is a bond which evidences a prorata ownership in a pool or group of consumer debt loans; the majority pay interest on a quarterly basis. There can be a great diversity in the type of collateral used to create and back these issues. An ABS might be backed by consumer installment loans such as VISA or MasterCharge loans, by installment contracts on personal property such as computers, by automobile loans, and even by liens on race horses. Payments of interest can be made on a monthly pass-through basis or on a quarterly basis. The issues are normally triple-A-rated instruments. This high rating can be achieved through an overcollateralization of the issue. Such is the case of ABSs backed by consumer loans. A $100MM issue would typically be backed with a minimum of $110MM in loans. This 10% overcollateralization (the minimum amount) adequately secures the loans which historically have a 3% to 5% default record. ABSs backed by real property, such as automobiles, frequently have some type of indirect insurance associated with the underlying loans and/or a surety bond which guarantees the distribution of principal and interest on the due dates. Figure 14–1 is the facing page of a prospectus issued in connection with the distribution of an ABS secured by new and used car loans and a surety bond. In a recent article, *The New York Times* indicated that we can expect to see a tremendous expansion in volume and collateral diversity relative to ABSs during the next several years.

CLEARANCE CONSIDERATIONS FOR ABSs

These issues are cleared either physically or through the book- entry facilities of The Depository Trust Company. For those securities which are handled physically, the rules are basically the same as those discussed in Chapter 12. All certificates delivered must be properly signed and guaranteed. Detached assignments are accomplished through the use of a corporate bond power as shown in Figure 14–2. Payment is made via a Fed funds wire. Most ABSs pay principal and interest on the 15th day of each month to holders of record on the last day of each month. The current month's factor is not available until a couple of days prior to payment date. Therefore, if a trade has a settlement date during the first two weeks of the month, the trade will settle on the previous month's factor. In calculating principal and interest on the previous month's factor, the principal amount will reflect an amount in excess of the true outstanding principal since each month the principal will pay down. When the current month's factor is available, the trade will have to be cancelled and corrected to reflect the proper amount of principal for the month in which the trade settles. The buyer must be reimbursed for the amount of the difference by the seller; provisions must be made for the prompt collection of these funds.

THE DEPOSITORY TRUST COMPANY

DTC is a book-entry clearing facility. Although its services are new to the MBS and ABS industry, DTC commenced its opera-

FIGURE 14–1. Prospectus for Auto Receivable-Backed Security

PROSECTUS

$87,500,000 (Approximate)

UST FASTBACs 1988-A Grantor Trust

7.85% Auto Receivable Backed Certificates

Series 1988-A, Final Distribution Date April 20, 1991

USTrust/Norfolk (Seller/Master Servicer)

Full and complete payment of the Interest Payment and the Principal Payment on each Distribution Date, and payment of the remaining Aggregate Scheduled Balance of the Contracts on the Final Distribution Date, is unconditionally and irrevocably guaranteed pursuant to a Surety Bond issued by

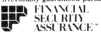

FINANCIAL
SECURITY
ASSURANCE ™

Interest, to the extent of the Pass-Through Rate of 7.85% per annum, will be distributed to Certificateholders on January 20, April 20, July 20, and October 20 of each year (the "Distribution Dates") commencing July 20, 1988 and ending April 20, 1991 (the "Final Distribution Date"). Principal Payments will be distributed to Certificateholders on each Distribution Date, to and including the Final Distribution Date, as described herein.

Each Certificate offered hereby will represent a fractional undivided interest in the UST FASTBACs 1988-A Grantor Trust (the "Trust") to be formed by USTrust/Norfolk (the "Bank"). The Trust property will include (i) a pool of retail installment sales contracts and installment loans secured by new and used automobiles (the "Contracts") and (ii) a Surety Bond issued by Financial Security Assurance Inc. ("Financial Security"). Each Contract was or will be originated by a motor vehicle dealer and purchased by the Bank. USTrust/Middlesex or USTrust/Essex or was or will be originated by one of such banks. In general, it is intended that Certificateholders receive on each Distribution Date (a) an Interest Payment equal to interest at the Pass-Through Rate on the Aggregate Scheduled Balance of the Contracts from the preceding Distribution Date (or from April 20, 1988 in the case of the first Distribution Date) and (b) a Principal Payment equal to the decline in the Scheduled Balances of the Contracts in respect of such Distribution Date as defined herein (including liquidations and full prepayments). Under the Surety Bond, Financial Security will unconditionally and irrevocably guarantee payment of the Interest Payment and the Principal Payment on each Distribution Date. In addition, on the Final Distribution Date Financial Security will be obligated under the Surety Bond to pay an amount equal to the Aggregate Scheduled Balance of the remaining Contracts for pass-through to Certificateholders. The Bank will act as master servicer of the Contracts and will have certain other limited obligations with respect thereto. Contracts not originated by the Bank will initially be subserviced by the respective banks that originated such Contracts.

The initial Aggregate Scheduled Balance of the Contracts will be approximately $87,500,000. The Final Distribution Date will be April 20, 1991. The Bank will have the option to repurchase all of the Contracts, and thereby cause early retirement of the Certificates, after the Aggregate Scheduled Balance of the Contracts is less than 10% of the aggregate initial principal amount of the Certificates. In addition, so long as no default under the Surety Bond has occurred and is continuing, if Financial Security has made a payment under the Surety Bond on at least two consecutive Distribution Dates and has not been reimbursed for the amount thereof from the funds in an account established by the Bank for the purpose of providing for such reimbursement or from other sources of funds available to cover losses. Financial Security shall have the right to purchase the Contracts and thereby cause early retirement of the Certificates.

It is a condition of issuance that the Certificates be rated "AAA" by Standard & Poor's Corporation and "Aaa" by Moody's Investors Service, Inc. on the basis of the issuance of the Surety Bond by Financial Security.
For a discussion of certain factors relating to this offering, see "Special Considerations."

THE CERTIFICATES REPRESENT INTERESTS IN THE TRUST AND ARE NOT INSURED OR GUARANTEED BY THE BANK, ANY OF ITS AFFILIATES, THE FEDERAL DEPOSIT INSURANCE CORPORATION, OR ANY OTHER PERSON OR ENTITY.
THESE SECURITIES HAVE NOT BEEN APPROVED OR DISAPPROVED BY THE SECURITIES AND EXCHANGE COMMISSION NOR HAS THE COMMISSION PASSED UPON THE ACCURACY OR ADEQUACY OF THIS PROSPECTUS. ANY REPRESENTATION TO THE CONTRARY IS A CRIMINAL OFFENSE.

	Price to Public(1)	Underwriting Discount	Proceeds to Bank(1)(2)
Per Certificate	99.890625%	.400%	99.490625%
Total (Approximate)	$87,404,296.88	$350,000	$87,054,296.88

(1) Plus accrued interest, if any, from and including April 20, 1988.
(2) Before deducting expenses payable by the Bank estimated to be $252,000.

The Certificates are offered by Drexel Burnham Lambert Incorporated (the "Underwriter"), subject to prior sale, when, as and if delivered to and accepted by the Underwriter and subject to approval of certain legal matters by counsel. It is expected that delivery of the Certificates will be made against payment therefor on or about April 20, 1988, at the offices of the Underwriter, 60 Broad Street, New York, New York.

Drexel Burnham Lambert
INCORPORATED

March 24, 1988

FIGURE 14–2. Detached Bond Power Assignment

OFF	ACCOUNT NO.	T	CK	RR #

IRREVOCABLE STOCK OR BOND POWER

FOR VALUE RECEIVED, the undersigned does (do) hereby sell, assign and transfer to

_____

_____

_____ | _____

(SOCIAL SECURITY OR TAXPAYER IDENTIFYING NO.)

IF STOCK, COMPLETE THIS PORTION
{ _____ shares of the _____ stock of _____

represented by Certificate(s) No(s). _____ inclusive,

standing in the name of the undersigned on the books of said Company.

IF BONDS, COMPLETE THIS PORTION
{ _____ bonds of _____

in the principal amount of $ _____ , No(s) _____ inclusive,

standing in the name of the undersigned on the books of said Company.

The undersigned does (do), hereby, irrevocably constitute and

appoint _____ attorney

to transfer the said stock or bond(s), as the case may be, on the books of said Company.

with full power of substitution in the premises.

Dated _____

IMPORTANT—READ CAREFULLY   Sign Here _____
The signature(s) to this Power must correspond with the name(s) as written upon the face of this certificate(s) or bond(s) in every particular without alteration or enlargement or any change whatever. Signature guarantee should be made by a member or member organization of the New York Stock Exchange, members of other Exchanges having signatures on file with transfer agent or by a commercial bank or trust company having its principal office or correspondent in the City of New York.

_____
(PERSON(S) EXECUTING THIS POWER SIGN(S) HERE)

SIGNATURE GUARANTEED

FC-125

tions in 1968 when it began to provide book-entry delivery of immobilized certificates for the corporate equity markets. Generally its services include:

❑ The acceptance of deposits which it holds in custody and services for its participants. Servicing of the positions includes the distribution of payments such as P&I.

❑ The execution of book-entry deliveries via valued accounting entries, debited and/or credited to its participants, which are netted and settled in a single transfer of monies at the end of the day.

❑ Pledging collateral for its participants' financing purposes.

❑ Providing for physical withdrawals from the system as required and permitted under terms of the original issuance.

DTC has two distinct systems: its Next-Day Funds Settlement (NDFS) system and its Same-Day Funds Settlement (SDFS) system. Participants must maintain a separate account for each system; each plays a role in the MBS/ABS industry. Before reviewing the use of each system, an explanation of the two-tiered monetary structure in the United States is appropriate.

Transactions in the U.S. securities market are settled in either clearinghouse funds (CHF) or in Fed funds (FF). The choice is not an optional one, it is predicated by the type of instrument traded. CHF represent funds which have next-day cash availability; regular bank checks are CHF instruments. Checks are nothing more than instructions to move cash balances from one banking location to another. Each evening checks undergo a clearing process whereby balances, represented by the checks negotiated during that day, are moved between the banking institutions involved. The "movements" are completed during the night-processing cycle and the funds are available as cash on the next business day. On the other hand, FF are considered to be immediately available funds; the clearing/collection process is unnecessary—they are the equivalent of cash and are what is used in the settlement of the check clearing process. Since FF are available as cash a day earlier than CHF, there is a premium attached to them. That premium is the equivalent of a full day's interest on the amount involved. So, if you were to pay for a delivery made to your firm in FF and redelivered the same securities that same day versus CHF, you would incur a loss equal to the value of one day's interest.

DTC's NEXT-DAY FUNDS SETTLEMENT (NDFS) SYSTEM

Asset-backed securities that have been issued in book-entry format are cleared within DTC's NDFS system. In this system instructions are given to DTC to deliver securities from the account of the member originating the instructions to another member's account. The contract value of the delivery is indicated on the instruction which is usually entered via DTC's on-line terminal system known as the participants terminal system (PTS). The delivery orders (DOs) will be executed provided the originator has a position sufficient to fulfill the order. If not, the order will pend until sufficient quantities are either received from other members or deposited by the originator of the instruction. Each settlement delivery will result in a credit being placed in the participant's account; each receipt generates a debit. At the end of the day a clearinghouse check will be paid to DTC if the participant's account contains a net debit for the day's activity; the participants receive a check for their credit balances. Balancing controls which have been previously described are applicable. An important note to make is that the normal cutoff time for NDFS deliveries is 11:30 A.M. EST; deliveries on the first day of issuance are extended to 1:15 P.M. EST. If an ABS issue is eligible for book-entry delivery, delivery must be accepted via NDFS unless otherwise agreed to by both parties at the time of the trade.

DTC's SAME-DAY FUNDS SETTLEMENT (SDFS) SYSTEM

Collateralized mortgage obligations which have been made eligible for DTC book entry will clear through the SDFS system. The services provided within SDFS are similar to those described in the DTC overview. Instructions must be processed through either the PTS or computer-to-computer facilities (CCFs). Instructions for normal deliveries will be accepted until 2:00 P.M. EST daily; an extra half hour is provided for recycling and repo deliveries. The major differences between SDFS and NDFS are twofold:

❑ SDFS is a same-day funds (Fed funds) settlement system, and final settlement occurs through the Fedwire via a settlement bank.

❑ Instructions will be executed only if a participant's net collateral within the system, which includes the value of the firm's proprietary positions, is sufficient to cover any net debit that would exist in its settlement account after the execution of the instruction.

We have already discussed the ramifications of Fed funds, so let us skip directly to the second point that relates to the risk-management features of SDFS. Because transactions are being executed on a "cash" basis, it is extremely important to insulate the system from the risk of failure by any of its members. Such a failure could possibly prevent DTC from paying other members the funds to which they were entitled, and would be catastrophic to the overall marketplace. In an effort to prevent such a situation from occurring, DTC requires each participant to make a cash and securities deposit to the SDFS fund, a sort of participants' omnibus fund whose assets are used to ensure the safety of the system. These assets would be used to satisfy the debt of a failing member. In addition to contributions to this fund, each participant is also subject to a net debit cap that effectively establishes a limit or a cap on the net debit settlement amount that each member can incur. The net debit cap is the lesser of

❑ 10 times the participant's mandatory and voluntary deposits to the SDFS fund **or**

❑ 75% of DTC's lines of credit with lenders, *or* and amount determined by the participant's settling bank, *or* an amount determined by DTC.

Obviously each participant can affect the amount of its net debit cap through increased voluntary contributions to the SDFS fund.

CONTROL FEATURES

In an effort to prevent entries that might create erroneous debits in the accounts of receiving participants, DTC has built the following controls into the SDFS system. The receiver authorized delivery (RAD) option can be used if a participant wishes to authorize all delivery and payment orders directed to his account or only those orders which exceed a certain dollar value. If a participant notifies DTC that he wishes to utilize this option, DTC sends an authorization request via PTS to the receiving participant each time an order is entered into the system which is subject to this control. The receiver can access on his PTS screen all transactions awaiting authorization; any which are not authorized will be dropped from the system at 2:45 P.M. EST. However, good transactions that are not authorized will subject the receiving participant to compensation claims.

SDFS also edits all DOs. It compares the settlement value of each delivery to its current market value. If the DO is not overvalued, the system will act on the delivery order. If there is a moderate overvaluation, a warning notification is sent to the receiver and the deliverer. If the DO is substantially overvalued, the receiver is sent an authorization message that must be acted upon before the delivery will be permitted.

15

Financing and Money Management

Having completed the chapters covering clearance, it is natural to expect that the next topic would be the control and management of fails, the settled trades that were not cleared on the settlement date. Before discussing fails, however, it is important to understand why so much emphasis is placed on fail controls. The primary goal of a fail control group is to reduce the financing requirements of the firm. What is financing? What is being financed?

No single answer to these questions will satisfy all situations. You can get a quick grasp on the matter, however, by thinking of yourself in the role of an entrepreneur with $15,000.00 available cash (equity) who is beginning a new business servicing home computers. Your working capital is sufficient to purchase necessary equipment and to rent a functional office for three months. You need $5,000.00 more to purchase replacement supplies to get started, so you get a loan from your friendly banker (she understands), using your newly purchased equipment as collateral. You've leveraged your $15,000.00 equity into $20,000.00 of working capital by financing the cost of your supplies; you're on your way to success. You are also in debt, and interest has to be paid on your $5,000.00 loan. The faster you get paid for your services, the faster you can pay off your debt to reduce your interest costs. More important, good cash flow will add equity to your firm, and that equity can also be leveraged by getting additional loans to expand your business. Now, you really are on your way!

All business organizations require capital—cash or its equivalent—to operate. All security investment firms are businesses. These businesses, particularly if the investment firm is a dealer organization, are some of the most highly leveraged businesses in the world. The greater the extent to which you have leveraged the equity of your firm through a series of successive loans and reinvestments, the greater will be your need to control the interest costs associated with those loans. Only an example can put this statement in focus with the impact that is absolutely necessary if you are to appreciate the importance of this topic.

Let us create a new mortgage-backed securities dealer firm that we will call BASIC MBS, Inc. After all start-up expenses for equipment, leases, and personnel have been met, BASIC has $10,000,000.00 (10MM) cash, representing the contributed equity of the investors in the firm. Being an MBS dealer, the firm's traders purchase with the available cash $10 million worth of MBS on their first day in business. The available cash is now depleted, but a 10MM inventory falls far short of being an adequate market-maker (dealer) base. BASIC needs to expand its ability to actively participate in the trading market by increasing the size of its trading inventory position.

On day two, therefore, the firm uses the fully paid securities in its inventory trading account as collateral for a loan. Using government guaranteed MBS, BASIC can obtain a loan equivalent to 95% of the market value of the collateral. The $10 million worth of inventory has a loan value of 9.5MM, which is borrowed. The original inventory is pledged as collateral, and the cash received is used to buy more MBS. Continuing with the same business philosophy, on day three BASIC "hocks" the additional 9.5MM worth of inventory, receiving a 9.025MM loan, and purchases an equivalent amount of securities. On day four, the amount involved is 8.574MM, and so on. If BASIC were to fully leverage its equity, a trading inventory valued at approximately 200MM could be attained from the original 10MM cash base.

In Table 15–1, the meanings of the abbreviated column heads are as follows:

COB	=	close of business (D1 = day one)
INVEN	=	market value of the trading account inventory (par value is assumed throughout example)
LV	=	loan value of securities in inventory (95%)
EOD LNS	=	end-of-day loan amount or cash borrowed
AVAIL	=	cash that can be borrowed (LV minus EOD LNS)
INT EXPNS	=	daily interest on outstanding loans that must be paid to the bank (assume a 7% interest rate throughout)
**	=	maximum amount of securities that can be purchased without bringing additional capital into the firm

Note: A scenario of successive daily loan increases has been depicted for the sake of clarity. In reality this process could and probably would take place over a much shorter period than indicated by the example.

TABLE 15–1. Ledger Balances of BASIC MBS, Inc. (Close of Business Daily) [a]

COB	INVEN	LV	EOD LNS	AVAIL	INT EXPNS
D1	10.000	9.500	00.000	9.500	$ 00
D2	19.500	18.525	9.500	9.025	$ 1,847
D3	28.525	27.099	18.525	8.574	$ 3,602
D4	37.099	35.244	27.099	8.145	$ 5,269
D5	45.244	42.982	35.244	7.738	$ 6,853
D6	52.982	50.333	42.982	7.351	$ 8,358
D7	60.333	57.316	50.333	6.983	$ 9,786
**	200.000 [b]	190.000	190.000	0.000	$36,944 [c]

[a] Figures expressed in millions (MM) except interest amounts.
[b] Standard margin calculations prove the validity of this figure:
Loan Value × Inverted Margin Requirement = Buying Power.
LV = 10MM × 0.95 = 9.5MM margin required = 5%.
Inverted = 100/5, or 20.
9,500,000 × 20 = 190,000,000 plus 10,000,000 cash purchase = 200MM**.
[c] Represents an interest cost of nearly $13.5 million per annum.

The illustration in Table 15–1 shows how a firm can take 10MM of equity and leverage that into a 200MM trading position. Financing is simply borrowing the capital required to operate; the interest due on the borrowed funds is *an expense that reduces profits*. From a dealer's standpoint, the major component of financing is the cost of carrying inventory (i.e., the trading positions). The firm does not have the available cash to purchase outright the hundreds of millions of dollars of inventory that it maintains in its role as a marketmaker. The annual interest cost associated with the borrowing in the example is $13.5 million.

OTHER FINANCING COMPONENTS
AND THE NEED FOR CONTROL

Financing costs do not stop with the interest costs associated with maintaining an inventory. There are other major components, including the following:

❑ Customers' debit balances in both cash and margin accounts.
❑ Uncollected funds resulting from fails to deliver.
❑ Cash receivables such as uncollected P&I payments.

Although substantial funds may be represented by customers' debits, the control of those balances and their impact on the P&L of a firm are not discussed in this book.

So, on to the second topic. Why do fails to deliver have an impact on financing? Because they represent uncollected cash that should be available to the firm. When securities are sold to another broker or dealer, payment for the sale is not received until the securities are delivered. Making certain that the delivery is made on the settlement date of the trade is the responsibility of the clearance division. The management and the traders of a firm know when the securities they sold are settling. On that day, they expect that the proceeds of the sales will be available for new investments or to pay off outstanding loans. Whenever cash is not available on the date it is due, the daily interest value on that cash is the minimum amount that is lost by the firm *each calendar day* that it is not received. Have you ever had the misfortune of being responsible for failing to deliver 25MM over a holiday weekend?

Even if the fail is cleaned up the next business day, that fail will have cost the firm four days' interest (Friday, Saturday, Sunday, and Monday). At a 7% rate of interest, that single fail will cost a firm nearly $14,500 in additional interest or carrying costs. That is the impact of a single item. What is the average dollar amount associated with the fail-to-deliver account at the firm for which you work? Is it $5MM, $10MM, $25MM, or $50MM? At 7%, the interest expense associated with these figures ranges from $350,000.00 to $3,500,000.00 per year. These amounts are additional expenses, losses. They are also, to a large extent, either avoidable or recoverable. The need to control fails is obvious.

All types of cash receivables represent funds that are past due. Again, had they been available on a timely basis, they would have been either reinvested or used to reduce outstanding loans. Consider the receivables associated with the monthly principal and interest payments due to your firm and its customers. As you will see when we discuss P&I processing, these receivables can become enormous if not tightly controlled. As a result of the abnormally high trading volume that took place in early 1987, more than one firm had P&I receivables in the tens of millions of dollars. Using the same ranges that were used in the preceding paragraph plus the interest costs for the inventory in the example, you can compile a staggering annual expense figure:

Interest on a 200MM inventory	$13,500,000.00
Interest on 50MM average fail to deliver	3,500,000.00
Interest on 50MM average P&I receivable	3,500,000.00
Total annual interest expense	$20,500,000.00

These are your major financing costs! The cost of financing your inventory is an expected cost. It can be reduced through proper money management, but it is an unavoidable cost of doing business. The balance of the interest expense shown, 34% of the total, is avoidable to a large extent. Methods for reducing these unnecessary costs are discussed in Chapter 16.

FINANCING METHODS AND MONEY MANAGEMENT

Now that you can readily identify where your financing needs originate, you need to understand some of the more common methods used to secure the funds required to operate a firm.

There are numerous methods of financing, and although each is an expense, certain methods are less costly than others and you should therefore use the cheapest source of funds to the fullest extent possible. It is important to reiterate that this discussion is about financing the firm and that the firm's, not customers' securities, are the collateral being used in each example. Rules for customer collateral are different and are not part of this material.

The cheapest source of funds are master note loan agreements. These loans are arranged through the trust investment division of a bank or through a parent organization, such as General Electric, which is the owner of Kidder Peabody. The interest rates on such notes can be considerably lower than the brokers' call rate. However, the notes must be negotiated for a minimum amount, so it is important to fully understand the trading goals of your firm to ensure that it is not overcommitted for funds that it does not require or for an amount that will have a negative impact on its ability to maintain relationships with a bank(s) brokers' loan division.

The most costly method of financing is borrowing through collateralized overnight bank loans. The interest rates on these loans is the brokers' call rate, a rate that is lower than prime. If this is the most expensive route to take, why use it at all? First, there is a significant interdependency within the banking/brokerage industry, and a certain number of these loans are maintained for reasons of business relationships. Furthermore, each day's final financing requirement is different, and the required amount is not known until the end of each day. All trade settlement, clearance, and money movement activities must be consolidated daily at the end of the clearance cycle. Only when all this activity has been accounted for does a firm know the exact amount of money it needs to borrow to meet its obligations. By that time of day, the collateral loan is probably the only source of funds available.

A large percentage of a dealer's financing requirements not covered by master note agreements will be met through the use of repos, which carry a lower interest cost than overnight collateralized bank loans. Although a repo is a financing vehicle, legally it is not considered a loan. A repo or repurchase agreement is the sale of a security for a stipulated dollar amount. Simultaneous to the sale, the seller *agrees to repurchase* from the buyer the same securities for the same dollar amount plus the equivalent of accrued interest based on a negotiated rate determined at the time of the original sale. This rate will be lower than the rate associated with an overnight loan because the funds that will be paid to the seller of the repo usually represent very short-term excess cash being invested by an institution that does not want to subject itself to the interest rate risks associated with money market investments. That safety and the length of the contract (many are overnight contracts) result in lower premiums to the lenders and less expensive financing for the dealer. The term of the repo (the length of time between the date of sale and the repurchase date) is also mutually agreed on at the time of sale. As stated, most repos are overnight contracts with extended terms of a week or a month being common. The value of the securities sold slightly exceeds the contract value of the repo; all repo contracts are for Fed funds and are "cash trades"—that is, they settle on the same day that the trade is executed. An important fact concerning repos is that the seller retains the beneficial rights to all P&I payments that accrue on the issue(s) sold under a repurchase agreement.

Figure 15–1 illustrates a repo sale having a contract value of 1MM.

On November 7, 1988, Dealer A will deliver the designated MBS to Institution B which will pay Dealer A $1,000,000.00. Dealer A has the use of this cash overnight and uses it to reduce his borrowing requirements at the end of the day. On the following day, the termination date of this contract, Institution B delivers the MBS back to Dealer A and receives payment in the amount of $1,000,184.03. This amount represents the contract value of the repo plus compensation for the use of Institution B's cash at the agreed-on rate of 6 5/8%.

A firm can also execute a reverse repo; funds will be paid out for securities received. Those securities can be used to generate cash by using them for a delivery that was temporarily tied up as a result of internal processing (e.g., a transfer). When using the securities in this manner, however, the purchaser must be sure of being able to return the same issue to the seller on the termination date of the reverse repo and to protect the seller on all P&I distributions. A major source of financing revenue comes from what is known as the "match book," in which repos and reverses of the same collateral are matched with income being derived from the rate spread.

FIGURE 15-1. Standard Repo Order Contract

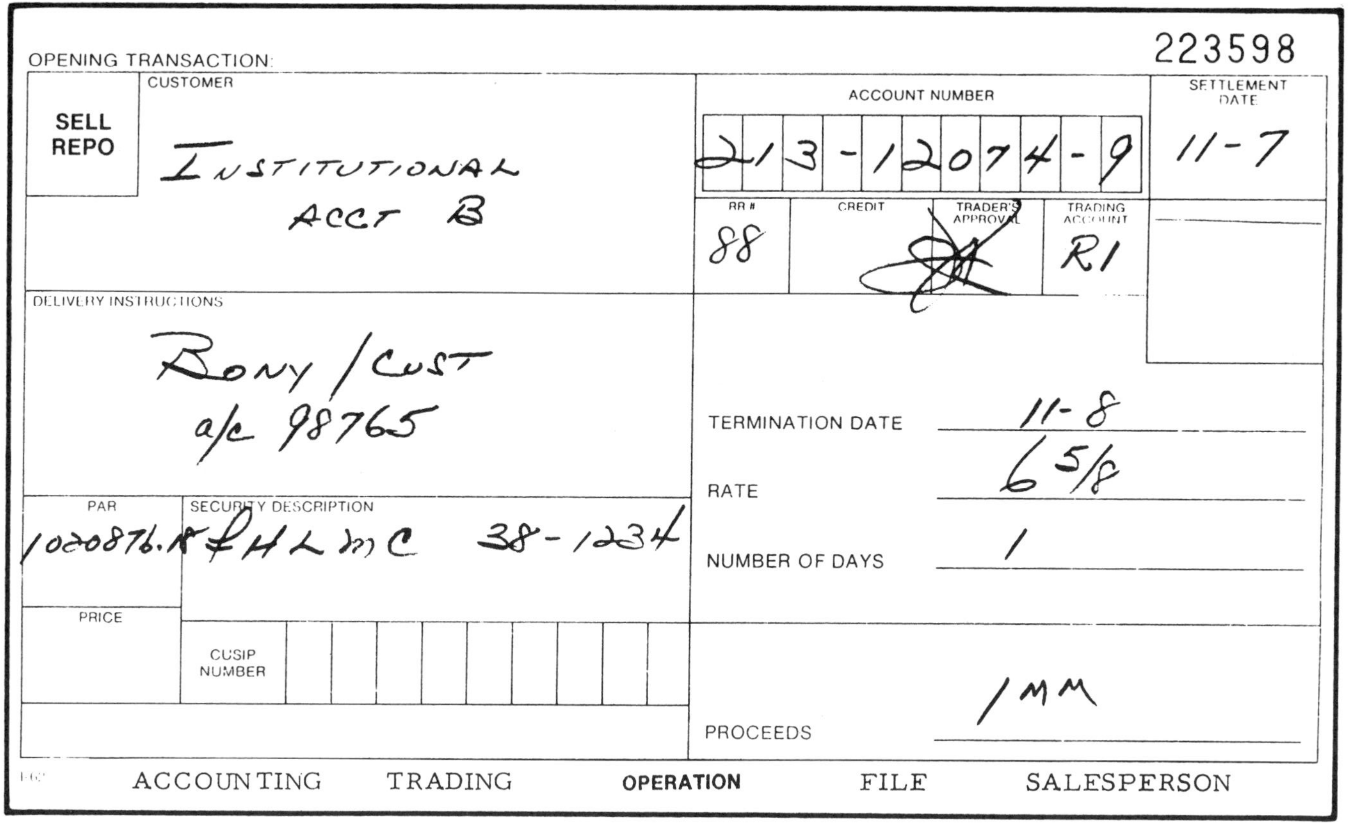

OPENING TRANSACTION:

223598

CUSTOMER

SELL
REPO

Institutional
Acct B

ACCOUNT NUMBER

2 / 3 - 1 2 0 7 4 - 9

RR #
88

CREDIT

TRADER'S
APPROVAL

TRADING
ACCOUNT
RI

SETTLEMENT
DATE
11-7

DELIVERY INSTRUCTIONS

Bony / Cust
_a/c 98765_

TERMINATION DATE   11-8

RATE   6 5/8

NUMBER OF DAYS   1

PAR
1020876.00

SECURITY DESCRIPTION
FHLMC   38-1234

PRICE

CUSIP
NUMBER

PROCEEDS   1 mm

ACCOUNTING   TRADING   OPERATION   FILE   SALESPERSON

257

Before leaving our discussion of repos, it is important to point out that although repos are not subject to the interest rate risk related to market losses, there are credit considerations to be kept in mind. The creditworthiness of the contra-side—that is, the ability of the contra-party to honor the terms of the contract—is crucial. Hand in hand with this consideration goes the decision on how to handle the clearance of the contract. There are three choices: (1) The repo trade can be cleared in the same manner in which any other type of trade would be cleared—namely, delivery versus payment. (2) Repos can be executed on a triparty basis. Under this arrangement, the seller instructs its clearance bank to remove the MBS sold under a repo contract from its own account and to place them in a special escrow account. Under this arrangement, the securities are not delivered to the purchaser; rather, they are segregated and under the control of a third party, the clearing bank. (3) Seg repos are executed that require no action on the part of the seller other than to segregate the sold securities on its own internal records. This type of repo contract should be permitted only with contra-parties who are known to be in a strong financial condition. The Government Securities Act of 1986 has created stringent controls governing the obligations and recordkeeping of firms engaging in repo transactions. A firm must have a written repo agreement signed by each account with whom it executes repos. The PSA has drafted a recommended standard repo contract (see Figure 15–2).

LETTERS OF CREDIT

Letters of credit are an alternative method of financing. They have many uses in other segments of the business but are relatively limited for MBS financing. A letter of credit involves an agreement between a broker or dealer and a commercial bank whereby the bank agrees to guarantee payment to a third party under certain circumstances. A common use of the letter of credit (LC) in MBS clearance is to use it in lieu of a cash or securities contingency deposit at a clearing corporation. A typical LC will guarantee that, in the absence of a deposit of required cash by the broker-dealer identified in the LC, the bank will make such a deposit on behalf of the broker-dealer up to the amount stipulated in the LC. Through these types of arrangements, cash funds that would otherwise be tied up in escrowed deposits are available to meet

FIGURE 15–2.

Public Securities Association
40 Broad Street, New York, NY 10004-2373
Telephone (212) 809-7000

MASTER REPURCHASE AGREEMENT

Dated as of _____ ____, _____

Between:

_____

and

_____

1. Applicability

From time to time the parties hereto may enter into transactions in which one party ("Seller") agrees to transfer to the other ("Buyer") securities or financial instruments ("Securities") against the transfer of funds by Buyer, with a simultaneous agreement by Buyer to transfer to Seller such Securities at a date certain or on demand, against the transfer of funds by Seller. Each such transaction shall be referred to herein as a "Transaction" and shall be governed by this Agreement, including any supplemental terms or conditions contained in Annex I hereto, unless otherwise agreed in writing.

2. Definitions

(a) "Act of Insolvency", with respect to any party, (i) the commencement by such party as debtor of any case or proceeding under any bankruptcy, insolvency, reorganization, liquidation, dissolution or similar law, or such party seeking the appointment of a receiver, trustee, custodian or similar official for such party or any substantial part of its property, or (ii) the commencement of any such case or proceeding against such party, or another seeking such an appointment, or the filing against a party of an application for a protective decree under the provisions of the Securities Investor Protection Act of 1970, which (A) is consented to or not timely contested by such party, (B) results in the entry of an order for relief, such an appointment, the issuance of such a protective decree or the entry of an order having a similar effect, or (C) is not dismissed within 15 days, (iii) the making by a party of a general assignment for the benefit of creditors, or (iv) the admission in writing by a party of such party's inability to pay such party's debts as they become due;

(b) "Additional Purchased Securities", securities provided by Seller to Buyer pursuant to Paragraph 4(a) hereof;

(c) "Buyer's Margin Amount", with respect to any Transaction as of any date, the amount obtained by application of a percentage (which may be equal to the percentage that is agreed to as the Seller's Margin Amount under subparagraph (q) of this Paragraph), agreed to by Buyer and Seller prior to entering into the Transaction, to the Repurchase Price for such Transaction as of such date;

(d) "Confirmation", the meaning specified in Paragraph 3(b) hereof;

(e) "Income", with respect to any Security at any time, any principal thereof then payable and all interest, dividends or other distributions thereon;

(f) "Margin Deficit", the meaning specified in Paragraph 4(a) hereof;

(g) "Margin Excess", the meaning specified in Paragraph 4(b) hereof;

(h) "Market Value", with respect to any Securities as of any date, the price for such Securities on such date obtained from a generally recognized source agreed to by the parties or the most recent closing bid quotation from such a source, plus accrued Income to the extent not included therein (other than any Income credited or transferred to, or applied to the obligations of, Seller pursuant to Paragraph 5 hereof) as of such date (unless contrary to market practice for such Securities);

FIGURE 15–2. (cont'd).

(i) "Price Differential", with respect to any Transaction hereunder as of any date, the aggregate amount obtained by daily application of the Pricing Rate for such Transaction to the Purchase Price for such Transaction on a 360 day per year basis for the actual number of days during the period commencing on (and including) the Purchase Date for such Transaction and ending on (but excluding) the date of determination (reduced by any amount of such Price Differential previously paid by Seller to Buyer with respect to such Transaction);

(j) "Pricing Rate", the per annum percentage rate for determination of the Price Differential;

(k) "Prime Rate", the prime rate of U.S. money center commercial banks as published in *The Wall Street Journal;*

(l) "Purchase Date", the date on which Purchased Securities are transferred by Seller to Buyer;

(m) "Purchase Price", (i) on the Purchase Date, the price at which Purchased Securities are transferred by Seller to Buyer, and (ii) thereafter, such price increased by the amount of any cash transferred by Buyer to Seller pursuant to Paragraph 4(b) hereof and decreased by the amount of any cash transferred by Seller to Buyer pursuant to Paragraph 4(a) hereof or applied to reduce Seller's obligations under clause (ii) of Paragraph 5 hereof;

(n) "Purchased Securities", the Securities transferred by Seller to Buyer in a Transaction hereunder, and any Securities substituted therefor in accordance with Paragraph 9 hereof. The term "Purchased Securities" with respect to any Transaction at any time also shall include Additional Purchased Securities delivered pursuant to Paragraph 4(a) and shall exclude Securities returned pursuant to Paragraph 4(b);

(o) "Repurchase Date", the date on which Seller is to repurchase the Purchased Securities from Buyer, including any date determined by application of the provisions of Paragraphs 3(c) or 11 hereof;

(p) "Repurchase Price", the price at which Purchased Securities are to be transferred from Buyer to Seller upon termination of a Transaction, which will be determined in each case (including transactions terminable upon demand) as the sum of the Purchase Price and the Price Differential as of the date of such determination, increased by any amount determined by the application of the provisions of Paragraph 11 hereof;

(q) "Seller's Margin Amount", with respect to any Transaction as of any date, the amount obtained by application of a percentage (which may be equal to the percentage that is agreed to as the Buyer's Margin Amount under subparagraph (c) of this Paragraph), agreed to by Buyer and Seller prior to entering into the Transaction, to the Repurchase Price for such Transaction as of such date.

3. Initiation; Confirmation; Termination

(a) An agreement to enter into a Transaction may be made orally or in writing at the initiation of either Buyer or Seller. On the Purchase Date for the Transaction, the Purchased Securities shall be transferred to Buyer or its agent against the transfer of the Purchase Price to an account of Seller.

(b) Upon agreeing to enter into a Transaction hereunder, Buyer or Seller (or both), as shall be agreed, shall promptly deliver to the other party a written confirmation of each Transaction (a "Confirmation"). The Confirmation shall describe the Purchased Securities (including CUSIP number, if any), identify Buyer and Seller and set forth (i) the Purchase Date, (ii) the Purchase Price, (iii) the Repurchase Date, unless the Transaction is to be terminable on demand, (iv) the Pricing Rate or Repurchase Price applicable to the Transaction, and (v) any additional terms or conditions of the Transaction not inconsistent with this Agreement. The Confirmation, together with this Agreement, shall constitute conclusive evidence of the terms agreed between Buyer and Seller with respect to the Transaction to which the Confirmation relates, unless with respect to the Confirmation specific objection is made promptly after receipt thereof. In the event of any conflict between the terms of such Confirmation and this Agreement, this Agreement shall prevail.

(c) In the case of Transactions terminable upon demand, such demand shall be made by Buyer or Seller, no later than such time as is customary in accordance with market practice, by telephone or otherwise on or prior to the business day on which such termination will be effective. On the date specified in such demand, or on the date fixed for termination in the case of Transactions having a fixed term, termination of the Transaction will be effected by transfer to Seller or its agent of the Purchased Securities and any Income in respect thereof received by Buyer (and not previously credited or transferred to, or applied to the obligations of, Seller pursuant to paragraph 5 hereof) against the transfer of the Repurchase Price to an account of Buyer.

4. Margin Maintenance

(a) If at any time the aggregate Market Value of all Purchased Securities subject to all Transactions in which a particular party hereto is acting as Buyer is less than the aggregate Buyer's Margin Amount for all such Transactions (a "Margin Deficit"), then Buyer may by notice to Seller require Seller in such Transactions, at Seller's option, to transfer to Buyer cash or additional Securities reasonably acceptable

2

FIGURE 15–2. (cont'd).

to Buyer ("Additional Purchased Securities"), so that the cash and aggregate Market Value of the Purchased Securities, including any such Additional Purchased Securities, will thereupon equal or exceed such aggregate Buyer's Margin Amount (decreased by the amount of any Margin Deficit as of such date arising from any Transactions in which such Buyer is acting as Seller).

(b) If at any time the aggregate Market Value of all Purchased Securities subject to all Transactions in which a particular party hereto is acting as Seller exceeds the aggregate Seller's Margin Amount for all such Transactions at such time (a "Margin Excess"), then Seller may by notice to Buyer require Buyer in such Transactions, at Buyer's option, to transfer cash or Purchased Securities to Seller, so that the aggregate Market Value of the Purchased Securities, after deduction of any such cash or any Purchased Securities so transferred, will thereupon not exceed such aggregate Seller's Margin Amount (increased by the amount of any Margin Excess as of such date arising from any Transactions in which such Seller is acting as Buyer).

(c) Any cash transferred pursuant to this Paragraph shall be attributed to such Transactions as shall be agreed upon by Buyer and Seller.

(d) Seller and Buyer may agree, with respect to any or all Transactions hereunder, that the respective rights of Buyer or Seller (or both) under subparagraphs (a) and (b) of this Paragraph may be exercised only where a Margin Deficit or Margin Excess exceeds a specified dollar amount or a specified percentage of the Repurchase Prices for such Transactions (which amount or percentage shall be agreed to by Buyer and Seller prior to entering into any such Transactions).

(e) Seller and Buyer may agree, with respect to any or all Transactions hereunder, that the respective rights of Buyer and Seller under subparagraphs (a) and (b) of this Paragraph to require the elimination of a Margin Deficit or a Margin Excess, as the case may be, may be exercised whenever such a Margin Deficit or Margin Excess exists with respect to any single Transaction hereunder (calculated without regard to any other Transaction outstanding under this Agreement).

5. Income Payments

Where a particular Transaction's term extends over an Income payment date on the Securities subject to that Transaction, Buyer shall, as the parties may agree with respect to such Transaction (or, in the absence of any agreement, as Buyer shall reasonably determine in its discretion), on the date such Income is payable either (i) transfer to or credit to the account of Seller an amount equal to such Income payment or payments with respect to any Purchased Securities subject to such Transaction or (ii) apply the Income payment or payments to reduce the amount to be transferred to Buyer by Seller upon termination of the Transaction. Buyer shall not be obligated to take any action pursuant to the preceding sentence to the extent that such action would result in the creation of a Margin Deficit, unless prior thereto or simultaneously therewith Seller transfers to Buyer cash or Additional Purchased Securities sufficient to eliminate such Margin Deficit.

6. Security Interest

Although the parties intend that all Transactions hereunder be sales and purchases and not loans, in the event any such Transactions are deemed to be loans, Seller shall be deemed to have pledged to Buyer as security for the performance by Seller of its obligations under each such Transaction, and shall be deemed to have granted to Buyer a security interest in, all of the Purchased Securities with respect to all Transactions hereunder and all proceeds thereof.

7. Payment and Transfer

Unless otherwise mutually agreed, all transfers of funds hereunder shall be in immediately available funds. All Securities transferred by one party hereto to the other party (i) shall be in suitable form for transfer or shall be accompanied by duly executed instruments of transfer or assignment in blank and such other documentation as the party receiving possession may reasonably request, (ii) shall be transferred on the book-entry system of a Federal Reserve Bank, or (iii) shall be transferred by any other method mutually acceptable to Seller and Buyer. As used herein with respect to Securities, "transfer" is intended to have the same meaning as when used in Section 8-313 of the New York Uniform Commercial Code.

8. Segregation of Purchased Securities

All Purchased Securities in the possession of Seller shall be segregated from other securities in its possession and shall be identified as subject to this Agreement. Segregation may be accomplished by appropriate identification on the books and records of the holder, including a financial intermediary or a clearing corporation. Title to all Purchased Securities shall pass to Buyer and, unless otherwise agreed by Buyer and Seller, nothing in this Agreement shall preclude Buyer from engaging in repurchase transactions with the Purchased Securities or otherwise pledging or hypothecating the Purchased Securities, but no such transaction shall relieve Buyer of its obligations to transfer Purchased Securities to Seller pursuant to Paragraphs 3, 4 or 11 hereof, or of Buyer's obligation to credit or pay Income to, or apply Income to the obligations of, Seller pursuant to Paragraph 5 hereof.

3

FIGURE 15–2. (cont'd).

9. Substitution

Seller may, subject to agreement with and acceptance by Buyer, substitute other Securities for any Purchased Securities. Such substitution shall be made by transfer to the Buyer of such other Securities against simultaneous transfer to the Seller of such Purchased Securities. After substitution, the substituted Securities shall be deemed to be Purchased Securities.

10. Representations

Each of Buyer and Seller represents and warrants to the other that (i) it is duly authorized to execute and deliver this Agreement, to enter into the Transactions contemplated hereunder and to perform its obligations hereunder and has taken all necessary action to authorize such execution, delivery and performance, (ii) it will engage in such Transactions as principal (or, if agreed in writing in advance of any Transaction by the other party hereto, as agent for a disclosed principal), (iii) the person signing this Agreement on its behalf is duly authorized to do so on its behalf (or on behalf of any such disclosed principal), (iv) it has obtained all authorizations of any governmental body required in connection with this Agreement and the Transactions hereunder and such authorizations are in full force and effect and (v) the execution, delivery and performance of this Agreement and the Transactions hereunder will not violate any law, ordinance, charter, by-law or rule applicable to it or any agreement by which it is bound or by which any of its assets are affected. On the Purchase Date for any Transaction Buyer and Seller shall each be deemed to repeat all the foregoing representations made by it.

11. Events of Default

In the event that (i) Seller fails to repurchase or Buyer fails to transfer Purchased Securities upon the applicable Repurchase Date, (ii) Seller or Buyer fails, after one business day's notice, to comply with Paragraph 4 hereof, (iii) Buyer fails to comply with Paragraph 5 hereof, (iv) an Act of Insolvency occurs with respect to Seller or Buyer, (v) any representation made by Seller or Buyer shall have been incorrect or untrue in any material respect when made or repeated or deemed to have been made or repeated, or (vi) Seller or Buyer shall admit to the other its inability to, or its intention not to, perform any of its obligations hereunder (each an "Event of Default"):

(a) At the option of the nondefaulting party, exercised by written notice to the defaulting party (which option shall be deemed to have been exercised, even if no notice is given, immediately upon the occurrence of an Act of Insolvency), the Repurchase Date for each Transaction hereunder shall be deemed immediately to occur.

(b) In all Transactions in which the defaulting party is acting as Seller, if the nondefaulting party exercises or is deemed to have exercised the option referred to in subparagraph (a) of this paragraph, (i) the defaulting party's obligations hereunder to repurchase all Purchased Securities in such Transactions shall thereupon become immediately due and payable, (ii) to the extent permitted by applicable law, the Repurchase Price with respect to each such Transaction shall be increased by the aggregate amount obtained by daily application of (x) the greater of the Pricing Rate for such Transaction or the Prime Rate to (y) the Repurchase Price for such Transaction as of the Repurchase Date as determined pursuant to subparagraph (a) of this Paragraph (decreased as of any day by (A) any amounts retained by the nondefaulting party with respect to such Repurchase Price pursuant to clause (iii) of this subparagraph, (B) any proceeds from the sale of Purchased Securities pursuant to subparagraph (d)(i) of this paragraph, and (C) any amounts credited to the account of the defaulting party pursuant to subparagraph (e) of this paragraph) on a 360 day per year basis for the actual number of days during the period from the date of the Event of Default giving rise to such option to the date of payment of the Repurchase Price as so increased, (iii) all Income paid after such exercise or deemed exercise shall be retained by the nondefaulting party and applied to the aggregate unpaid Repurchase Prices owed by the defaulting party, and (iv) the defaulting party shall immediately deliver to the nondefaulting party any Purchased Securities subject to such Transactions then in the defaulting party's possession.

(c) In all Transactions in which the defaulting party is acting as Buyer, upon tender by the nondefaulting Party of payment of the aggregate Repurchase Prices for all such Transactions, the defaulting party's right, title and interest in all Purchased Securities subject to such Transaction shall be deemed transferred to the nondefaulting party, and the defaulting party shall deliver all such Purchased Securities to the nondefaulting party.

(d) After one business day's notice to the defaulting party (which notice need not be given if an Act of Insolvency shall have occurred, and which may be the notice given under subparagraph (a) of this Paragraph or the notice referred to in clause (ii) of the first sentence of this Paragraph), the nondefaulting party may:

(i) as to Transactions in which the defaulting party is acting as Seller, (A) immediately sell, in a recognized market at such price or prices as the nondefaulting party may reasonably deem satisfactory, any or all Purchased Securities subject to such Transactions and apply the proceeds thereof to the aggregate unpaid Repurchase Prices and any other amounts owing by the defaulting party hereunder

4

FIGURE 15–2. (cont'd).

or (B) in its sole discretion elect, in lieu of selling all or a portion of such Purchased Securities, to give the defaulting party credit for such Purchased Securities in an amount equal to the price therefor on such date, obtained from a generally recognized source or the most recent closing bid quotation from such a source, against the aggregate unpaid Repurchase Prices and any other amounts owing by the defaulting party hereunder; and

(ii) as to Transactions in which the defaulting party is acting as Buyer, (A) purchase securities ("Replacement Securities") of the same class and amount as any Purchased Securities that are not delivered by the defaulting party to the nondefaulting party as required hereunder or (B) in its sole discretion elect, in lieu of purchasing Replacement Securities, to be deemed to have purchased Replacement Securities at the price therefor on such date, obtained from a generally recognized source or the most recent closing bid quotation from such a source.

(e) As to Transactions in which the defaulting party is acting as Buyer, the defaulting party shall be liable to the nondefaulting party (i) with respect to Purchased Securities (other than Additional Purchased Securities), for any excess of the price paid (or deemed paid) by the nondefaulting party for Replacement Securities therefor over the Repurchase Price for such Purchased Securities and (ii) with respect to Additional Purchased Securities, for the price paid (or deemed paid) by the nondefaulting party for the Replacement Securities therefor. In addition, the defaulting party shall be liable to the nondefaulting party for interest on such remaining liability with respect to each such purchase (or deemed purchase) of Replacement Securities from the date of such purchase (or deemed purchase) until paid in full by Buyer. Such interest shall be at a rate equal to the greater of the Pricing Rate for such Transaction or the Prime Rate.

(f) For purposes of this Paragraph 11, the Repurchase Price for each Transaction hereunder in respect of which the defaulting party is acting as Buyer shall not increase above the amount of such Repurchase Price for such Transaction determined as of the date of the exercise or deemed exercise by the nondefaulting party of its option under subparagraph (a) of this paragraph.

(g) The defaulting party shall be liable to the nondefaulting party for the amount of all reasonable legal or other expenses incurred by the nondefaulting party in connection with or as a consequence of an Event of Default, together with interest thereon at a rate equal to the greater of the Pricing Rate for the relevant Transaction or the Prime Rate.

(h) The nondefaulting party shall have, in addition to its rights hereunder, any rights otherwise available to it under any other agreement or applicable law.

12. Single Agreement

Buyer and Seller acknowledge that, and have entered hereinto and will enter into each Transaction hereunder in consideration of and in reliance upon the fact that, all Transactions hereunder constitute a single business and contractual relationship and have been made in consideration of each other. Accordingly, each of Buyer and Seller agrees (i) to perform all of its obligations in respect of each Transaction hereunder, and that a default in the performance of any such obligations shall constitute a default by it in respect of all Transactions hereunder, (ii) that each of them shall be entitled to set off claims and apply property held by them in respect of any Transaction against obligations owing to them in respect of any other Transactions hereunder and (iii) that payments, deliveries and other transfers made by either of them in respect of any Transaction shall be deemed to have been made in consideration of payments, deliveries and other Transactions hereunder, and the obligations to make any such payments, deliveries and other transfers may be applied against each other and netted.

13. Notices and Other Communications

Unless another address is specified in writing by the respective party to whom any notice or other communication is to be given hereunder, all such notices or communications shall be in writing or confirmed in writing and delivered at the respective addresses set forth in Annex II attached hereto.

14. Entire Agreement; Severability

This Agreement shall supersede any existing agreements between the parties containing general terms and conditions for repurchase transactions. Each provision and agreement herein shall be treated as separate and independent from any other provision or agreement herein and shall be enforceable notwithstanding the unenforceability of any such other provision or agreement.

15. Non-assignability; Termination

The rights and obligations of the parties under this Agreement and under any Transaction shall not be assigned by either party without the prior written consent of the other party. Subject to the foregoing, this Agreement and any Transactions shall be binding upon and shall inure to the benefit of the parties and their respective successors and assigns. This Agreement may be cancelled by either party upon giving written notice to the other, except that this Agreement shall, notwithstanding such notice, remain applicable to any Transactions then outstanding.

5

FIGURE 15–2. (cont'd).

16. **Governing Law**
This Agreement shall be governed by the laws of the State of New York without giving effect to the conflict of law principles thereof.

17. **No Waivers, Etc.**
No express or implied waiver of any Event of Default by either party shall constitute a waiver of any other Event of Default and no exercise of any remedy hereunder by any party shall constitute a waiver of its right to exercise any other remedy hereunder. No modification or waiver of any provision of this Agreement and no consent by any party to a departure herefrom shall be effective unless and until such shall be in writing and duly executed by both of the parties hereto. Without limitation on any of the foregoing, the failure to give a notice pursuant to subparagraphs 4(a) or 4(b) hereof will not constitute a waiver of any right to do so at a later date.

18. **Use of Employee Plan Assets**
(a) If assets of an employee benefit plan subject to any provision of the Employee Retirement Income Security Act of 1974 ("ERISA") are intended to be used by either party hereto (the "Plan Party") in a Transaction, the Plan Party shall so notify the other party prior to the Transaction. The Plan Party shall represent in writing to the other party that the Transaction does not constitute a prohibited transaction under ERISA or is otherwise exempt therefrom, and the other party may proceed in reliance thereon but shall not be required so to proceed.

(b) Subject to the last sentence of subparagraph (a) of this paragraph, any such Transaction shall proceed only if Seller furnishes or has furnished to Buyer its most recent available audited statement of its financial condition and its most recent subsequent unaudited statement of its financial condition.

(c) By entering into a Transaction pursuant to this paragraph, Seller shall be deemed (i) to represent to Buyer that since the date of Seller's latest such financial statements, there has been no material adverse change in Seller's financial condition which Seller has not disclosed to Buyer, and (ii) to agree to provide Buyer with future audited and unaudited statements of its financial condition as they are issued, so long as it is a Seller in any outstanding Transaction involving a Plan Party.

19. **Intent**
(a) The parties recognize that each Transaction is a "repurchase agreement" as that term is defined in Section 101(39) of Title 11 of the United States Code, as amended (except insofar as the type of Securities subject to such Transaction or the term of such Transaction would render such definition inapplicable), and a "securities contract" as that term is defined in Section 741(7) of Title 11 of the United States Code, as amended.

(b) It is understood that either party's right to liquidate securities delivered to it in connection with Transactions hereunder or to exercise any other remedies pursuant to Paragraph 11 hereof, is a contractual right to liquidate such Transaction as described in Sections 555 and 559 of Title 11 of the United States Code, as amended.

[Name of Party]   [Name of Party]

By _____   By _____

Title _____   Title _____

Date _____   Date _____

ANNEX I

Supplemental Terms and Conditions

ANNEX II

Names and Addresses for Communications Between Parties

6

normal business requirements. The bank receives a fee for its guarantee. Letters of credit may be collateralized or uncollateralized.

FIGURE 15–3. Letter of Credit

D. Form of Letter of Credit for Use as Collateral in Connection with VA Vendee Loans.*

(Issuing Bank's Letterhead)

IRREVOCABLE UNCONDITIONAL LETTER OF CREDIT

(1) To: Government National   Letter of Credit No. _____
         Mortgage Association   Date _____
         451 Seventh St., S.W.   GNMA Commitment No. _____
         Washington, D.C. 20410

Gentlemen:

     For the account of _____, we hereby authorize you to draw on us at sight up to an aggregate amount of _____ dollars ($_____).

     This letter of credit is irrevocable and unconditional.

     Drafts drawn under this letter of credit must specify the letter of credit number and be presented at the office identified below not later than _____.

     This letter of credit sets forth in full the terms of our obligations to you, and such undertaking shall not in any way be modified or amplified by any agreement in which this letter is referred to or to which this letter of credit relates, and any such reference shall not be deemed to incorporate herein by reference any agreement.

     We engage with you that sight drafts drawn under, and in compliance with, the terms of this letter of credit will be duly honored at _____.

                              Yours very truly,

                              [Issuing Bank]

                              By:_____
                                 [   ]

                                 [   ]

---
*To be used in connection with VA vendee account mortgages, or installment contracts guaranteed pursuant to VA Regulation 4600.

16

Fail Control

Now that you understand financing and the tremendous costs associated with it, you can appreciate why a primary goal of all clearance departments is to maximize cash flow. The only way to achieve this goal is to establish procedures that tightly control fails. Fails are trades that have not been delivered (i.e., cleared) by the close of business on the settlement date of the trade. When a trade is executed between two securities firms and the securities traded are not cleared (delivered and paid for) on the settlement date, the broker-dealer that bought the securities has a *fail to receive* and the seller has a *fail to deliver*. Trading involves a constant turnover of inventory through daily buying and selling. When a firm sells to the street, the securities sold must be delivered before payment will be received from the contra-broker-dealer. If the funds due on the sale are not available to pay for securities purchased, a firm experiences a negative cash flow, which must be compensated for through the expense of additional financing.

On the basis of these facts, you come to the conclusion that procedures must be established to ensure that all sales are delivered on the settlement date of the trade. Anyone who has worked in securities operations for more than a week knows that that's nirvana, not the real world. And so, we have to discuss fail control. Any such discussion must be addressed from the standpoints of both prevention and cure, as follows:

- ❏ Presettlement fail control.
- ❏ Postsettlement fail control.

PRESETTLEMENT FAIL CONTROL

Cliche' time! "An ounce of prevention is worth a pound of cure." Prevent fails! If you want to ensure maximum cash flow, prevent fails! Don't react to a disease, and negative cash flow is just that. *Prevent it*! Before you can prevent something from occurring, however, you have to understand what causes the occurrence. We will discuss some of the common reasons that prevent a firm from delivering sold securities on the settlement date and the steps to be taken in each situation.

- ❏ The securities were not available because they were being used to collateralize a repo or a bank loan.

Although pool or group numbers may differ, securities of a similar type are equally acceptable to a bank or a dealer for the purposes of collateralization of a repo or a loan. When an issue that has been sold is being used as collateral, that issue must be recovered through a substitution. *Substitution* is the process of replacing an issue that is collateralizing an open contract with a different issue, presumably one that has not been sold. Subs should always be executed for bank loans, and whenever possible for repos. The Government Securities Act of 1986 requires that you obtain a customer's permission before executing a repo substitution.

- ❏ The securities were bought from one or more dealers or institutional COD accounts, one or more of whom have failed to deliver them.

Here you can exercise only marginal control. Before settlement date, contact the contra-dealer or the customer's agent and explain that the securities owed to you are needed for turnaround. Try to arrange for an early guaranteed delivery. In the absence of such an arrangement, use securities that are available in some other free location. A free location is one from which securities can be delivered without creating a regulatory compliance problem.

❑ The securities that were bought were received too late on the day of sale to be redelivered (turned around) on the same day.

There is no control that you can exercise in this situation. If you have taken the steps described in the previous paragraph and the delivery is made just at the delivery cutoff time (refer to clearance schedules in Chapter 10), you will have no additional time to redeliver the securities. When cutoff time is reached, no further deliveries can be made that day *unless* special mutually agreed-on arrangements can be obtained. Always make the effort to make these arrangements if a large fail is at stake.

❑ The retail customer for whom the broker-dealer sold the securities has not yet deposited them in his or her account.

Again there is little control that can be exercised. It is the margin department's responsibility to ensure that the customer is not paid for the sale until the securities have been received and verified as negotiable.

❑ The securities were in transit from an out-of-town branch office.

This situation can occur when a retail customer has delivered securities to a branch office. The branch then forwards the certificates by an armored carrier service to the main office for clearance of the customer's trade. Securities in transit are always received at a central area, usually the vault. If securities in transit are needed for redelivery, they should be flagged at the point of receipt to ensure prompt routing to the clearance area or immediate deposit at the MBS depository or the Fed.

❑   The securities were not negotiable.

Usually this situation involves certificates that did not contain the proper endorsement of the holder(s) or the endorsements were not properly guaranteed. If signatures are required, immediately contact the operations manager at the branch responsible for the account. The manager should immediately forward, by messenger or express mail if the contract value of the resulting fail calls for that type of expense, a HUD form for endorsement. A supply of blank HUD forms should be available at all branches; signed forms should be returned to the main office by the quickest means available. Unendorsed certificates should be booked into an account or by a method that will clearly identify the shares as securities that are "sold, not signed" to facilitate monitoring unresolved items. This is imperative in a high-volume retail environment. If securities were improperly guaranteed (see Chapter 12), the person responsible should be advised of the guarantee requirements for mortgage-backeds.

❑   The securities were in transfer.

The GNMA issues that are not yet subject to mandatory book-entry clearance are physically transferred into either the firm's name or a customer's name. Securities that have been sold but are being transferred cannot be delivered because the certificates are at Chemical Bank, the transfer agent. Certificates being transferred to the firm's name can be obtained more quickly for redelivery by paying a rush transfer fee to the agent. If certificates are being transferred to a customer who has subsequently sold them, an effort should be made to stop the transfer process. If it has already been accomplished, a signed HUD form should be obtained immediately from the client. If you know there will be a serious and/or costly delay in obtaining the required signatures, a guaranteed letter of correction should be returned to the agent with the certificates. The agent will cancel and replace the certificate with one in the firm's name. The required delivery can then be made.

❑ The securities required a P&I due bill that was not obtained in a timely manner.

This is a fully controllable situation. All trades that settle on or before the P&I record date but are cleared after the record date require a due bill. Clearance personnel should make certain that they immediately contact the dividend department to obtain the required due bills for their physical deliveries. PSA rules state that, in the case of wireable deliveries, the Fedwire message is an acceptable due-bill substitute.

❑ The trading account sold short.

Clearance can do nothing to prevent a fail under this circumstance. Clearance must advise the trader, or a trader's assistant, however, that the firm is in a fail position because of the short in the inventory account. It is then up to the trader to execute a sub, a buy-back, or a dollar roll, or simply to continue to fail until the market permits covering the short at a satisfactory price.

❑ The securities were in a suspense account as the result of an earlier internal misallocation or error.

Suspense accounts are used to book unresolved errors or differences. The major problem with these accounts is complacency. In many instances, the account is not under the direction or control of the clearance department, and there is the tendency to think that there is nothing that can be done to rectify the problem. Suspense positions that contribute to fails should be brought to the attention of the clearance manager immediately. That person should immediately contact the area responsible for the account and coordinate the prompt resolution of the difference.

The Delivery Requirement Analysis (DRA)

The keys to presettlement fail control are the following:

❑ Identify all delivery requirements.
❑ Identify the source of the securities to be delivered.

❑ If the source is indicative of a possible fail, take immediate steps to prevent it or to minimize it.

These three steps should be started two days before settlement date. The question is: How do you accomplish them? The tool or report needed is a delivery requirement analysis (DRA) similar to the one shown in Figure 16–1 (see p. 272). Assume that you are an employee in the clearance department of the firm that issued this report. Before looking at the analysis of the report that follows the explanation of the illustration, answer the following questions yourself:

1. Are there any delivery requirements for today (October 21, 1988)?
2. Will you be able to make this delivery today? Does the stock record suspense position come into play?
3. If you do deliver, where will you get the securities?
4. Do you have concerns that are based on future settlement activity?
5. How will you use the securities you could receive on October 23? What steps should you take today relative to them?
6. How will you satisfy your delivery requirements on October 24?

FIGURE 16–1. A Delivery Requirement Analysis (DRA)

```
Mtg Backed Securites Clearance Department      ①Dated 10-21-88
                              ②
 GNMA Pool 185850  9% 10-15-16    CUSIP 362167L71   Factor .52324929

        **DELIVER**                          **RECEIVE**

  SD    ACCT   QTY/VALUE    INSTRUX    SD    ACCT   QTY/VALUE   INSTRUX
       ④        ⑤          ⑥
③ 1021 4444  1000,000.00F  US TRUST  1021 5432 1000,000.00F  CHASEBK
⑦ Prin Trd    523,249.29A  130 John  Prin Trd   523,249.29A  1 NYP
⑧ #6543      $499,010.42   5flr CUS  #5213      494,123.01   BLvl TR
⑨                          ac 77777                          ac68686

  1024 1225  2500,000.00F  BKRS TR   1023  0614 150,000.00F  BKRS TR
  Prin Trd   1308,123.23A  1BT PLZ   Prin Trd    78,487.39A  1BT PLZ
  #8892      $1295,041.90  Trust     #8857      $77,715.22   Retail

 OPEN ITEM RECAP (CONTRACT VAL)      LOCATION RECAP COB 10-20-88

                Deliver  Receive      Account    Face Amt  Mkt Value
  COD BLOT       499M     494M        SUSPN P&S
  RTL BLOT                            SUSPN CAGE
  BKR BLOT                            SUSPN SR    100M       53M
  COD FAIL                            DK
  RTL FAIL                            RECLAIM
  BKR FAIL                            TRD AC SHORT
  SubTotal       499M     494M        OVERNITE BKLN 350M     183M
                                      OVERNITE REPO
⑩ NEXT DAY                            TERM BANK LN         ⑪
                                      TERM REPO   2000M     1046M
  COD                                 FREE BOX PHYS
  RETAIL                  78M         FREE BOX DEP
  BROKER                              FREE BOX FED
                                      FIRM TFR
  FUTURE                              CUST TFR
                                      TRANSIT     150M       78M
  COD           1295M                 EXCESS SEG
  RETAIL
  BROKER

  TOTALS        1794M    572M                     2600M     1360M
```

Explanation of the DRA:

1. Date of the report is the date the report is received.

2. A complete analysis is shown for every issue in which a delivery versus payment must be made, either currently or in the future. This is a full description and current month's factor of each reported issue. The report itself is divided into four quadrants. All sales that have to be cleared are under the "DELIVER" section; purchases are under the "RECEIVE" section. The "OPEN ITEM RECAP" provides a summary of the contract values of all pending deliveries and receipts. The "LOCATION RECAP" is a listing of internal accounts and shows where available inventory (inventory previously delivered to the firm) is presently located.

3. The original settlement date of the trade being described.

4. The firm's internal account number of the customer for whom the trade was executed.

5. The trade details. F = the original face amount. A = the amortized amount of the trade based on the factor in effect at time of execution (not necessarily the current factor).

6. The delivery/receive instructions. Should include the name and address (or ABA number or depository number, whichever is applicable) of the agent, the identity of the department at the agent responsible for processing (trust, custody, etc.), and the agent's internal account number for the customer.

7. Prin Trd = principal transaction. Agn Trd = agency transaction. Identification facilitates analysis of the report.

8. The internal reference number of the transaction used for processing and look-up purposes.

9. A P&I due-bill indicator. If the open trade must have a due bill accompanying the delivery, the payable date (PD) and an actual or estimated amount due will be printed. No DBs were required in this report; an example can be seen in Figure 10–2.

10. The OPEN ITEM RECAP provides a "snapshot" of current, next-day, and future requirements. In the example, you quickly see that current delivery requirements are offset by current receivables. There are no next-day deliveries. The future requirements indicate that a large delivery must be made, but it shows no offsetting purchase, which means that the locations have to be reviewed to determine where you will get the securities. COD = an institutional DVP or RVP trade. RTL = a retail trade. BKR = a trade done with another broker or dealer. BLOT = trade blotter items, purchases and sales, that settle today. FAIL = trades settled on a previous day that did not clear. NEXT DAY = all trades settling on the next business day. FUTURE = all trades settling two or more business days into the future.

11. The LOCATION RECAP is an identified listing of every internal account containing securities that could possibly be used to make a pending delivery. Location accounts containing securities that may not be used for delivery are simply not listed (e.g., the seg account). SUSPN = suspense account; an unreconciled difference temporarily booked to an interim account for balancing purposes. Suspenses potentially represent available securities, or they can represent an invalid trade. Suspense positions require immediate research (SUSPN SR = a stock record suspense). DK = Don't know. A separate account should be established for the control of previous deliveries returned by agents and customers because they don't agree with the contract terms. RECLAIM = the reclamation account. It contains all deliveries returned for a reason other than a DK (e.g., wrong quantity or money). TRD AC SHORT = the uncovered short position in the firm trading account(s). OVERNITE BK LN = securities being used to collateralize a bank loan that must be paid off the first business day following the inception of the loan. Assuming the loan is paid, the securities come back under your control, and you need take no action to obtain possession for delivery. OVERNITE REPO = securities being used

to collateralize an overnight (one business day) repurchase agreement; handled in the same manner as an overnight loan. TERM LOAN & TERM REPO = securities being used to collateralize loan and repo agreements that have extended maturities. Action must be taken to substitute other collateral to ensure the availability of these securities on the date that delivery is to be made. FREE BOX is a storage location for securities readily available for delivery or any other purpose. The three categories differentiate between securities that are being held physically in the firm's own vault, held in the firm's account at an MBS book-entry depository facility, or held in the Federal Reserve's book-entry wire system. FIRM TFR = securities being transferred into the firm's (street) name; these securities are usually available 72 hours after the date they were submitted to the agent. CUST TFR = securities being registered in a client's name. Should a customer sell securities while they are in the process of being registered to that customer's name, immediate steps should be taken to cancel the reregistration so that the certificates are available to clear the sale. TRANSIT = securities in the process of being shipped from an out-of-town branch to the central office; receipt can be anticipated within one business day. EXCESS SEG = securities belonging to customers that have not been fully paid for and therefore can be used for firm needs.

PRESETTLEMENT ANALYSIS OF THE DRA

Let's look now at the six questions presented on page 271 and compare your findings to those that follow:

Q. Are there any delivery requirements for today (October 21, 1988)?

A. Yes. One million face amount must be delivered to US Trust Company for account #4444 versus payment of $499,010.42

Q. Will you be able to make this delivery today? Does the stock record suspense position come into play?

A. The delivery can be made today. Suspense entries should always be reconciled immediately, but in this case there doesn't appear to be a problem with the delivery but, rather, an unposted entry from the day before.

Q. If you do deliver, where will you get the securities?

A. You have two choices. You can wait to see if the 1MM that you bought the same day (the receive for account 5432) comes in and then use those securities for your delivery. Or you can use securities that are easily obtained—namely, the securities that are collateralizing a term repo. Advise the repo trading desk that you need to substitute a different issue as collateral for the outstanding repo. You can then use the securities that get returned when the sub is completed to accomplish your delivery to US Trust. Unless you are *certain* that you will receive the 1MM from Chase, the substitution route is preferable. It guarantees your ability to avoid a Friday night fail (three days of interest is involved on a weekend fail). Should the 1MM you bought come in later in the day, you can always use it as collateral for a bank loan. You will incur a rate disadvantage between the repo rate and the bank loan rate, but that amounts to only $20 to $30 (plus transaction and clearance fees for two trades) as opposed to a potential interest loss of several hundred dollars if you fail.

Q. Do you have concerns that are based on future settlement activity?

A. Assuming that the transactions settling on October 21 cleared on the settlement date, the next delivery must be made on October 24. On that day you have to deliver 2.5MM face value to Bankers for account #1225. A quick review of upcoming purchases reveals that only 150M face are due to be received. You need to locate another 2,350M face to complete this delivery. The location recap discloses that there are 350M in an overnight loan. Overnight loans are paid off daily, and the collateral used to secure them is returned to your control each morning.

You need have no concern about the availability of those certificates. The remaining 2MM face is collateralizing a term repo. The concern here is the date of termination of the repo. If it terminates after October 24, take immediate steps to have the traders replace (substitute) Pool 185850 with one or more pools that have not been sold. If the repo terminates on the settlement date of the sale, October 24, you will want to flag the repo buy-back with some kind of indicator to alert the traders not to roll (i.e., renew the repo).

Q. How will you use the securities you could receive on October 23? What steps should you take today relative to them?

A. These securities will be needed to complete the 2.5MM delivery scheduled for the next day. The DRA indicates that the account sold is a retail account, and a review of the location recap discloses that the certificates are in transit (from an out-of-town branch). Because they are in transit, you know two things. First, they will be available for delivery on the settlement date; transit locations usually clean up on a next-day basis. Second, if they are in transit, you know that they are physical and in the name of a customer. This 150M is the weakest link in this chain and could easily cause you to fail on 2.5MM unless you take preliminary precautions. Today, 10-21-88, the day before settlement date, contact the department that takes in securities from transit and ask them to examine the incoming certificates to ensure that they have been properly signed and are negotiable. If they are not, make an immediate phone call and follow it up with a wire to the branch office operations manager at the branch handling the account. A HUD form, the bond power required for MBS, should be hand-delivered or sent by Express Mail to the client and returned directly to the main office by Express Mail so that the certificates can be delivered on settlement date. But you're still not out of the woods! The delivery has a ticket value of 78M; in the overall scheme of things it is not a high priority item. If October 23 and 24 are exceptionally hectic, there is a chance that a small delivery such as this will not be made. The final step, therefore, is to contact the bank clearing your retail trades and tell them to place an "urgent requirement" on the trade so that you can be ensured of its receipt.

Q. How will you satisfy your delivery requirements on October 24?

A. You have done everything you could to ensure delivery and prevent a costly fail. You have 2MM coming back from repo, 350M from an overnight loan, and the 150MM coming from a customer. "Ya done good!"

This is the kind of *presettlement analysis* that must be done for every sale made by the firm. It is what makes the difference between an efficient clearance operation and a poor one.

What could have happened? Assume that when the 150M in transit came into the main office, it was discovered that the certificate was in joint name and that only one party had signed it (not an uncommon occurrence). On 10-24 you now realize that you need this 150MM to make your delivery, and you begin to inquire about it. At this point, it is going to take at least three days to rectify the problem, which means that at minimum you will incur interest costs on the equivalent of $3,885,125.70 ($1,295,041.90 contract value × 3 days = $3,885,125.70). Failure to protect yourself from the potential fail would cost your firm a *minimum loss of $755* at a 7% interest rate because, since you failed to make your delivery and secure payment on settlement date, you would have to borrow the cash you did not receive.

POSTSETTLEMENT FAIL CONTROL

Despite the fact that you have carefully prepared for every settlement date, situations will always arise that result in the inability to clear a transaction on the settlement date. Regardless of the reason for a fail, you must control for all fails. Controlling fails means ensuring that the total dollar contract value of all fails stays within reasonable parameters and that individual fails get delivered, "cleaned up," within a reasonable time. The only way to control open fails is to be constantly aware of them. This can be accomplished through two means:

❑ A daily review of the open fail file.
❑ The use of specific accounts to book transactions that contribute to the fail figures.

Reviewing the Open Fail File

The open fail file is the basic source of information available to a fail control group. This file contains the details of every trade that has settled but not cleared. To receive the optimum benefits from a fail file, separate the fails to receive and fails to deliver and sort the records in each into the following sequences:

❑ Security number sequence.
❑ Contract value sequence (highest to lowest).
❑ Aged sequence (oldest to most current).
❑ Contra-party sequence (account group).

Security Number Sequence. The security number sequence is of little value in controlling fails, but it is important to have because it provides an easy method of looking up information from a general standpoint.

Contract Value Sequence. By sequencing fails in the order of their contract value, you can immediately identify those fails that are costing your firm the most money to finance. Under ordinary circumstances, these are the items to which you should give priority attention so that they can be delivered as quickly as possible and turned into cash. Use available and incoming securities to the best advantage. Examine the open fails in Figure 16–2, keeping in mind that there are 1MM in the free box which were received too late to turn around on the previous day.

In this scenario you have a customer delivery requirement for 3MM plus a broker delivery of 1MM. You have 1MM in the box that can be immediately delivered, and you have three lots of 1MM coming in from various sources.

FIGURE 16–2. An Analysis of Open Fails

| Open Fail-to-Deliver File | | | | COB 10-24-88 |
SD	Quantity	Description	Contra-Party	Contract Value
10-23-88	3000,000.00	GNMA Pool 185850	Acct 5432	$3,187,260.73
10-21-88	1000,000.00	GNMA Pool 185850	Broker C	$1,021,116.46
Open Fail-to-Receive File				COB 10-24-88
SD	Quantity	Description	Contra-Party	Contract Value
10-23-88	1000,000.00	GNMA Pool 185850	Broker A	$1,030,111.67
10-21-88	1000,000.00	GNMA Pool 185850	Broker D	$1,019,006.64
10-21-88	1000,000.00	GNMA Pool 185850	Acct 4444	$1,017,850.76

Because you cannot deliver a partial to the customer (unless it has been mutually agreed that you can), hold the 1MM in the box until later in the day in an attempt to accumulate enough securities to make the 3MM delivery. You can always make the 1MM before cutoff time. But if you immediately delivered the 1MM and subsequently only $2 million out of the 3MM open receives cleaned up, you would be forced to finance the 2MM because of not having enough securities to make your delivery. This is fail management through the use of a value-sequenced file.

You should age the fail files for both business and regulatory reasons. From a business viewpoint, the older an item becomes, the more difficult it is to clear the trade satisfactorily. Everyone wants their money ASAP. So when a fail becomes aged, it is a safe assumption that something is wrong that requires immediate special attention.

Aged Sequence. From a regulatory viewpoint, special accounting procedures are mandated for street fails more than 30 calendar days old. On November 10, 1972, the Securities and Exchange Commission adopted SEC Rule 15c3–3: "(To insure) that customer funds and securities not be exposed to risk of loss through broker-dealer insolvency." To this end, every broker-dealer is required to maintain a special reserve (bank) account for the exclusive benefit of customers. The special handling of aged fails under this ruling effectively requires a deposit of cash into this special reserve account. Because this deposit is escrowed for customers, its effect is to reduce the working capital and cash flow of the firm. You know the effect that has! The administration of

Rule 15c3–3 is complicated, and this brief discussion is a gross oversimplification. It is important, however, that you recognize the existence of the rule and the potential impact of aged fails.

Contra-Party Sequence. The last sort of the fail files involves sequencing the open contracts by the identity of the contra-party. If the system used by your firm is capable of identifying related and subsidiary accounts, all of these should be grouped together in the report under a master account title. There are three advantages to this type of an analysis. *First,* potential pair-off situations can be quickly identified. Fails to receive and fails to deliver can occur on different settlement dates and involve the same party for the same issue. On mutual agreement, these can be offset by means of internal accounting entries, and settlement can be completed by the payment of the net money difference between the two contracts—thus reducing your open fails. *Second,* sorting by contra-party groupings enables management to determine the overall exposure, the open commitments, that a firm has with a single entity or group. Cliché time again! "Never put all your eggs in one basket." Whenever the total value of open contracts with a single entity or group approaches the limits established internally by your firm, you must notify your management. The head trader will consider prohibiting additional trades with the account(s), and clearance will take steps to clear immediately as many outstanding contracts with the account(s) as possible. Historically, the monitoring of firm exposure on an account-by-account basis has proven to be a necessary precaution that must be done on a continuing basis. The *third* advantage of a contra-party sequence sort is closely related to the second. Most firms maintain a credit committee whose responsibility it is to monitor the financial stability of the firms with which their organization does business. There are times when the committee will advise that all open contracts with a particular firm be immediately cleared or closed out by some other means. Whenever this occurs, clearance personnel need to have a consolidated list of all open contracts with the firm in question.

The focus thus far has been placed on determining priorities for the purpose of controlling fails to deliver. What about fails to receive, especially when the securities to be received are not needed for a turnaround delivery? If there are no extenuating circumstances calling for immediate action, normal follow-up procedures should start no later than the tenth business day after settlement. Regardless of the fact that there is no delivery requirement, there is still a risk to the firm connected with these fails. A fail to receive represents a purchase made by your firm either for a customer or for the firm's own inventory account. That purchase was made at a specific price. Assume that the current market price is now 4 points higher than the original purchase price. Should the contra-party default or DK this trade, your firm faces a potential loss of the 4-point profit it is expecting. On a 1MM trade, that would amount to a $40,000.00 loss!

EXPEDITING THE CLEANUP OF OPEN FAIL CONTRACTS

There is a major difference between mortgage-backed issues and most other security issues that increases the difficulty of clearing open fails. That difference is the specificity of the individual MBS issues. If you are failing to deliver 1MM IBM 9.375% Debentures due 2004, you could deliver any certificate in your possession or borrow the bonds for delivery. If you are failing to deliver $1 million FHLMC PC 25–000037 10% due 2017, however, you could not deliver just any FHLMC PC having a 10% coupon maturing in 2017. You need the specific pool, 25–000037. There may be an enormous number of 10%s of 2017; there are only a few with the required pool number. The seller must produce the securities before delivery can be made. This is not the case with other instruments, which can be easily borrowed for delivery because they are not constrained by this type of specificity. So how do you clean up your fails? You identify the cause or reason for your inability to make a delivery, and then work to eliminate the cause.

If you are failing to receive, contact the contra-party. Indicate that you have an urgent need for the securities owed to you, and get a commitment for a delivery date. Record the name, phone number, date, and time, and briefly summarize *every* conversation. Follow up with the person you spoke to if the commitment to make a promised delivery is not honored. Try to find out what is preventing delivery, and notify a manager in your office if you are unable to get the required results. Because of the specificity of pool numbers, fails that have been acknowledged but remain open for long periods should be suspect as being part of a chain of fails associated with that pool. Such a chain is known as a *round robin*. The same pool was bought and sold several times over, and multiple fails are involved in a chain that ultimately can be traced to the original transaction. When the contra-side of a very old trade continues to indicate that its delivery is being held up because of a fail, find out who *their* contra-side is. Attempt to follow the chain. In this kind of situation, the brokers in the middle of the chain will frequently be able to pair off between themselves versus net checks.

Another way to resolve aged fails is to try a temporary substitute delivery of pools with the same coupon and maturity, or a substitution of Treasuries. When executing a sub, you generate cash for the securities delivered. The contra-party receives the substituted securities, which it holds as collateral against the original transaction. When you get the original securities, you must contact the contra-party and make arrangements to simultaneously receive and deliver (swap) the two open contracts against payment. Permission to do a sub must be obtained from the contra-party. It may be difficult, but it's not impossible. Always try. Remember that substitutions of pools collateralizing a loan or term repo can and should always be done.

Always try to get permission to make a late delivery or a partial delivery. A late delivery is one that is made after the normal cutoff time for the day. A partial consists of delivering part of the original contract. Take, for example, the open fails for GNMA Pool 185850 shown in Figure 16–2. In such a situation you may have $1 or $2 million at the end of the day against your open contract of 3MM for account 5432. Request the account to accept part of the contract now and the balance when you receive it. Otherwise, you will have paid out $2 million that must be financed as a result of your inability to redeliver to the purchaser.

Two other methods of fail control can be used, but they must be coordinated between operations management and trading. They can be used when you are in a situation involving a fail that will be open for an extended period (e.g., a large sale has been made by an estate and legal papers are pending). The first is the use of a reverse repo. The securities received as the collateral on the reverse can be used to make delivery on an open fail. It is imperative, however, that you know that you will be able to roll the reverse for an extended period and that you will be able to protect the P&I payments you will owe to the party who repoed the securities to you. The second is a trading agreement to execute a buy-back/sell-back. The securities that were originally sold are bought back from the purchaser, and the fail is paired off with the purchase. A simultaneous agreement is made to resell the securities at the then prevailing market price to the same contra-party when they ultimately become available. This permits your firm to continue to accrue interest on the securities during the extended fail period in exchange for the market risk that may be sustained at the time of the sell-back. This strategy is very similar to the trading strategy involved in TBA dollar rolls.

REVIEWING SPECIFIC ACCOUNTS TO REDUCE FAILS

A number of separate accounts should be established to assist in controlling fails: a DK account, a reclamation account, a turnaround bank loan account, and a turnaround box account. Although each is used for a unique reason, each reflects positions with delivery requirements that were not satisfied on the day the securities were available. The purpose of setting up separate accounts is to provide an opportunity to do a thorough analysis of the entries that are made to these accounts. Such an analysis can help to determine patterns or chronic problems that can be corrected, thereby improving the fail financing picture.

The DK Account

A DK is the return of a previously delivered transaction by the contra-party with the claim that they "Don't Know" the transaction. Every DK results in an additional financing charge because the contract value of the trade has to be paid back to the party returning the securities. Whenever an item is returned DK, clearance operations must take immediate steps to determine if all details of the trade were correctly processed internally. Once that is ascertained, contact the purchaser's clearance operations group to determine if they have an internal difference. If neither of these efforts is successful in resolving the DK, the transaction must be referred to the trading desk for resolution between the traders involved in the transaction. The purpose of maintaining a separate DK account is to provide management with quick access to all DKed trades; each should be resolved within one business day. Another reason for maintaining this account is to enable the firm to build a history file of all DKed trades. It is useful to be able to identify all DKs on an account-by-account basis and also on a clearing agent basis. Such an historical analysis will reveal if any patterns exist for which corrective measures can be taken. Codes should also be provided within this file to permit the recording of information relative to compensation claims. A compensation claim is a formal request to be reimbursed for interest charges associated with financing the returned securities. Such a claim should be made when it is proven that the original delivery was valid as per the terms of the trade. Records should also be maintained regarding DKs on which no compensation was claimed, the reason for the failure to seek compensation, and the identity of the person authorizing the financing loss.

The Reclamation Account

The use of a reclamation account is very similar in scope to the DK account. A reclamation is a delivery being returned for any reason other than a DK. Again, a reclamation file provides the capability to identify transactions that are being unnecessarily financed. What was the cause of the reclamation? Could it have been avoided? Do the circumstances indicate that a change in procedures or a shift in manpower is required? Should compensation be sought? As you can see, the scope of the DK account and the reclamation account are very similar; many firms choose to use a single account for book purposes.

The Turnaround Bank Loan and Box Accounts

The turnaround bank loan account and the turnaround box account are also similar to each other. Each contains securities that were received during the day but that were not used to reduce a settled pending delivery requirement. If the redelivery requirement does not settle until the following or some subsequent business day, loans and box deposits should not be booked to these accounts. These accounts also isolate the transactions that contributed to the previous day's financing costs. They enable management to analyze the reason for a firm's fails and the efficiency of its clearance operations.

THE FAIL SPREAD (FAIL RATIO)

As you can see, a careful postsettlement analysis of your open fails and their offsetting positions will accurately reveal exactly how efficient a clearance operation is in converting its open contracts to cash. A far quicker method of determining this efficiency can be achieved by calculating the fail spread (also known as the fail ratio). When a firm buys from the street, a fail to receive is set up on its records. Cash must be paid out when the item is received. If that item is sold, a fail to deliver is set up and must be cleared before payment will be made by the contra-broker or contra-dealer. The fail spread, or fail ratio, is a comparison of the dollar value in the fail-to-receive account versus the dollar value in the fail-to-deliver account. If the FR figure is consistently higher than the FD figure, the cash flow objective is most likely being met.

When a fail to receive is cleaned up, the dollar value in the account (which from an accounting standpoint is a credit or payable) is reduced. There has been an outflow of cash. When the security is delivered, the fail to deliver is cleaned up and the dollar value (which is a debit or receivable) is reduced. At this point, cash outflow has been offset by cash intake. If the securities received were not turned around to the street, the fail ratio would be negatively impacted. There is an open fail to deliver with a debit amount. That amount is now offset by a credit to cash, the payment made when the FR was cleaned up. That cash has to be replaced and because it has not been (the FD is still open), the cash must be borrowed at the current financing rate. This is an outright expense. A negative fail ratio may result.

Communications and networking are among the most effective tools available to an MBS clearance and fail control group. Fails can be prevented by communicating possible problems to the people who are in a position to take immediate steps to resolve the potential problem. Actions such as arranging for late deliveries, partial deliveries, substitutions, and so on all involve communicating with your peers in other organizations. This is your network; use it! Cliché time! "One hand washes the other." If you have the opportunity to help someone at another firm without negatively impacting the P&L of your own firm and without infringing on confidential relationships and/or information, then help out! MBS clearance is difficult. There are many pieces that have to come together, and efficiency is dependent on the cooperation among all the players. How important is that cooperation to you and your firm? If it is done right, you will *save millions*! If not, ...

17

Principal and Interest (P&I) Processing

Payments on outstanding mortgages must be made on a monthly basis. The payments have two components: (1) a portion of the principal (or outstanding) amount of the loan and (2) interest on the principal amount outstanding during the previous month. A mortgage-backed security represents an investment, evidenced by a certificate or a book-entry equivalent thereof, in a package or pool of individual mortgages. Because the MBS holders effectively own a proportionate share of all the mortgages in a pool, when the mortgagors make their monthly payments on their individual mortgages, the total amounts received, less servicing and guarantee fees, are passed through to the security holders. This is the monthly P&I.

GENERAL CONCEPTS AND DEFINITIONS

Mortgage-backed securities are registered instruments, and the registered holders of these securities are the individuals and institutions who receive the P&I distribution. The purpose of registration is to be able to determine who owns a security. An issuer or central paying agent will always pay current P&I distributions to the current registered owner.

Trading is active and registrations constantly change, however, so there must be a particular time when the books of the transfer agent are "recorded" to determine who will receive the current distribution. The date that this is done is known as the *record date*. On the close of business on the record date (RD), whoever is registered on the books of the agent (Chemical Bank for all physical GNMA, and the FedNY for all FHLMC and FNMA issues) will be the one who will receive the current month's distribution. The book closing process is repeated every month, generally on the last business day of each month. Registration information on the books of the agent corresponds to the registration information as shown on the outstanding certificates.

The registered owner is frequently an agent for the true, or beneficial, owner of the securities. The beneficial owner is the party who has invested its funds in a particular MBS, the party to whom all benefits from that investment should flow. Typically, there is a layering of beneficial ownership in today's investment community. Think about an eligible GNMA issue on deposit at the MBSCC depository. The physical certificates are registered in the name of the depository's nominee, MBSCC & Co. The depository holds the certificates on behalf of its members, the first layer of beneficial ownership. Its members, the brokerage and banking community, have made many of their deposits on behalf of their customer base, the second layer of benefical ownership. The typical flow of a P&I distribution under a GNMA II program is as follows:

Mortgagor → Mortgagee → Chemical Bank (transfer agent) → MBSCC → Bank/ Broker/Dealer → Customer

The *mortgagor* is the debtor who must make monthly loan payments. The *mortgagee* is the institution that supplied the mortgages that it subsequently pooled and sold. The mortagee must continue to perform all accounting functions, including receipt and disbursement of monthly P&I payments, in its capacity as the servicer of the pool. The *transfer agent* receives the passed-through P&I payments from the servicer and distributes the payments to the registered owner recorded on the mortagee's registration and transfer records, the MBSCC & Co. The MBSCC & Co. distributes the P&I payment to the banks, brokers, and dealers which the depository knows, according to its accounting records, to be the beneficial owners of the securities registered in its name. The P&I is then credited to the true beneficial owners, the customers of record on the books of the banks, brokers, and dealers.

The date on which an investor can actually expect to receive the P&I distribution is known as the *payable date* (PD). There is a monthly record date and a monthly payable date. Normally, an investor can expect to receive a distribution every 30 days, but you should be aware of the fact that there is a payment delay (see Figure 17–1). The First Boston Corporation explains this delay as follows:

Payment delay refers to the time lag between the date on which the homeowners are scheduled to make their mortgage payments and the date the servicing institution pays the pool investors. The payment delay differs for each pass-through type. Since interest is calculated monthly, the payment delays result in interest-free delay periods of 14, 19, 24, and 44 days for GNMA-I, GNMA-II, FNMA and FHLMC, respectively, reflecting the actual number of days elapsed. For example, under the GNMA-I program, the homeowner is scheduled to pay the servicer on the first of the month, and the servicer subsequently pays the investor on the fifteenth of the month regardless of whether or not the homeowner's payment has been received. Payment delays are usually stated in a misleading fashion. The stated delay is 45 days for GNMA-I, 50 days for GNMA-II, 55 days for FNMA and 75 days for FHLMC pools. The stated delay is the time lag from the issue date of the pass-through until the date of the first payment from the servicer to the investor. The number of days stated includes both the issue date and the first payment date. Subsequent principal and interest payments are passed through to the investor monthly on the same day of month.

CALCULATION OF MONTHLY P&I AMOUNTS

The calculation of monthly P&I amounts is another facet of MBS processing that is unique. The simplistic realm of dividend and interest processing disappears. You *cannot* simply multiply a coupon rate by face value to determine the annual interest amount that will accrue on a fixed income issue for the life of the security. You *can* expect that payable amounts will differ monthly, sometimes drastically. You *can* expect that it will be necessary to calculate both a principal payout and an interest payout each month.

Assume that you own $250,000.00 face value of mortgage pool 123456 9.50% due 08-15-2011 on the record date of 6-30. It is now 7-10, and you want to know the exact P&I distribution you

FIGURE 17-1. How Payment Delays Work

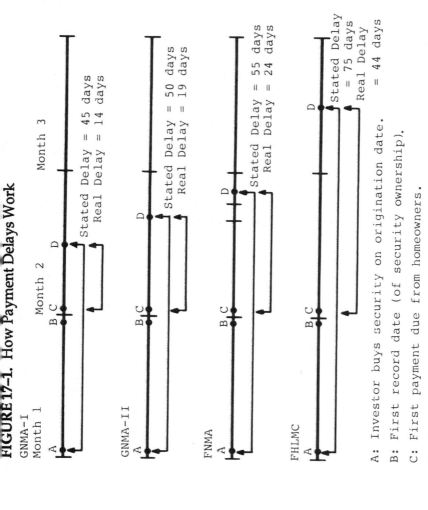

A: Investor buys security on origination date.

B: First record date (of security ownership).

C: First payment due from homeowners.

D: First payment actually made to pass-through investor.

Source: First Boston Fixed Income

will receive on 7-15. What do you have to do to arrive at the total amount of the distribution? You have to calculate two different amounts: a separate principal amount and a separate interest amount. Let's look at the interest amount of the distribution first. Interest is paid on the outstanding amount of a debt, the amortized amount of the pool. You already know that to calculate the current amortized amount of any MBS you multiply the face value of the pool by the current factor. For the pool in this example, the factor announced on 6-8 was .87654321, and the factor announced on 7-8 was .87312341. The interest that will be paid on 7-15 is the interest that accumulated during the month of June. It is the factor that was announced in June that reflects the amortized value of the pool during that period. Therefore the June factor must be used to calculate the amortized amount, or outstanding principal value, of the loan on which interest is payable.

Formula for Calculating Monthly Interest

Face amount	×	factor		=	amortized amt	×	coupon	/#mos.yr.	=	interest
$250,000.00	×	.87654321	=		$219,135.80	×	.095	/ 12	=	$1,734.83

The next step is the calculation of the principal paydown amount for the month. Factors represent the percentage of the currently outstanding amount of the original aggregate value of the mortgage loans collateralizing a pool. The percentage is expressed as an eight decimal place integer. Looking at our example, if 87.654321% of the original loans were outstanding in June and 87.412341% were outstanding in July, simple subtraction reveals that .341980% of the outstanding mortgages were paid down as of July 1. That translates into a factor of .00341980. In the following formula, "RD Mo Factor" equates to the factor applicable during the month in which the record date occurred and "PD Mo Factor" equates to the factor applicable during the month in which the payable date occurred.

Formula for Calculating Monthly Principal Paydown

(RD Mo Factor	–	PD Mo Factor)	×	Orignal Face	=	Principal Paydown
(.87654321	–	.87412341)	×	$250,000.00	=	Principal Paydown
	.00341980		×	$250,000.00	=	$854.95

The July 15 P&I distribution for the pool just calculated will be $2,589.78, consisting of $854.95 principal and $1,734.83 interest. The principal amount represents a return of investment capital and as such is nontaxable, excluding considerations for a discounted purchase price. The interest portion of the distribution must be reported to the customer and to the IRS at the end of the year as taxable income.

P&I PROCESSING

Now that you understand how P&I distributions originate and how they are calculated, let's review the processing cycle. Most mortgage-backed issues and asset-backed issues have the same record date, the last business day of the month. That fact should be ingrained in everyone's mind, not just in the minds of the people who are responsible for P&I processing. Remember how important presettlement planning is to the clearance operation. Prerecord date planning is just as important to P&I processing. If a firm owns an MBS on the record date, either on its own behalf or on behalf of its customers, it is entitled to receive a P&I distribution. The actual distributions, however, are distributed to the registered owner on the close of business on the record date. Knowing this, everyone in any operational department should make every effort to ensure that the firm's record date position is "clean."

A clean record date position means that all certificates are properly registered in the firm's name or deposited at a depository, open transactions have been cleared on settlement date, and there are no pending items that will prevent timely and full receipt of the total distribution to which the firm is entitled. In many instances, it is possible to achieve this position if everyone keeps alert to the fact that the last business day of the month is the record date. Clearance people should deliver all open contracts on or before the record date; any open fails, customer or streetside, should be identified for the P&I department. People in the vault should examine all their physical inventory. If it is eligible for a depository, they should make the deposit. Deposits made on the actual record date must be so marked; they may also be used that same day for delivery purposes. If certificates are for a nondepository issue and they are not registered in the firm's name, they should be sent to the transfer agent for reregistration no later than noon on the record date, preferably a day or two before the record date when possible. People in charge of stock record balancing should make sure that all open "breaks" are resolved by the end of day so that the records will reflect an accurate picture on the RD. Preparatory record date processing is extremely important.

Having successfully jumped that hurdle, what comes next? Each of the following has to be considered:

- ❑ Determining your record date position.
- ❑ Balancing your record date position.
- ❑ Accounting for open repo positions.
- ❑ Due-bill and payable date processing.
- ❑ Controlling receivables.

Determining Your Record Date Position

A record date position is a balanced accounting record that reflects the identity of all accounts to which the P&I distribution must be paid as well as all accounts from which payment will be received. A record date position is a stock record (SR) extract.

What is a stock record? It is the official accounting ledger on which all security holdings and movements are recorded. It does not reflect any cash values associated with a transaction, only the share, or quantity, amount of the security involved. As such, it contains the total long and short positions in every security for which the firm maintains a position for either itself or its customers. A long position is a debit position; a short position is a credit position. Basic accounting mandates that, in any accounting ledger, total debits must equal total credits. Therefore, there are equal amounts of long and short positions for each security listed on the stock record. A stock record is posted on a settlement date basis. Executed trades that have not reached settlement date will not appear on the stock record. The quantity values should always reflect original face, not current amortized, amounts.

Long positions are always indicative of beneficial ownership. Any account with a long position owns the securities recorded on the SR and is entitled to all the benefits of ownership, including P&I payments. If a customer purchased an issue and the trade has settled but not delivered, the customer's account will have a long position. Sales to other brokers and dealers that have not been cleared are fails to deliver and are always long positions.

Short positions represent either a receivable or a location. If a customer has a short position, that customer owes the firm the securities listed as well as any P&I that might accrue while the position remains short. Fails to receive and securities bought from other brokers and dealers that have not been cleared are always short positions on the SR. Locations are addresses (accounts) where security holdings are stored. Examples of these accounts are the box account, the depository account, the omnibus clearing account, the firm transfer account, the customer transfer account, and the safekeeping account. Each of these represents the physical location of securities that the firm is holding on either its own behalf or that of its customers. P&I payments are expected on all positions in location accounts, but you have to understand the purpose of each location account to be able to determine the manner in which they will be received and, more important, by whom they will be received. The customer transfer account reflects securities physically located at the transfer agent for the purpose of being reregistered into the name of a customer. The safekeeping account represents securities registered in the customer's own name that are being held in custody on behalf of the client. In both these instances, the customers will appear with long positions on the stock record. Because the securities are registered in the customers' names, however, the firm carrying their accounts will not credit them with the P&I since they will receive it direct from the issuer. The specific customer accounts with securities in one of these location accounts can be easily identified through the use of a memo field on the SR which clearly indicates the portion of each customer's long position that is in safekeeping or transfer.

Balancing Your Record Date Position

Yes, you are right! Your record date position is a stock record extract; the P&I department should not have to balance it. That should have already been done by the SR department. The issue, however, is making certain that all P&I credits (payables) are offset by an equal amount of P&I debits (receivables). Furthermore, it is ensuring that all required steps have been taken to ensure receipt of incoming funds on a timely basis. This includes recording the certificate numbers and registering all physical securities

FIGURE 17–2.   Stock Record Position Listing

ISSUE: MBS Pool 123456			CUSIP: 888888MB1			COB: 06-30
D-L-A	LONG	SHORT	ACCOUNT	SEG	SK	TFR
06-30	5MM		Firm Trading			
06-29	3MM		DVP Customer A			
05-07	1MM		Retail Customer B		1MM	
06-29	2MM		DVP Customer C			
03-16	2MM		Retail Customer D	2MM		
06-14	2MM		Retail Customer E			1M
06-30		10MM	Fail to Receive			
06-30		1MM	Repo Financing Acct			
03-20		2MM	Segregation (SEG)			
05-07		1MM	Safekeeping (SK)			
06-28		1MM	Customer Transfer (TFR)			
TOTALS	15MM	15MM		2MM	1MM	1M

Note: D-L-A is the date the latest activity was posted to each account.

(other than those on deposit at a book-entry depository), issuing due bills for physical deliveries, setting up receivables for fails to receive and open repo positions, and preparing any manual adjustments that might be required.

Let's assume that the SR position shown in Figure 17–2 is to be balanced; for simplicity, every 1MM in holdings is entitled to $10,000.00 (10M) in P&I. We will go through the steps illustrated in Figure 17–3.

FIGURE 17–3. A Dividend Department P&I Takeoff

```
ISSUE: MBS Pool 123456                          CUSIP: 888888MB1

Record: 06-30-xx        Payable: 07-15-xx        Rate: 10.00
```

LONG	SHORT	ACCOUNT	DEBIT	CREDIT	MEMOS
5MM		Firm Trading		① 50M	
3MM		DVP Customer A		② 30M	
1MM		Retail Customer B		③	1MM SK
2MM		DVP Customer C		④ 20M	
2MM		Retail Customer D		⑤ 20M	
2MM		Retail Customer E		⑥ 10M	1MM TFR
	10MM	Fail to Receive ⑦	100M		
	1MM	Repo Financing Acct ⑧	10M		
	2MM	Segregation (SEG) ⑨	20M		
⑩	1MM	Safekeeping (SK)			
⑪	1MM	Customer Transfer (TFR)			
15MM	15MM		130M	130M	

⑫

Explanation of P&I Takeoff Listing (Figure 17–3):

1. The system has calculated a $50,000.00 P&I credit for this account. This account contains a firm's trading inventory and is entitled to P&I distributions just like any other customer. Had the account been short on the RD, a cash debit would be charged to the account reflecting the P&I due to the firm.

2. Since this is a DVP account, the P&I credit for the long position will be journaled into a due-bill payable account for subsequent payment to the account's clearing agent. A DVP trade that is open over the RD cannot be delivered without a due bill. Because the due bill must subsequently be honored, the system credit is voided to preclude duplication of payment.

3. Although this customer has a long position, no credit will be given because the entire long position is offset by an SK memo-field entry. This means that the certificates are in the customer's name and that the P&I payment will be

made directly to the registered owner by the issuer/agent.

4. Same explanation as the second item.

5. This customer will receive credit on its entire position because the customer's certificates are being held in seg. Segregated certificates have to be registered in the name of the firm. When the firm receives the P&I distribution on them, it must credit the amount to the customers for whom the seg position is being maintained. It is not necessary for the dividend takeoff to reflect the seg memo entry; all long positions will be credited unless the system identifies a reason not to do so as in items 2, 3, 4, and 6.

6. In this case the credit to be processed reflects a credit on 1MM of a 2MM position. The transfer memo field indicates that on or before the record date (6-28 in this case as per the SR) 1MM of this issue was presented to the transfer agent for registration into the customer's name. For set-up balancing purposes, it is always assumed that the transfer will be accomplished on a timely basis; the dated date of the new certificate will be the record date or earlier. Therefore, the customer should receive the P&I direct from the issuer/agent. Part of the balancing process in this instance involves notifying the firm's transfer personnel that the issue in transfer went record. When the certificate is received back from the transfer agent, this group must examine the dated date to confirm that it did "make transfer" (i.e., that it was reregistered on or before the RD). If the date of the new certificate is a date later than the RD, the transfer department should advise the dividend department immediately. Copies of the old certificates, the ones forwarded to the agent for reregistration, must be obtained to determine who the registered owner was. This is the party that will receive the P&I; a formal claim for the return of the P&I must be made to the person or entity involved. Once it is realized that customer transfer missed the record date, the account involved must be set up to receive the credit to which it is entitled regardless of whether the claim has been or will be paid. Transfers processed on the record

date can be "iffy"; try to get them to the agent before the RD.

7. This position could represent a single FR of 10MM or 10 fails of 1MM each. Receivables must be set up for each separate fail contract. The cage must be notified that the open fails went record so that they know that they must receive due bills when the deliveries are made by the failing brokers. Once received, the due bills should be transmitted to the dividend department for redemption on the payable date.

8. The repo account serves as a location account. The identity of each individual repo contract comprising the total repo position must be identified and a receivable established for each. Repos will be discussed further in the following pages.

9. Segregation is an account that identifies the location of certificates held in firm name for customers. Whenever there is a position in a box or a seg location, it is necessary to obtain a photocopy or microfilm record of the certificates. The copies should be examined first to ensure that the quantity of the photostats received equals the takeoff position. If you do not have complete registration information available, you will never be able to determine how to secure payment should you come up with a shortage on payable date. *Certificate numbers are indispensable.* For all certificates registered in the name of another firm or customer name, claims must be initiated.

10. It is not necessary to obtain copies of the certificates in this location. The individual certificates that comprise this position are relatively immobile and easily researched should a problem arise with the position. All these certificates are registered in a customer's name; payment will be made direct to each customer by the issuer/agent.

11. This is the location account for certificates physically at the offices of the transfer agent. The handling of this account was explained in item 6.

12. These cash figures represent the total P&I debits that
must be received to offset the total credits to be paid out
to customers and other firms.

Accounting for Open Repo Positions

When repos were discussed, it was indicated that, from a
trade origination and clearance standpoint, a repo is treated like
a sell trade. When a sale is executed, the seller gives up all beneficial rights to the security on settlement date in exchange for the
cash contract value of the transaction. This is not true of repo
sales. All beneficial rights of ownership, including the right to
receive accrued P&I payments, are retained by the seller. That's
logical when you realize that the securities sold in a repo trade are
treated similarly to securities collateralizing a loan. When you
make a loan, the collateral serves as the lender's security. The
lender has no rights to the collateral unless the borrower defaults.
Repos can present peculiar, sometimes serious, control
problems relative to the collection of P&I. Repo trading has a high
volume activity at a large dealer firm. The identity of the party
with whom the repo was executed is not discernible from the
dividend takeoff. Many firms record a repo on their records like
any other sale. The first entry to the contra-party's account reflects
the sale, and the second entry reflects the delivery of the collateral
leaving the customer's account flat at the end of the day. If there
is no position, you can't identify the customer. This problem is
exasperated when the collateral being used is either an FHLMC
or an FNMA and the delivery must be executed through the Fed.
When the delivery is made, the Fed reduces the position in the
deliverer s account and increases the receiver's account. If the
repo is outstanding on the record date, the Fed, reacting to the
long position in the receiver's account, will record that account as
the holder of record and will credit that account with the P&I on
the payable date. It is now up to the originator of the repo to claim
back the P&I to which it is entitled. So unless there is separate
automated support providing subsidiary listings showing the
customer details relative to open repo account positions, clerks
must manually review every repo trade and settlement to determine "who's doing what to whom and when?" If activity is normal, the situation is still controllable. In early 1987, however,
extraordinary volume was experienced in MBS. Since practically

every position was going record on the same day, clerks fell behind in obtaining repo contract information and depended on the
contra-party to pay the P&I due. These people were themselves
backlogged, and the problem snowballed with the result that individual firms had tens of millions of dollars in P&I receivables
as the result of unreconciled repo trading accounts.

The PTC depository provides its users with an excellent system for repo accounting. It involves the use of an interim account
used exclusively for repo clearance. Instead of melding regular
and repo activities into a single position, repo trading deliveries
are posted only to the interim account so that the true beneficial
ownership of the position can be determined and credited to the
proper party on the payable date. Internal repo codes and
separate system support for this process are musts.

The last repo-related P&I problem for discussion involves
repos cleared by the physical delivery of the underlying securities.
Firms receiving securities collateralizing repos should not be
reregistering the certificates in their name, but for a variety of
reasons they frequently do. The delivering firm will be showing
the original certificates as part of their open inventory. When this
occurs, the delivering firm will naturally be underpaid by the is-
suer/agent. Whenever an underpayment occurs and your
records reflect an open "physical" repo on the RD, you should first
verify that payment was or was not received on the certificates in
question. Many problems are quickly resolved by making this
your first step.

Due-Bill and Payable Date Processing

Due bills are nontransferable promissory notes indicating
that the recipient is entitled to the P&I payment described in the
due bill. Due bills are intended to protect the rights of the purchaser. When a customer, a bank, or a broker purchases an MBS
for settlement on or before a record date, the buyer is entitled to
receive the P&I that will be distributed on a future date. If the
seller delivers the securities after the record date, it is impossible
for the buyer to transfer the securities into its name in time to be
a holder of record. Because the seller failed to clear the contract
on or before the record date, the seller must pay the P&I to the
buyer. To ensure that this payment is made, the buyer does not
have to accept a delivery after the record date unless a due bill is

attached to the certificates (we'll talk about book entry shortly). A physical due bill must accompany the physical delivery. And if the delivery is delayed until after the actual payment date, a check for the amount of the distribution must accompany the delivery or it will be rejected. It is important to protect your firm on all incoming items requiring due bills. Failure to obtain will definitely result in a loss of cash flow; at worst it could result in substantial capital losses.

With so many MBS eligible for the Fedwire or a depository, how do you issue and/or obtain due bills through these systems? You don't! However, the PSA has ruled that for book-entry security receipts that require a due bill, copies of the messages from book-entry entities may be used as if they were a due bill. The copy is to be presented to the deliverer along with the details of the payment and a signed standard indemnification statement. The PSA has specific guidelines for redemption; consult these regulations and follow them in order to prevent a DK of your redemption.

Due bills and due-bill substitutes must be properly redeemed within 60 days after issuance. They are null and void after that time, and the formal claim process must be pursued in order to collect payment. Due bills should always be redeemed promptly; redemption payments are due no later than three business days after receipt. So, if you redeem your due bills three days or more before the payable date, you are entitled to receive your payment on the payable date; interest compensation may be claimed for payments that are not timely.

On the payable dates, all the prebalanced debit and credit entries relative to each P&I distribution should be processed. Payments on a firm's positions will originate from various sources. FHLMCs are paid on the fifteenth of each month, and payments will be in the form of a wire payment message through the Fed. The same is true for FNMA issues except that the payable date is the twenty-fifth of each month. Payments for PTC depository positions will be in the form of a credit to each participant's account; the credit becomes part of the overall money settlement figure with PTC for the day. GNMA I payments are made on the fifteenth of each month, and GNMA II payments are made on the twentieth of each month. If the payments are being made on physical certificates, there is a more significant difference in the payment method. Payments for GNMA II physicals are made by a single check processed by the transfer and disbursing agent, Chemical Bank. Payments for GNMA I distributions are made directly by each issuer, and a separate check is issued for each certificate. Each check is accompanied by a HUD form that discloses all details concerning the distribution and the remaining amortized balance of the certificate (see Figure 17–4). Aside from the problem of having to process multiple P&I checks, there is another serious problem associated with processing GNMA I P&I. While Chemical Bank is the transfer agent for GNMA I issues, there are occasions when a regional issuer will make its monthly distribution before it receives information on record date reregistrations from Chemical. In these cases, underpayments result even though certificates were in your firm's name on the record date. If it appears that your firm has been underpaid on a GNMA I distribution, first check certificates that were registered on or near the record date against the certificate number on the HUD form; it may save a lot of work.

Controlling Receivables

We're really beating a dead horse here, but the best control of receivables takes place during your prerecord date processing. Securities eligible for book entry should be deposited. All due bills should be accounted for. Clearance should be advised of all the Fed and PTC depository messages that will be needed to execute proper redemptions. All physicals not registered in the firm's name should be sent to the transfer agent. Should you fail to accomplish this and there are certificates registered in the name of another party, a P&I claim must be prepared and presented. There have been times when volume was so heavy that it was impossible to get every certificate to the agent on time to make transfer by the record date. Book entry should eliminate this problem, but if it ever occurs, choose the certificates that will not be reregistered. Choose those registered in the name of recognized, financially stable, banks and brokers. When you process your claim, you won't have to worry about payment. Make sure that certificates in the names of individuals and other unknown entities are the ones that receive the priority attention needed to get them transferred on time.

Receivables are costly. Because you are obliged to pay out the credit side, these debits must be financed until payment is

FIGURE 17–4. HUD Form that Accompanies GNMA I P&I Payments

U.S. Department of Housing and Urban Development	ISS. NO.
Government National Mortgage Association	72400
MORTGAGE BACKED SECURITIES PROGRAM	
ISSUER'S MONTHLY REMITTANCE ADVICE	

TO THE FOLLOWING SECURITY HOLDER:

GNMA POOL NUMBER	DATE
4881CD	JUN. 15, 1931

CERTIFICATE NUMBER	REPORTING MONTH
716583SF	MAY. 1981

SECURITY INTEREST RATE	PRO RATA SHARE PERCENTAGE
12.5	2.22100577

This remittance advice covers the above security holder's proportional share of the distribution in the indicated pool of mortgages for the above reporting month. ☒ The check is enclosed. ☐ The check will be forwarded separately but no later than the 15th of the current month

A.	CASH DISTRIBUTION DUE HOLDER FOR SCHEDULED PRINCIPAL AMORTIZATION	$	262.36
B.	CASH DISTRIBUTION DUE HOLDER FOR INTEREST		10,380.97
C.	CASH DISTRIBUTION OF ADDITIONAL PRINCIPAL COLLECTIONS		13.78
D.	ADJUSTMENTS (+ or –) (Explain)		.14
E.	TOTAL CASH DISTRIBUTION DUE HOLDER	$	10,657.25
F.	OUTSTANDING BALANCE OF THIS CERTIFICATE AFTER CREDIT OF ABOVE DISTRIBUTION	$	996,296.92

EXPLANATION FOR ITEM D:
      PAYOFF OR LIQUIDATION

I hereby certify that the information contained herein is true to the best of my knowledge and belief.

Dunbar Associates	*Fred Dahl*
(Issuer)	(Authorized Signature)
SECURITIES ACCOUNTING SECTION	
P.O. Box 132	Riviera, New Mexico
(Street)	(City and State)

In the event of transfer of the security, the most recent Remittance Advice must accompany the certificate.

Hud 1714

received. There is no guarantee that the receivables will be honored, especially if the claim is against an unassociated party who does not understand the industry. Have you ever tried to explain to a customer that the securities the customer sold and delivered weeks before the record date were really outstanding and that the P&I should be given to a brokerage firm the customer never heard of before?

Give P&I receivables the same kind of attention you give to fails. The receivable file should be sorted into several sequences according to amount, age, and contra-party. All conversations relative to their payment should be notated with names and dates. Claims should be processed through NSCC's dividend settlement service to expedite payment, and management should be advised immediately of any situation that appears to have the potential to become a write-off.

Appendix

PSA Guidelines to Reduce Daylight Overdraft and Payments System Risk

As a result of ongoing concern with problems generated by
daylight overdrafts and unnecessary fails, PSA recommends the
following good delivery guidelines.

I.   GENERAL CONSIDERATIONS

Brokers, dealers and clearing banks should comply with PSA
guidelines implementing the Federal Reserve Board's $50 million
transfer size limit, as well as with the Federal Reserve Bank of
New York's statement regarding dealer clearance behavior and the
reduction of payments system risk. Accordingly, dealers should
establish procedures designed to ensure that large deliveries of
securities are not delayed until late in the day. In particular,
delivery instructions should be given to clearing banks as soon as
practicable after a trade is entered into and deliveries of
securities should be made as soon as $50 million lots of
securities are in position. A dealer acts contrary to the intent
of these guidelines where it creates artificial shorts in its
position by transferring securities to its customer/seg account or
where it holds incoming deliveries in an unvalidated/unmatched
queue, or does not promptly instruct its clearing bank on same-day
trades.

II.   INSTRUCTIONS AND RELEASE OF ACCOUNT "HOLDS"

For all next-day trades (trades other than those done for
same-day settlement), sending and receiving dealers should have
instructions pended with their clearing banks by 12:00 p.m. (New
York time) on the settlement date. Notwithstanding when
instructions were pended or any dealer instructions to the
contrary, clearing banks' automated systems will release all
"holds" at the account, CUSIP and trade levels at 2:00 p.m. (New
York time).

For all same-day (cash) trades, dealers should have
instructions pended with their clearing banks as soon as
practicable after entering into a trade. Additionally, the
following principles will apply:

    Trades done before 2:00 p.m. (New York time) - clearing
    banks will release all "holds" at the account, CUSIP and
    trade levels at 2:00 p.m. (New York time).

    Trades done between 2:00 p.m. and 2:30 p.m. (New York
    time) - will be subject to the 2:00 p.m. (New York time)
    release "holds" rule.

    Trades done after 2:30 p.m. (New York time) - will be
    done as conditional trades, subject to the terms agreed
    to by the parties, and will be subject to the 2:00 p.m.
    (New York time) release "holds" rule.

To assist all market participants in monitoring compliance
with these guidelines, clearing banks and self-clearing dealers
must include the following information on lines six and seven of
the Fedwire messages for all (next-day and cash) trades:

    - the time and date when delivery instructions were
    pended; and

- the time when the clearing bank released the "hold", if
the delivery occurred on or after 2:00 p.m. (New York
time).

All existing time stamps will continue to be in effect.

III.   WIRE DEADLINES

The wire deadlines will be implemented in three stages, as
described below. The Federal Reserve will make the 15-minute
dealer turn-around time applicable nationwide from the effective
date of these guidelines.

A.   FIRST 60 DAYS - NATIONWIDE DEALER TURN-AROUND TIME

During the first 60 days that these guidelines are in effect,
the current Fedwire deadlines will continue to apply, with the
exception that dealer turn-around time will be expanded to apply
nationwide. The current Fedwire deadlines are as follows:

Customer-to-Dealer cut-off time.....2:15 p.m. (New York time)

Dealer-to-Dealer cut-off time.......2:30 p.m. (New York time)

Dealer-to-Customer cut-off time.....2:45 p.m. (New York time)

Reversals...........................Can be done at any
                                    time during the day,
                                    but 2:45 p.m. to
                                    3:00 p.m. (New York time)
                                    is reserved exclusively
                                    for reversals
                                    (Type Code 2002)
The Federal Reserve will continue to apply their current
guidelines in granting wire extensions. As a result of the
securities traffic problems caused by dealers' building their
securities positions until late in the day, the year-to-date
average close, given extensions, for the Federal Reserve's
securities wire is 4:18 p.m. (New York time). It is contemplated
that improved delivery practices under these guidelines may
ultimately permit a 3:30 p.m. (New York time) firm overall close
of the Fedwire.

B.   AFTER 60 DAYS - EVALUATE FEASIBILITY OF FIRM FEDWIRE CLOSE

After the first 60 days, the Federal Reserve with the
involvement of PSA's Government and Federal Agency Securities
Division Operations Committee will consider instituting a firm
closing hour for regular securities traffic. This consideration
will involve a determination of whether the guidelines have been
effective and have had their intended effect of reducing daylight
overdraft and payments system risk as well as eliminating abuses
in the Fedwire system. The Customer-to-Dealer cut-off time will
be 15 minutes before the Dealer-to-Dealer cut-off time. The
nationwide Dealer-to-Customer cut-off time will be 15 minutes

after the Dealer-to-Dealer cut-off time. The last 15 minutes before the overall close of the Fedwire will continue to be reserved exclusively for reversals (Type Code 2002). Fedwire closing will not be extended, except under extraordinary circumstances.

C. FUTURE - 3:30 P.M. FIRM FEDWIRE CLOSE

After sufficient time has elapsed and all parties have experience and are comfortable with a fixed closing time, the <u>firm closing hour</u> for regular securities traffic will be moved to 3:00 p.m. (New York time), followed by a firm 3:30 p.m. (New York time) overall close of the Fedwire system. The Federal Reserve will continue to make the 15-minute dealer turnaround time applicable nationwide. Fedwire closing will not be extended, except under extraordinary circumstances.

In addition, the following cut-off times will control:

Customer-to-Dealer cut-off time......2:45 p.m. (New York time)

Dealer-to-Dealer cut-off time........3:00 p.m. (New York time)

Dealer-to-Customer cut-off time......3:15 p.m. (New York time)

Reversals...........................Can be done at any time during the day, but 3:15 p.m. to 3:30 p.m. (New York time) is reserved exclusively for reversals (Type Code 2002)

For all stages of these wire deadlines, a dealer acts contrary to the intent of these guidelines if it uses the reversal code for any transactions but reversals.

Although these guidelines identify different delivery cut-off times for dealers and customers, they do not determine who is a dealer or a customer. Each firm, as part of the conditions upon which it is willing to do business, determines whether its counterparties receive dealer or customer time.

IV. <u>REMEDIES FOR NON-COMPLIANCE</u>

After sufficient time for implementation of these guidelines, PSA will work to develop practicable industry guidelines for compensation by dealers who do not comply with these guidelines.

V. <u>IMPLEMENTATION</u>

In order to afford clearing banks the opportunity to adjust their systems to comply with these guidelines, these guidelines will become effective three months after their approval by the Primary Dealers Committee.

Glossary

ACCRETION The process of accumulating the amount of interest that has accrued on a debt instrument since the last payable date of the coupon up to, but not including, the current date. This amount is usually added to the outstanding principal (amortized) amount of the issue to determine a true current market valuation.

ACCRUED INTEREST Interest that has been earned but not yet paid. This amount is based on the current amortized amount of an issue and is debited to the purchaser, credited to the seller. *See* ACCRETION.

ADJUSTABLE RATE MORTGAGE (ARM) A mortgage loan in which the interest rate is adjusted periodically in synchronization with movements in a predetermined index, such as the Treasury bill rate or prime rate. *See* CAP.

AE CREDIT A soft dollar amount credited to an account executive in payment of his order; the amount to be paid is based on the amortized amount of the trade. The hard dollars received by the AE are a percentage of that amount. This rule is not applicable if the AE is salaried as in the case of discount brokerage firms.

AGENT The role of a broker/dealer firm when it acts as an intermediary, or finder, between its customer and a marketmaker or contra-broker.

ALLOCATION The function of assigning specific pools, or groups, to a previous trade that was executed on a forward, or TBA, basis. *See* TO BE ANNOUNCED.

AMORTIZE To pay down a loan through numerous periodic payments.

AMORTIZED AMOUNT The outstanding principal, or loan amount, of the mortgages in a pool. The amount is obtained by multiplying the original face value by the current factor value as announced by the issuer, GNMA, or other agencies of the government. *See* BOND BUYER.

APPROVED LENDER A lending organization, such as a commercial bank, a savings and loan association, or a mortgage banker, whose operations and financials are reviewed by an MBS issuer. Satisfactory review means that the organization is eligible (approved) to participate in the programs offered by the issuer (e.g., the FHLMC).

ARBITRAGE The process of hedging purchase and sale transactions resulting in a relatively risk-free investment. Profits are realized either as net price or as a net interest rate spread.

ARM A variable, or floating, rate mortgage. *See* ADJUST-ABLE RATE MORTGAGE.

ASKED PRICE The price at which a trader is willing to sell a security.

ASSET-BACKED SECURITY (ABS) A security similar in principal to an MBS. The underlying collateral for an ABS could consist of personal loans such as car loans and credit card loans.

AVERAGE LIFE The anticipated time that will elapse before the entire outstanding principal amount of an MBS is repaid to the holders. Because of numerous prepayments of mortgage loan principal, the average life (not the maturity date) becomes a primary valuation or pricing consideration for mortgage-backed issues. *See* DURATION and HALF-LIFE.

BALLOON MORTGAGE   A mortgage in which the scheduled principal payments will not fully amortize the loan by its maturity date. The amount of outstanding principal at the maturity date of the loan is payable in one bulk sum at maturity.

BASIS POINT   A measure of changes in prices or yields for fixed-income securities. One basis point equals 1/100 of 1 percent (0.0001). In terms of dollar pricing, it is the equivalent of $100 on a $1 million transaction.

BENEFICIAL OWNER   The true owner of a security as opposed to the person or entity who is maintaining custody of the issue. It is the person or entity to whom all benefits (e.g., principal and interest payments) of the security flow.

BID PRICE   The price at which a trader is willing to buy a security.

BOND   An interest-bearing security evidencing long-term debt and having a specified maturity date, usually 30 years.

BOND BUYER   A monthly informational service available in various formats which lists all outstanding pools and their current month's factor. *See* FACTOR and AMORTIZED AMOUNT.

BOND RECORD   The official accounting records of a broker-dealer that reflect the beneficial owner (long) and the contra-location or receivable (short) for every security. It is a fully identified inventory ledger.

BOOK ENTRY   The method used most frequently by securities firms to accomplish interfirm deliveries. Movements are accomplished by electronic instructions that become accounting entries recording the transfer of beneficial ownership on the records of a centralized depository. There is no delivery of physical certificates. *See* BENEFICIAL OWNER and DEPOSITORY.

BOX   A section of a broker-dealer's cashiering department where securities are temporarily stored.   In today's book-entry environment, the "box" is principally considered an "accounting" location rather than an actual physical location (which does continue to exist).

BRANCH WIRE   A trade order or administrative message that originates from a branch or regional office.

BROKER   An agent who acts as an intermediary between two customers. For this service, the firm receives a stated commission or fee. A broker does not position securities.

BROKER-DEALER   A registered securities firm that executes trades on behalf of its customers as either broker or dealer. See BROKER and DEALER.

BROKER'S BROKER   A broker specializing in providing electronic quotation, execution, and comparison systems to the dealer community. Subscribing dealers enter their quotes into a broker's broker system, and other dealers execute their orders with the broker's broker who then compares the trade and ultimately gives up the name of the true contra-side of the transaction. The broker's broker receives a fee per trade for providing its services—namely, a centralized quotation system and dealer anonymity during the execution process. See GIVE UP.

BULLET LOAN   A short-term financing method that provides for repayment of the entire principal in one amount, or "bullet." See BALLOON MORTGAGE.

BUYDOWN   A type of mortgage loan whereby a seller or homebuilder pays an amount "up front" to a lender who then gives the buyer a loan with a rate below the market rate. This rate is either for a specified period or for the life of the loan.

BUY-IN   The process of repurchasing a security previously bought from a broker or dealer who failed to deliver the security to the purchasing broker or dealer. Any losses incurred in closing out the original trade are passed along to the original seller who has failed to deliver.

CALL OPTION   A contract giving its holder the right to purchase securities at a specified price within the specified period of the option.

CALL PROTECTION   A feature built into certain MBS that is designed to minimize the risk of prepayment of the underlying mortgages. Issues may be structured so that if the mortgage loans are prepaid, the funds are not passed immediately through to the investor. This protection provides the more consistent cash flow desired by some investors. *See* COLLATERALIZED MORTGAGE OBLIGATION.

CALL PROVISION   The right of the lender of funds to ask for prompt repayment.

CAP (INTEREST)   A ceiling placed on interest rates to limit the extent to which the rates can be raised during a specific period. ARMs usually have both an annual cap and a lifetime cap.

CAPITAL   Cash used for investment purposes—that is, to earn income.

CARRY   The interest costs associated with the funds borrowed to purchase securities. When these costs exceed the cash flow realized from the interest payments received on the purchased inventory, there is a negative carry. If the interest income exceeds the financing charges, there is a positive carry. *See* CURRENT YIELD.

CASH FLOW YIELD   A monthly internal rate of return of an investment in a projected stream of monthly payments of principal and interest. The yield varies with the prepayment assumption that determines the cash flow pattern.

CERTIFICATE   The actual document, registered in the name of the holder, that serves as proof of ownership by the investor. *See* BENEFICIAL OWNER.

CLAIM   The process of filing a written request for payment of a P&I payment erroneously received by a party other than the beneficial owner. The claim is made against the recipient of the P&I.

CLEAR (CLEARED) A term synonymous with settlement. It refers to the receipt and/or delivery of securities against full payment on or after the contracted settlement date of a trade.

CLEARING AGENT An organization that provides various services for customers and customers' accounts such as holding inventory positions, receiving and delivering securities, and disbursing funds.

CLEARINGHOUSE FUNDS (CHFs) One of the two types of funds used in settlement of securities transactions in the United States. These funds have the connotation of next-day availability because they are usually transferred (paid) by means of checks that must go through an overnight collection process before the cash they represent can be released. Most MBS transactions may not be paid for in CHFs; payment is due in cash-equivalent same-day funds. *See* FED FUNDS.

CLOSING The official (legal) creation of a mortgage loan. It is at the closing that the property deed changes hands, the mortgage and other loan documents are signed, and the loan proceeds are disbursed for payment to the seller of the property.

COLLATERALIZED MORTGAGE OBLIGATION (CMO) An MBS that is structured much like a corporate bond. On issuance, there are usually several different classes, called tranches, each of which differs in coupon, maturity, and price. Each tranche in a particular CMO issue pays down the principal portion of the tranche serially (i.e., in maturity order). No tranche receives a distribution of principal before all earlier maturities have been fully paid down (redeemed). The underlying collateral for a CMO could be a GNMA I or II, GPM, FNMA, FHLMC, or conventional mortgages. Principal and interest payments are usually paid on a semiannual basis. *See* CALL PROTECTION and REMIC.

COMMITMENT FEE A fee paid by lenders to an MBS dealer for the dealer's commitment or promise to buy an MBS from the lender at a future date in accordance with the provisions of the commitment letter. *See* STANDBY CONTRACT.

CONDITIONAL PREPAYMENT RATE (CPR) A measure of prepayment which assumes that each month a constant proportion of the outstanding mortgages will prepay. [Cardiac pulmonary respiration (CPR) is also the first-aid treatment to be given an MBS trader who completed positioning $100 million current coupons an hour before interest rates rose 50 basis points!]

CONDOMINIUM A form of property ownership whereby the purchaser receives title to a particular unit in a multiple-unit structure and a proportionate interest in common areas of the property.

CONFIRMATION A statement of the terms and conditions of a trade executed by a broker-dealer on behalf of a customer. The confirm serves as a bill for purchases and as an advisory notice for sales.

CONFORMING LOAN AMOUNT The maximum loan amount allowable applied individually to each mortgage loan being used to create a new MBS. If the outstanding principal amount of the loan exceeds this amount, it will be rejected as MBS collateral.

CONSTRUCTION LOAN A short-term debt instrument the proceeds of which are used during the development phase of a project—that is, from the start to the completion of construction, before opening. Funds are advanced as needed to pay contractors, and interest is paid only on the funds used. On completion of the project, the construction loan usually is replaced by a long-term project loan.

CONTINGENT RATE A rate of interest that is subject to change on the occurrence of some event that can be defined but that is not certain to occur.

CONTRA-SIDE A term used to describe the other side with whom a trade was executed (i.e., the buyer versus the seller, or vice versa). The term is usually used in the context of the street-side of a trade but can also refer to a customer's trade.

CONVENTIONAL MORTGAGE A mortgage that is not insured by the Federal Housing Administration (FHA) or the Farmers Home Administration (FmHA) or guaranteed by the Veterans Administration (VA). It is called a conventional loan because it conforms to industry standards.

CONVENTIONAL PASS-THROUGH SECURITY An MBS, the underlying collateral of which consists of conventional mortgages. *See* CONVENTIONAL MORTGAGE.

CONVERTIBLE ADJUSTABLE RATE MORTGAGE An ARM that gives the borrower the option to convert to a fixed-rate mortgage. The conversion is made at the current market rate, and the privilege must be exercised within the stipulated time frames of the option agreement (usually the time of the first scheduled rate adjustment).

COOPERATIVE A form of property ownership in which a corporation holds the actual title to the property and conveys units to individuals through the issuance of shares and occupancy agreements.

CORPORATE BOND EQUIVALENT YIELD An upward adjustment to reflect the effects of monthly payment of interest rather than semiannual payment of interest, which is the convention in the corporate and government bond markets. The corporate bond equivalent yield adjustment for mortgages compensates for monthly compounding.

CORRESPONDENT The mortgage banker or other issuer who services the mortgage loans collateralizing an MBS.

CO-SERVICER A lender who participates in a joint pool and performs the ongoing servicing activities under the supervision of a master servicer.

COUPON The rate of interest recorded on the face of a certificate.

COUPON INTEREST The coupon rate multiplied by the amortized value.

CUMULATIVE The provision in an agreement that the benefits prescribed for one of the parties will accumulate until paid.

CURRENT COUPON *See* GUARANTEED COUPON.

CURRENT FACE *See* AMORTIZED AMOUNT.

CURRENT YIELD The percentage of annual interest received on an investment based on the coupon rate times the principal amount of the purchase (i.e., the amortized value times the price).

CUSIP The standard identification number assigned to securities that must be used during the confirmation, comparison, and clearance processes because it is the only uniform method of identifying issues. The acronym stands for "Committee on Uniform Securities Identification Procedures."

CUSTODIAN In the clearing process, an organization, usually a bank or a clearing broker, that holds securities under its own name or under its control on behalf of its customers. In the origination of an MBS, the organization that maintains physical possession of the original mortgage documents that serve as the underlying collateral for an issued MBS. Custodian services are provided under the terms of an official custodial agreement involving the custodian, the mortgagee, and the MBS issuer.

DK ("DON'T KNOW") An operational term associated with either the clearance or comparison of trades. It implies that the contra-side of the trade has no knowledge of the trade or has trade detail in which fundamental data (coupon, pool number, price, net trade value, etc.) differ from those of the submitting party.

DEALER A registered trading organization that creates a marketplace for securities, buying and selling for the account and risk of the firm.

DEBENTURE   An unsecured debt security backed only by the good faith and repayment ability of the issuer.

DEEP DISCOUNT   A trading price that is well below the par price. For mortgage-backed securities, a deep discount is given to make low coupon securities more attractive to the investor.

DEFAULT   The failure by the mortgagor to complete payments as prescribed by the terms of the mortgage contract.

DELAY   The "stated" delay time that elapses before the first payment of principal and interest (GNMA I is 45 days, GNMA II is 50 days, FHLMC PC is 75 days, FNMA MBS is 54 days, conventional pass-through is 54 days). The actual delay, or penalty, is 30 days less than the stated delay.

DELINQUENT PAYMENT   A late payment(s) of the principal and interest due in accordance with the terms of a mortgage loan.

DELIVERY INSTRUCTIONS   Delivery information accompanying each trade; it is used in settlement procedures. These instructions indicate the location to or from which securities should be delivered or received. They should include the name and address (or ABA number if wireable to a bank) of the receiving firm, the specific area that is to receive the securities (i.e., trust or custody), and all pertinent trade data.

DELIVERY VERSUS PAYMENT (DVP)   The process whereby payment for a securities trade is made either simultaneous with or subsequent to the actual delivery or receipt of the traded securities.

DEMINIMUS PUD   A planned unit development in which the common property has little effect on the value of the property securing the PUD unit mortgage.

DEPOSITORY   A limited-purpose trust company chartered for the purpose of providing settlement and custodial service for securities that are maintained in a book-entry environment. *See* BOOK ENTRY.

DEPRESSED MORTGAGE MARKET A market in which the value of whole loans is less than their outstanding principal value. Such a market can occur when the interest rates on the outstanding mortgages are below the current interest rates.

DISCOUNT PRICE A price that results in a principal amount which is less than the current outstanding principal or amortized amount of the issue being traded. *See* DEPRESSED MORTGAGE MARKET.

DISCOUNT RATE The rate that the Federal Reserve charges to its member banks when they borrow funds from the Fed.

DISINTERMEDIATION The withdrawal of funds from savings institutions for use in other investments that yield a higher current income. In the mortgage market, it decreases the amount of funds available for real estate loans.

DON'T KNOW *See* DK.

DRAFT The process of physically delivering securities to an out-of-town location using the services of a third party, usually a bank and/or an armored carrier. Payment is made on receipt of the securities.

DUE BILL A legal document that evidences the indebtedness of one party to another with regard to dividend, interest, or other distribution. A due bill must accompany all deliveries of securities that have a settlement date equal to or earlier than a given record date when delivery and payment occur between the record date and the principal and interest/dividend payment date. If delivery occurs after the payment date, a due bill is not acceptable; a full payment check is required.

DUE-BILL CHECK A postdated check issued before, but not negotiable until, the payment date of a dividend, interest, or other distribution.

DUE DATE   The day of the month, referred to as the remittance date, on which the monthly payment is due on a mortgage loan.

DURATION   A measure of an instrument's price volatility relative to current interest yields. *See* AVERAGE LIFE.

DURATION VARIABILITY   A measure of the extent to which the duration of a cash flow may vary from its expected value owing to fluctuation in yields and/or prepayment rates.

EFFECTIVE YIELD   The percentage of return, or interest income, being realized on an investment. It is derived by using the principal cost and coupon as a basis of determination. Effective yield, also known as nominal yield, is determined by dividing the interest income by the amortized amount of the MBS and multiplying by 12 (assuming the MBS pays monthly).

ENDORSEMENT   The signing of an instrument by the registered holder, usually for the purpose of assigning or transferring ownership.

EQUITY   The value of property in excess of all claims or liens against it.

ESCROW PAYMENTS   The amounts constituting ground rents, taxes, assessments, water rates, mortgage insurance premiums, fire and hazard insurance premiums, and other payments required to be deposited by the mortgagor with the mortgagee before subsequent payment by the mortgagee.

EXECUTION REPORT   An information report confirming the details of a completed (executed) trade order.

EXERCISE   To exercise an option is to require the buyer or seller of an option to perform a securities transaction as agreed on in the terms of the option contract.

EXERCISE PRICE   *See* STRIKE PRICE.

FACE   Original principal amount (issuance value) of a debt security. Also referred to as *par value*. It is the quantity value that is printed on the face of a physical MBS.

FACTOR   The percentage of the original principal balance of an MBS, expressed in a decimal format (eight places), that is currently outstanding.

FACTOR TAPE   A magnetic tape published and updated monthly for each guarantor or program (e.g., GNMA, FNMA, or FHLMC) that lists all pools issued in their respective markets and the current month's factor for each pool.

FAIL   A securities transaction not cleared (i.e., received or delivered) versus payment on the settlement date.

FANNIE MAE (FNMA)   *See* FEDERAL NATIONAL MORTGAGE ASSOCIATION.

FARMERS HOME ADMINISTRATION   A government agency within the Department of Agriculture that operates under the Consolidated Farm and Rural Development Act of 1921 and Title V of the Housing Act of 1949. It provides financing to farmers and other qualified borrowers.

FAST-PAY BONDS   Bonds with a high redemption priority over other bonds in an issue. As a result of their high priority, such bonds are redeemed at a faster rate than others in the same issue. The first, or "A," tranche of a CMO is a fast-pay bond.

FED FUNDS   One of the two types of currency exchanges used in the United States. They are the excess reserve balances of a member bank on deposit at a central bank in the Federal Reserve System and are 100% collected funds. Therefore, they are the equivalent of cash. Fed funds are used for settlement of money market instruments, U.S. government securities, and most MBS transactions. *See* CLEARINGHOUSE FUNDS.

FED FUNDS RATE   A rate of interest associated with borrowing a member bank's excess reserves. The rate is determined by the forces of supply and demand and current interest rates.

FEDWIRE The computer system of the Federal Reserve System that is used to make interbank book-entry movements of eligible securities and Fed funds. Notifications of these movements are made by Fedwire messages. FHLMC and FNMA are the MBS presently delivered through the Fed system. Only Federal Reserve member banks are permitted to have direct access to this system.

FEDERAL DEPOSIT INSURANCE CORPORATION An agency established by the Banking Act of 1933 to insure the deposits of banks.

FEDERAL HOME LOAN BANK (FHLB) A government-sponsored system of 12 regional banks chartered to provide credit facilities and liquidity to its members. All federally chartered S&Ls must be members, and state-chartered organizations may join. The FHL banks are owned by their members.

FEDERAL HOME LOAN BANK BOARD A regulatory and supervisory agency for S&Ls chartered by the FHLB. The board also oversees the operations of the Federal Home Loan Mortgage Corporation.

FEDERAL HOME LOAN MORTGAGE CORPORATION (FHLMC) Known as "Freddie Mac," the FHLMC is a private corporation authorized by Congress to sell participation certificates and collateralized mortgage obligations backed by pools of conventional mortgage loans.

FEDERAL HOUSING ADMINISTRATION (FHA) A division of the Housing and Urban Development Department (HUD). Its main activity is the insuring of residential mortgage loans made by private lenders. It sets standards of construction and underwriting. The FHA does not lend money or construct housing.

FEDERAL NATIONAL MORTGAGE ASSOCIATION (FNMA) Known as "Fannie Mae," this agency was created by Congress to support the secondary mortgage market. It is a private corporation, buying and selling residential mortgages insured by the FHA or guaranteed by the VA. The FNMA also issues mortgage-backed securities backed by conventional mortgages.

FEDERAL RESERVE SYSTEM The central banking system of the United States. It consists of the Federal Reserve Board, 12 Federal Reserve Banks and two Federal Reserve facilities. Functions of the FRS include setting monetary policy and the discount rate, influencing the cost and availability of credit, supervising bank regulations and bank holding companies, and overseeing international banking operations.

FEDERAL SAVINGS AND LOAN INSURANCE COR-PORATION (FSLIC) A corporation established in 1934 by the National Housing Act. It insures savings account deposits in the nation's S&Ls.

FEE A negotiated sum of money paid to an investor or a securities dealer in exchange for a letter of commitment or a standby agreement to purchase a stipulated amount of an MBS at a future date.

FHA EXPERIENCE A statistical table, revised periodically, used to calculate prepayment estimates. It represents the percentage of an original pool of mortgages that is expected to survive at the end of each year over the life of an MBS. A 300% FHA translates into a "fast" paydown of principal.

FHA INSURED MORTGAGE *See* FEDERAL HOUSING ADMINISTRATION.

FHLMC (FREDDIE MAC) *See* FEDERAL HOME LOAN MORTGAGE CORPORATION.

FHLMC PARTICIPATION CERTIFICATES Securities backed by a pool of mortgages owned by the FHLMC. Certificates certify ownership interests in a specific pool of mortgages.

FINAL MONEY The net amount, including accrued interest, to be paid by or paid to the contra-side of a securities transaction on delivery on the settlement date of the trade.

FIRM POSITION The inventory, or trading, position of a dealer firm.

FIRM YIELD MAINTENANCE A condition specified at the time of execution of a TBA trade. A FYM trade guarantees a specific yield to a customer instead of guaranteeing a specific coupon. For example, 10% TBA at par may be settled by any coupon traded during the TBA period. However, the price of the transaction will be changed to maintain a 10% yield.

FIXED RATE An interest rate that does not vary. A fixed-rate mortgage is one on which the interest rate is set for the entire term of the loan.

FIXED-RATE OPTION *See* CONVERTIBLE ADJUSTABLE RATE MORTGAGE.

FLAT An order that is executed with no accrued interest. Normally, an issue is traded flat four business days before the payable date.

FLOATING RATE *See* ADJUSTABLE RATE MORTGAGE.

FLOOR The lowest level to which interest rates may decline on an adjustable rate mortgage.

FNMA *See* FEDERAL NATIONAL MORTGAGE ASSOCIATION.

FORTY-EIGHT HOUR RULE A term associated with the allocation process for TBA contracts. Specific pool (delivery) information must be transmitted by the seller to the buyer no later than 3:00 P.M. EST, of the second business day before the contracted settlement date. If the information is not transmitted in time, the delivery date for the pool is moved forward one more day. However, there is no adjustment in the calculation of the accrued interest of the trade.

FORWARD COMMITMENT A commitment to purchase loans at a fixed yield or on a floating rate basis, within a specified time that usually does not exceed 12 months. It is also referred to as a standby commitment.

FORWARD TRANSACTION *See* TO BE ANNOUNCED.

FULLY MODIFIED PASS-THROUGH An MBS for which the full and timely payment of principal and interest is guaranteed by the issuer. A GNMA pool is an example of a fully modified pass-through because GNMA guarantees that if there is a shortage of collections for any month(s), the amounts passed through to the investor will be adjusted or modified to equal the full anticipated paydown.

FUNDING The actual transfer of funds to the seller.

GEM *See* GROWING EQUITY MORTGAGE.

GENERIC TRADE A TBA transaction with no specific instructions or requirements. *See* SPECIFIED TRANSACTION.

GIANT An MBS issued under a FHLMC program that aggregates existing or newly created guarantor program PCs, thereby creating a single giant participation certificate. Giants are intended to enhance the liquidity and market price of securities issued under the 15-year guarantor or swap program (non-Gnomes).

GIVE UP The process of disclosing the true identity of the contra-side of a securities transaction. Relative to MBS trades, this process is performed by broker's brokers through the clearing division of the MBSCC. *See* BROKER'S BROKER.

GNMA *See* GOVERNMENT NATIONAL MORTGAGE ASSOCIATION.

GNOME A participation certificate, issued under FHLMC's cash program, that has a 15-year maturity. Gnomes have a pool prefix number of either 21 or 38 and trade at a premium to FHLMC's 15-year participation certificates, which are issued under the guarantor or swap program.

GOOD DELIVERY A term referring to the fact that a delivery is being made in conformity with all applicable rules and within the required time frames of the agencies that oversee the clearance and settlement of MBS.

GOOD FUNDS *See* FED FUNDS.

GOVERNMENT NATIONAL MORTGAGE ASSOCIATION (GNMA) (GINNIE MAE) On September 1, 1968, Congress enacted legislation to partition the FNMA into two continuing corporate entities. The GNMA assumed responsibility for the special assistance loan program and the management and liquidation functions of the older FNMA. The GNMA also administers and guarantees mortgage-backed securities, which channel new sources of funds into residential financing through the sale of privately issued mortgage-backed securities. The term *pass-throughs* is often used to describe Ginnie Maes. The GNMA is a wholly owned U.S. government corporation and is part of the Department of Housing and Urban Development.

GRADUATED PAYMENT MORTGAGE (GPM) A type of mortgage in which the monthly payments increase for a period of up to five years at which time they level off. This type of mortgage results in negative amortization because early payments are insufficient to cover the interest due on the mortgage. A GPM is frequently used by a first-time homebuyer who presently has a relatively low income that is expected to increase over the years.

GRANTOR TRUST A trust in which the grantor (certificate holder) retains control over the income or assets, or both, to such an extent that for tax purposes the grantor will be treated as the owner of the property (mortgage assets) and its income. The result is to make the income from a grantor trust taxable to the grantor but not to the trust that receives it.

GROWING EQUITY MORTGAGE (GEM) A type of mortgage loan in which annual increases in monthly payments are used to reduce the outstanding principal amount of the loan, thereby shortening the life of the mortgage. GEMs are typically 15-year loans.

GUARANTEED COUPON One of the conditions specified at the time of a TBA trade. The term refers to the fact that a specific coupon rate is guaranteed to a customer at the time pools are allocated to the TBA.

GUARANTOR PROGRAM An FHLMC program under which lenders sell or swap loans in exchange for participation certificates guaranteed by the FHLMC.

GUARANTY A promise by a third party to pay the principal and interest due to the holders of the MBS in the event that the original obligor fails to make the payments due under the terms of the mortgage loan contract. Many MBS have multiple layers of guarantees.

HAIRCUT A percentage reduction in the actual market value of an MBS. Haircuts are common in transactions such as repos and are used to provide the cash lender with some margin of protection against market depreciation.

HALF-LIFE The point in time when half of the original principal amount of an MBS is expected to be repaid. *See* DURATION and AVERAGE LIFE.

HEDGING The purchase or sale of mortgage futures contracts to offset cash market transactions. The offsetting of assets with liabilities of a similar nature for the purpose of limiting investment position risk.

HIGH-RATIO LOAN A loan that exceeds 80% of the sales price or the market value of the real estate, whichever is less.

HUD The U.S. Department of Housing and Urban Development, established by the Housing and Urban Development Act of 1965 to replace the Housing and Home Financing Agency. The department is responsible for the implementation and administration of government housing and urban development programs including GNMA. HUD programs cover community planning and development, housing production, the extension of mortgage credit (FHA), and ensuring equal opportunity in housing.

INCOME LIMITS The maximum amount of income that a family may realize in order to be eligible for rent supplements or for admission into low- and moderate-income housing projects.

INCOME PROPERTY Real estate owned and operated to produce income.

INSURED LOAN A mortgage loan in which payment of a portion of the outstanding principal amount of the loan has been guaranteed by an issuer of an MBS in the case of loan foreclosure(s).

INTEREST DISTRIBUTION AMOUNT The aggregate interest portions, adjusted to the pass-through rate, of the monthly installments paid to the holders of MBS.

INTEREST ONLY (I/O) One of the two security types produced by "stripping" an MBS. It represents ownership of the interest portion of the monthly payments being made on the underlying collateral of the stripped MBS. Frequently, I/Os are structured to incorporate a portion of the principal payments into the I/O distribution in an effort to make this a more stable investment. *See* NOTIONAL AMOUNT.

INTEREST RATE The coupon rate as recorded on the face of an MBS. The percentage rate charged for the use of money (e.g. , a mortgage).

INTEREST TO DATE Interest that has accrued on a repurchase agreement (repo) or reverse repurchase agreement (reverse repo).

ISSUE DATE The date on which an issuer places a security in the marketplace; the first day in which a debt instrument begins to accrue interest. In terms of physical certificates, the day on which the transfer agent issues and registers a new certificate; that date is imprinted on the face side of every physical certificate.

ISSUE DATE PRINCIPAL BALANCE The principal balances of the underlying mortgage loans after crediting the principal portions of the monthly installments due on or before the issue date of the related MBS, whether or not collected, plus all principal prepayments.

ISSUER The originator of the MBS. The party, such as a mortgage banker, who writes and services mortgage loans and then pools them together as collateral for an MBS which, when issued, carries the additional guaranty of the agency under whose name the MBS is issued.

JOINT POOL A pool created when two or more FNMA-approved lenders participate under the same pool purchase contract.

JUMBO POOL A pool issued under the GNMA II program that contains the mortgages originated by multiple issuers. These pools are very large and frequently contain mortgages from a diverse geographic area. This tends to make their pay down rate more predictable, and therefore the pool itself is more liquid, or marketable.

LEVEL PAYMENT MORTGAGE A mortgage loan that calls payments of a fixed unchanging amount each payment period throughout the life of the mortgage contract. A portion of each payment is applied against the outstanding principal amount of the loan. The amount allocated to the paydown of principal is extremely low in the early years of this type of mortgage but progressively increases with each payment.

LEVERAGING The process of borrowing money for the purpose of investing the funds to yield a greater rate of return than the cost associated with the loan.

LIBOR The London Interbank Offering Rate of interest for U.S. dollar loans transacted between members in the London Euromarket.

LIQUIDATION PROCEEDS The cash received in connection with the liquidation of defaulted mortgage loans.

LOAN INFORMATION SHEET A listing of the loans that will serve as collateral for an MBS and used in the formation of a new MBS. For each loan, it shows the principal balance, term, loan-to-value ratio, and other pertinent information.

LOAN-TO-VALUE (LTV)   The ratio, expressed as a percentage, of the mortgage loan amount divided by the lower of the appraised value or the current purchase price of the mortgaged property. *See* HIGH-RATIO LOAN.

MAJORS   The FNMA program for the creation of large, multi-issuer, guaranteed mortgage-backed securities similar to the GNMA II Jumbo program and the FHLMC Giants program.

MARGIN   The amount paid to a brokerage firm by the customer when he or she borrows funds from the broker to purchase a security. *See* HAIRCUT.

MARGIN CALL   The cash or security equivalent amount being requested as collateral or protection for the firm pending final payment or liquidation of a transaction margined by a customer.

MARK TO THE MARKET   A process of updating the price valuation of a particular issue, or all issues contained in inventory, to reflect the current market value of the issue(s). This mark is used to ensure that the value of securities collateralizing outstanding loans is still adequate and to calculate current profit and loss figures for securities in inventory.

MARKET VALUE   The amortized value of an MBS multiplied by the current market, or bid, price.

MASTER SERVICER   A lender who coordinates the packaging of a joint pool and supervises the ongoing servicing activities of co-servicers. *See* JOINT POOL.

MATCHED BOOK   The records of the accounts used to identify reverse repo trades made specifically for the purpose of "reselling" the purchased collateral under a repo contract. Income is realized from the difference in the rate receivable on the reverse repo contract and payable under the matched repo contract. *See*

REPURCHASE AGREEMENT and REVERSE REPURCHASE AGREEMENT.

MATCHED TRADE   A condition that exists when both sides (trader and customer) of a trade agree on the details of the transaction.

MATURITY DATE The date on which the final principal and interest payments on a security are due to the investor(s).

MBSCC *See* MORTGAGE-BACKED SECURITIES CLEARING CORPORATION.

MIDGET A GNMA pass-through security with an intermediate term of 15 years that is similar in structure to the original 30-year GNMA security.

MOBILE HOME PASS-THROUGH An MBS collateralized by mobile homes or by mobile home units and their development lots. Four types of mobile home pass-throughs are guaranteed by GNMA.

MODIFIED PASS-THROUGH A pass-through security that provides investors with a guarantee of full and timely payment of interest plus a pro rated share of the principal as paid by the mortgagor plus a guarantee of ultimate full collection of principal.

MONTHLY PAYMENT The scheduled monthly payment of principal or interest on a mortgage loan.

MONTHLY REMITTANCE The total of the principal and interest amounts distributed to MBS holders on each remittance or payable date. *See* PASS-THROUGH SECURITY.

MORTGAGE A legal document in which real estate is pledged as collateral for the loan used to purchase the property.

MORTGAGE-BACKED BOND An MBS formatted to appear and act like a corporate bond rather than a pass-through or participation certificate inasmuch as the interest is paid semiannually at a fixed rate and the principal is paid at maturity. The ownership of the underlying mortgages collateralizing the bond is retained by the issuer of the bond.

MORTGAGE-BACKED SECURITIES CLEARING COR-PORATION (MBSCC) The MBSCC was established in 1979 by the Midwest Stock Exchange, Inc. to standardize and reduce the cost and potential risk associated with forward (TBA) trading activity in MBS. The MBSCC provides centralized trade comparison, margin consolidation, and settlement services for dealers, brokers, mortgage bankers, commercial banks, and thrift institutions active in the forward markets in FHLMC, FNMA, and GNMA issues.

MORTGAGE-BACKED SECURITY (MBS) A generic term for a debt security collateralized or backed by mortgage loans issued by mortgage bankers, commercial banks, savings banks, and other institutions on real estate. The monthly principal and interest payments paid to the mortgagees are passed through to the holders of the MBS. Many of these securities are backed by the full faith and credit of the U.S. government or one of its agencies.

MORTGAGE BANKER A company that specializes in originating mortgage loans for sale to investors in the form of an MBS. It frequently continues to service the loans it has sold. As the local representative of regional or national institutional lenders, it acts as a correspondent between lenders and borrowers.

MORTGAGE GUARANTY INSURANCE Insurance obtained from a nongovernmental agency, guaranteeing payment of a predetermined principal amount of an outstanding mortgage loan, thus affording the lender protection against foreclosure caused by prolonged illness, serious injury, or death of the borrower.

MORTGAGE LOAN SCHEDULE A document that identifies the individual mortgage loans of an MBS and that sets forth their principal balances as of the close of business on the cutoff date (after deducting any payment of principal due on or before such date), loan number, original principal amount, appraised value, payment date, date of origination, the mortgage interest rate, the monthly payment, the type of dwelling unit, state and county codes, and the maturity of the mortgage loan.

MORTGAGE PAY-THROUGH BONDS An MBS that has the features of both a participation certificate and a mortgage-backed bond. The collateral securing the bond remains the property of the issuer, and the payments received on the underlying mortgages are passed through to the holders of the pay-through bond.

MORTGAGE YIELD A device for measuring the rate of return on a mortgage; calculation is based on an assumed 12-year life for mortgages with a 30-year term.

MORTGAGEE An institution, group, or person who originates a loan to an individual or organization for the purpose of purchasing real estate property. A first lien on the property is conveyed to the mortgagee (creditor) as collateral for the loan.

MORTGAGOR The person or organization who receives a cash loan for the purchase of real estate property and who mortgages (assigns) that property as collateral for the loan.

MULTIFAMILY MORTGAGE A mortgage agreement issued for the purchase of a development containing more than four family dwellings. Generally associated wtih garden apartments, townhouses, and high-rise apartment buildings but does not include nursing homes or hospitals.

MULTIPLE POOL An MBS consisting of mortgages issued and/or purchased from more than one lender. See GIANT, JUMBO POOL, and MAJORS.

MUTUAL SAVINGS BANK A state-chartered financial institution that invests principally in mortgages.

NAME AND ADDRESS FILE A computer file that contains the account numbers and the corresponding names and addresses of every customer of a firm. The file also contains all pertinent data concerning each customer, including settlement instructions, records of trading authorizations, margin agreements, and the like as well as codes used for both the categorization of accounts and as indicators that initiate programmed services. The file can be accessed by either an account number or an abbreviated version (short name) of the account name.

NATIONWIDE LENDER A seller originating, selling, and servicing mortgages in states other than, and in addition to, the state in which its principal office is located.

NEGATIVE AMORTIZATION The process of adding unpaid interest amounts to the current outstanding principal amount (amortized amount) of an MBS security, thus effectively increasing the outstanding amount of the mortgage loan. The underpayment of the interest is a deliberate process that is associated with GPMs and certain adjustable rate mortgages. *See* GRADUATED PAYMENT MORTGAGE.

NET YIELD The amount of the gross coupon associated with the actual mortgage loans collateralizing an MBS less the servicing fees. It is the interest yield to be received by the MBS investor. *See* PASS-THROUGH SECURITY.

NOMINAL YIELD *See* EFFECTIVE YIELD.

NOMINEE NAME A fictitious name, registered and authorized with the transfer agent(s), used as a common registration name for physical registered certificates being held in trust or custody. Used to facilitate transactions that would otherwise require the filing of various legal documents with each certificate reregistration.

NOTIONAL AMOUNT A fictitious par amount representing the underlying principal amount of an interest-only stripped security. Used both as a reference in determining pricing and for use in the calculation of actual periodic payments.

ODD LOT A unit of trading below the normal (round lot) trading unit. An odd lot for mortgage-backed securities is anything below $500,000.00 or $1,000,000.00, depending on the instrument traded.

OFFERING PRICE *See* ASKED PRICE.

OMNIBUS ACCOUNT NUMBER A general ledger account number serving as a reference in grouping and balancing multiple similar transactions.

OPTION A contract whereby one party (the option writer) grants a second party (buyer) the right to buy or sell certain securities at a specified time and price. *See* STANDBY CONTRACT.

OPTIONAL REDEMPTION An optional call provision reserved by the issuer that becomes exercisable after a certain number of years from issue date. This provision allows the "clean-up" of small amounts of remaining principal with thin marketability.

ORIGINAL FACE AMOUNT The principal amount of an MBS on its date of issuance.

ORIGINATION The process whereby a mortgage-backed security, backed by approved mortgages in a pool, is issued.

ORIGINATION FEE The sum charged to the mortgagor for processing the mortgage loan.

ORIGINATOR One whose function is to originate (issue) mortgage-backed securities. Builders, brokers, and others are solicited to obtain applications for mortgage loans. The individual mortgage banker who performs this function is also designated as the originator (the issuer).

PAIR-OFF The elimination of the receiving and delivering process by matching buys and sells of similar TBAs settling in the same month and/or identical MBS settled trades. The process facilitates securities settlement. In the pair-off process there is usually a net money difference between the value of the buy and sell transactions that is paid (collected) at the end of the day.

PAR A price equal to 100% of the amortized value of an MBS.

PAR CAP A provision made by the trader that limits the price change on a TBA transaction to par. This limitation is associated with firm yield maintenance contracts that are not currently being traded.

PARTICIPANTS TRUST COMPANY The proposed name for the GNMA depository that is currently the Depository Division of the MBSCC.

PARTICIPATING MORTGAGE A loan agreement that provides that the lender receive a share of the revenue (profits) or a portion of some other defined amount regularly received by the borrower in addition to normal debt service.

PARTICIPATION CERTIFICATE (PC) A modified pass-through security, issued and guaranteed by the FHLMC, representing a pro-rated share in the conventional and agency-guaranteed mortgages that collateralize the PC. *See* MODIFIED PASS-THROUGH.

PAR VALUE *See* FACE.

PASS-THROUGH SECURITY A form of an MBS representing an undivided interest in an underlying pool of mortgages. The monthly principal and interest payments made by the mortgagors are passed monthly to the investor, net of the servicing fee of the issuer and any applicable agency guaranty fee. The sum of these fees is usually 50 basis points. *See* FULLY MODIFIED PASS-THROUGH and MODIFIED PASS-THROUGH.

PAYABLE DATE The date on which principal and interest are due to be paid to the registered and beneficial owners of a mortgage-backed security. This monthly date varies according to the programs of the guaranteeing agencies.

P&I *See* PRINCIPAL AND INTEREST.

PIECE The size of a physical certificate; the quantitative expression or denomination of each physical certificate held in inventory. The denominations imprinted on the certificates are expressed as original principal amounts. They must be amortized using the current factor to determine their current value.

PLANNED UNIT DEVELOPMENT (PUD)   A one- to four-family individually owned unit situated on a parcel of land that is common property for the benefit and use of the individual PUD owners. The common property is maintained and owned by a homeowners' association, corporation, or trust.

PLEDGED ACCOUNT MORTGAGE (PAM)   A graduated payment mortgage in which part of the mortgagor's down payment is deposited into a savings account. Funds are drawn from the account to supplement the mortgagor's monthly payments in the early years of the loan.

P/O   *See* PRINCIPAL ONLY.

POINT   An amount equal to 1% of the principal of the loan. In the context of trade pricing, a point is the equivalent of 100 basis points or 0.01. *See* BASIS POINT.

POOL   The conglomerate of individual mortgages that are packaged (bundled) into groups by primary lenders such as banks, savings and loan associations, and mortgage companies to serve as the underlying collateral for mortgage-backed securities.

POOL NUMBER   The specific number referencing the pool of mortgages that collateralizes an MBS.

PREMIUM   An amount paid over and above the current outstanding amortized value of an MBS. Issues are traded at a premium during times of depreciating interest rates.

PREPAYMENT   A partial or total payment of the principal amount of an outstanding mortgage loan before the date required for that payment under the terms of the loan.

PRICE   The dollar amount to be paid for securities. The price for an MBS is expressed as a percentage of the amortized amount.

PRICE CAP   A provision made by the trader that limits the price on the allocation of a TBA trade executed with a firm yield maintenance provision. It is not currently applicable. *See* FIRM YIELD MAINTENANCE and PAR CAP.

PRIMARY MARKET Offerings in newly issued securities; the TBA market.

PRIME RATE The interest rate charged by banks to their preferred customers. One of the barometers used for predicting general trends in interest rates.

PRINCIPAL AND INTEREST (P&I) The monthly payments made by mortgagors and passed through to the holders of an MBS. The payments consist of interest on the outstanding principal amount of the loan and a portion of the principal.

PRINCIPAL BALANCE The unpaid balance of an obligation exclusive of accrued interest.

PRINCIPAL ONLY (P/O) One of the products resulting from the stripping of an MBS. It is the portion of a strippped MBS that represents only the principal amount of the mortgage loans. P/Os are traded at a discount because investors receive either none or a small percentage of the interest payments being made on the underlying mortgages. The difference between the purchase price and the total principal repaid by maturity represents the investors' income.

PRINCIPAL TRADE A securities transaction in which the buying and/or selling dealers are trading the inventory of their firm for their firm's own account and risk. Profits are made from the differences realized between the buy price and the sell price.

PRIVATE PASS-THROUGH SECURITIES MBS securities that carry no federal agency guarantee.

PUT OPTION A contract giving its holder the right to sell securities in the future at a specified price within a specified time.

REAL ESTATE INVESTMENT TRUST (REIT) An investment vehicle established for the benefit of a group of real estate investors and managed by a group of trustees who hold title to the assets on behalf of the trust and who also control its acquisitions and investments.

REALIZED PROFIT & LOSS (P&L)   The profit and loss associated with each sale of inventory. Realized P&L is calculated on both a trade date basis and a settlement date basis.

RECLAMATION   Occurs when the seller in a transaction exercises the privilege of recovering his or her certificates and returning the contract money, or when a buyer exercises the privilege of recovering his or her contract money and returning the certificates, should any irregularity be discovered on delivery and settlement of the contract. *See* GOOD DELIVERY.

RECORD DATE   The date on which you must be either the registered holder or beneficial owner of an MBS to be entitled to payment of principal and interest. The record date for the majority of MBS falls on the last business day of the month. You are not considered a holder of record unless the settlement date of your purchase falls on or before the record date.

REFINANCING   The repayment of an outstanding debt from the proceeds of a new loan using the same real estate property as collateral. Refinancing frequently occurs when interest rates drop.

REGISTERED HOLDER   The name in which a certificate is registered (i.e., the name imprinted on the certificate by the transfer agent). The registered holder will always receive the P&I payments although the registered owner may not be the true beneficial owner.

REGULAR SERVICING OPTION   A guaranty fee option, usually 25 basis points, selected by the lender when requesting the issuance of an MBS. Under this option, the lender assumes the entire risk of loss from a borrower default.

REMIC   An acronym for Real Estate Mortgage Investment Conduit. A REMIC is a nontaxable entity (a corporation, partnership, or trust) formed under the Tax Reform Act of 1986 to create multiple-class mortgage-backed securities. The concept is similar to that used in the creation of CMOs. Any agency or issuer can become a REMIC. The securities issued under this program are known as REMICs.

RENEGOTIABLE RATE   The rate of interest on a mortgage loan that is subject to change at certain periods during its life. The renegotiation timetable is stated in the mortgage contract and is usually pegged onto another rate such as Treasury bills. *See* ADJUSTABLE RATE MORTGAGE.

REPURCHASE AGREEMENT (REPO)   A sale of securities that is accompanied by a simultaneous agreement of the seller to buy back the securities at a later date for the same contract value of the original sale plus an amount calculated on the basis of an agreed rate stipulated at the time of the original sale. A repo is a short-term financing vehicle.

REVERSE ANNUITY MORTGAGE (RAM)   A type of mortgage on which the lender makes periodic payments to the mortgagor using the mortgagor's home equity as security. The payments result in negative amortization.

REVERSE REPURCHASE AGREEMENT (REVERSE REPO)   An agreement to purchase securities and a simultaneous agreement to resell the securities on an agreed-on date to the original seller for the same contract value plus an amount based on a rate agreed on at the time of the original purchase. It is a vehicle for realizing income on short-term uninvested funds. *See* MATCHED BOOK.

ROLLOVER MORTGAGE (ROM)   A type of mortgage that provides for renegotiation of the interest rate and payment terms, usually at each five-year period during the term of the loan.

ROUND LOT   A unit of trading or a multiple thereof. The normal round lot for mortgage-backed securities is $500,000.00 and above.

SAFEKEEPING   A general ledger account on the books of a broker or dealer that is used to show the location of the physical securities held in the name of and on behalf of the firm's customers. A separate physical location in a firm's vault used to store securities registered in the names of the firm's individual customers.

SAVINGS AND LOAN ASSOCIATION (S&L)   A mutual or stock association chartered and regulated by either federal or state government. S&L associations accept time deposits that have traditionally been invested in residential mortgage loans, but their lending powers have now been expanded beyond that.

SEASONED ISSUES   Pools or PCs that have been outstanding for at least two years. Seasoned issues have usually had a greater market value than new issues because enough time has elapsed since issuance to fairly accurately determine their paydown rate.

SEASONING   The aging of a mortgage; the amount of time that has elapsed since origination. A seasoned mortgage is one that has been outstanding for a year, which is the time deemed necessary to determine the creditworthiness of the mortgagor.

SECOND MORTGAGE   A lien against a property that has lower priority than the primary (first) mortgage.

SECONDARY MARKET   The resale market for established MBS.

SECURITY   A certificate evidencing any one of the guaranteed mortgage pass-through instruments executed by the FNMA and authenticated by the certificate registrar.

SECURITY MASTER FILE   A computer file that contains the descriptive information about specific securities, including factor information for MBS. Access to the file for MBS information should be through use of a pool number index, a CUSIP index, or any other internal indexing method desired by the traders and operations personnel of the firm.

SEGREGATION   A general ledger account on the books of a broker or dealer that shows the location of securities registered in the firm's name but held beneficially for its customers. A separate physical location in the vault to store fully paid customer securities.

SELLER The term for an approved organization that sells and services mortgages.

SERIAL BONDS Bonds issued with multiple sequential maturity dates and said to mature "serially" as they reach maturity. *See* COLLATERALIZED MORTGAGE OBLIGATION.

SERVICER A mortgagee who performs the ongoing servicing activities for the mortgage loans used to create an MBS.

SERVICING The collection of payments and management of operational procedures related to a mortgage, including all bookkeeping and loan analysis studies.

SERVICING FEE An amount paid to the original mortgagors in consideration for the duties performed as a servicer of the mortgages underlying the MBS. The fee is a portion of the interest amount paid each month by the individual mortgagors. The usual fee is 0.00375% of the outstanding principal amounts of each loan at the time the P&I payments are due from the mortgagor and are contingent on payment by the mortgagor of the amount of P&I that is due.

SETTLEMENT BALANCE ORDER (SBO) An irrevocable instruction to settle or clear (receive or deliver) a TBA trade of specific quantity and of a particular class to a specific contra-party (not necessarily the same party with whom the trade was originally executed). The SBO is the end product of the comparison and netting functions performed by the MBSCC clearing division on behalf of its participants. The SBO must be used during the allocation process to determine the exact pools that are to be delivered under the SBO contract.

SETTLEMENT DATE The date agreed on by the involved parties for the actual payment of funds and the delivery of mortgage-backed securities in which the terms of trade are specified. Five settlement dates each month are assigned, according to security type, for the clearance of TBA trades. Normal settlement date for a secondary trade done for a specific pool is five business days after the trade date.

SETTLEMENT DATE POSITION   The inventory position of
the firm on settlement date. It reflects those trades that have settled, but it does not necessarily mean that the trades have cleared.

SHARED APPRECIATION MORTGAGE (SAM)   A
mortgage loan in which the mortgagor receives a below-market
interest rate in return for which the mortgagee receives a portion
of the future appreciation in the value of the property.

SINGLE-FAMILY LOAN   A mortgage loan secured by one-
to four-family housing properties.

SINKING FUND   The obligation to retire liabilities according to a schedule, which results in a substantial partial redemption of the issue before final maturity.

SLOW-PAY BONDS   Bonds in a low priority class compared with bonds in other classes with respect to the order of
redemption. The low priority results in slow redemption (principal paydown) when such bonds are compared to bonds in other
classes.

SPECIFIED POOL TRADE   A contract for the purchase or
sale of mortgage-backed securities in which the terms of the contract are clearly defined and include the identity of the pool to be
delivered in settlement of the trade.

SPECIFIED TRANSACTION   A forward (TBA) transaction
that stipulates limitations, other than those called for under PSA's
Uniform Practices, on the MBS that may be allocated to that particular TBA. Such limitations must be agreed on by both the buyer
and seller. Examples include a below-normal limitation on the
number of pools that may be allocated to the TBA, requiring only
seasoned pools, and so on.

SPREAD   The difference between the rate at which money
can be borrowed and the rate at which it can be loaned. *See*
MATCHED BOOK.

STANDBY CONTRACT An option (or standby commitment) to buy or sell a specified amount of mortgage-backed securities by or on a specified date.

STANDBY NOTIFICATION DATE The date by which the buyer or seller of a standby agreement (option) must acknowledge whether or not he or she wishes to exercise the contract.

STANDBY OPTION FEE The fee paid to the writer of an option.

STANDING INSTRUCTIONS Delivery instructions established for each account. These instructions are located within the master name and address file of every broker-dealer. They can apply to all transactions executed on behalf of an account, regardless of security type, or there can be a different set of instructions for each security type or MBS program.

STOCK RECORD See BOND RECORD.

STREET NAME Registration of physical securities in the broker-dealer's own firm name. See SEGREGATION.

STRIKE PRICE The price at which an options or standby contract will be executed (exercised).

STRIPPED MORTGAGE-BACKED SECURITY An MBS that is used to create two or more new securities that are sold separately to investors. The newly created securities represent a participation in the cash flow realized from either the principal portion of the monthly MBS payments or the interest portion of the monthly MBS payments. Usually, the new securities represent ownership in the cash flow of a specified percentage of both principal and interest payments. See INTEREST ONLY and PRINCIPAL ONLY.

SUSPENSE ACCOUNT A general ledger account used to record and reflect unreconciled money and/or security differences. It should be a Julian-dated account for control and reconciliation purposes.

TAIL   That portion of the original face amount of a GNMA pool that is not evenly divisible by $5,000.00.

TBA   *See* TO BE ANNOUNCED.

TBA CONTRACT   A commitment letter confirming the details of a TBA contract. This letter is usually sent only to institutional accounts in order to reduce the potential exposure of a DK when the time comes to settle the TBA. The commitment letter should be signed and returned to the originator.

TERM LOAN   A short-term debt that has either no amortization or low amortization provisions, so that the principal is paid in one lump sum. A term loan is generally a secondary lien at high interest rates.

TO BE ANNOUNCED (TBA)   A forward transaction in mortgage-backed securities. A trade in which only the generic terms of the contract, such as the coupon and MBS program (e.g., FHLMC, FNMA, or GNMA) are known at the time of execution. The specific terms of the contract are provided by the seller to the buyer during the allocation period, a process governed by the Uniform Practices of the Public Securities Association (PSA).

TRADE DATE   The contractual date of execution of a securities transaction. The date on which two parties enter into an agreement for the purchase or sale of mortgage-backed securities, regardless of the date on which such securities are to be delivered.

TRADE DATE POSITION   The inventory position of the firm on trade date.

TRADE-FOR-TRADE (T/T)   A designation for TBA trades that precludes them from the netting cycle at the MBSCC. Odd lot transactions must be done on a trade-for-trade basis.

TRADER'S POSITION   The inventory position of every security traded on the trading desk of an MBS dealer. These positions must be maintained on a real-time basis, and therefore many firms maintain the trader's inventory manually or on microcomputers. This inventory must be constantly reconciled against the official inventory ledgers of the firm.

TRANCHE   One of the individual issues of a CMO. *See* COLLATERALIZED MORTGAGE OBLIGATION.

TRANSFER AGENT   Retains a record of each holder of a security and provides services for the reregistration of outstanding physical certificates as well as replacements for lost and stolen certificates.

TWELVE-YEAR AVERAGE LIFE   The assumption that, given an MBS with a stated maturity of 30 years, the principal balance of the issue will be paid down in full by the end of 12 years.

UNMATCHED TRADE   A condition in which the contra-side of a transaction has not agreed to the details of the trade.

UNREALIZED PROFIT AND LOSS   The profit and loss associated with the unsold portion of a firm's inventory. Determined by comparing the current market value of the inventory to its purchase cost.

VARIABLE RATE   *See* ADJUSTABLE RATE MORTGAGE.

VARIANCE   The amount by which the amortized value of the pools allocated to a TBA transaction can differ from the face amount of the TBA trade. The variance, currently 2.499999% plus or minus, is determined by the Uniform Practices of the PSA.

VETERANS ADMINISTRATION (VA)   An independent agency of the federal government created in 1930. The Servicemen's Readjustment Act of 1944 authorized the agency to administer a variety of benefit programs designed to facilitate the adjustment of returning veterans to civilian life. The VA home loan guaranty program is designed to encourage lenders to offer long- term, low-down-payment mortgages to eligible veterans by guaranteeing the lenders against loss. The VA also guarantees mobile home loans to eligible veterans.

WEIGHTED AVERAGE COUPON (WAC) The arithmetic mean of the coupon rate of the underlying mortgages of an MBS.

WEIGHTED AVERAGE MATURITY (WAM) The arithmetic mean of the remaining term of the underlying mortgages of an MBS.

WHEN ISSUED As applied to mortgage-backed securities only, a trade for which the applicable current factor has not been released. Because the factor information is not available, the final money on the transaction cannot be calculated and is designated "when issued." As soon as the factors become available, all WI trades are recalculated and settled.

WHOLE LOAN Mortgage loans that have not been pooled to collateralize a mortgage-backed security.

YIELD The annual percentage of return earned on a security.

ZERO COUPON CMO Bonds that are either true zero coupon instruments or accrual bonds. An accrual bond (or compound interest bond) is a coupon bond that during some part of its life accumulates accrued interest as increased principal rather than as cash paid. This accumulation is called *accretion*.

Index

Registered clearing corporation, role of in settlement process, 81
Registered holder, 340
Registered holders of GNMA securities, guarantees to, 7
Regular servicing coupon, 340
REMICs, 15, 190. See also "Real estate mortgage investment conduits."
Renegotiable rate, 341
Repo order contract, 257
Repo positions, accounting for open, 300-301
Repo trade, 258
Repos, 69, 256-258
Retail accounts, other names for, 173
Retail orders, 66-67
  as source of order origination, 66-68
Retail trader, role of order origination, 68
Retail trades, comparison process of, 123
Reversal code, Fedwire, 200-201
Reverse annuity mortgage, 341
Reverse repos, 69, 258
Risk, 4, 5, 6, 107-118
  capital, 4
  definition of, 5
  limiting capital exposure, 6
  limiting in corporate investing, 3-4
  securitization of mortgages and, 5-6
  ways of controlling, 107-108
RMJ trading systems, as broker's broker, 63
Rollover mortgage, 341
Rollovers, 69
Round lot trades, 68
RVP, see "Receive-versus-payment transactions."
RVP/DVP, see "Receive versus payment/deliver versus payment."

S

Safekeeping accounts, 173, 341
Sale of MBS, three entitities involved in, 9
Same-day funds settlement (SDFS), 246, 247-248
SBO, see "Balance Order Settlement System."
SBO instruction process and netting, 147-152
SBO market differential (SBOMD), 144
SBO processing, 146-154
SBOMD, see "SBO market differential."
Scheduling, cutoff for Fedwire processing, 195-196
SDFS, see "Same-day funds settlement."
SECMST, see "Security master file."
Second mortgage, 342
Secondary market trade, see "When issued."
Secondary market, 342
Securitization process, mortgage, 6-8
Security master file, 70, 88-91, 101
Security number, 70, 279
  importance of in trade processing, 70
  sequence, use of in sorting fails, 279
Security, vault, 231-232
Segregation, 342
Self-clearing firms, 208, 209
Sequences sorting fails into, 279-282
Serial bonds, 343
Servicer, 343
Servicing fee, 343
Settlement amount, definition of, 144
Settlement balance order (SBO) option, 125, 144
Settlement date, TBA market, 122
Settlement netting services, 141-146
Settlement options, physical, 208-211
Settlement processing, 81-82, 125. See also "Clearance...."
  as defined by MBSCC, 125
SF, see "Single-family mortgages."
Shared appreciation mortgage, 344
Single-family mortgages (SF), 118
Sinking fund, 344
Skeletal orders, 92-93
Skeletal trade, 70, 92. See also "Skeletal orders."
  definition of, 70.
Slates, definition of, 69
Slow-pay bonds, 344
Specialist, role of, 61
Specified pool trade, 344
Spread, 344
SR, see "Stock record extract."
Standby agreement, execution of by mortgage bankers, 11
Standby contract, 345
Standby option fee, 345